Applying C For The IoT With Linux

First Edition

Harry Fairhead

I/O Press
I Programmer Library

Harry Fairhead Applying C For The IoT With Linux

1st Edition

ISBN Paperback: 978-1871962611

First Printing, 2019
Revision 1

Published by IO Press   www.iopress.info

In association with I Programmer   www.i-programmer.info

Preface

C is an important language because, despite what many will tell you, it is still the closest we have to a machine-independent assembler. This makes it ideal for working closely with the hardware and hence it is ideal for most low-level programming. Today's small embedded processors are no longer as small as they once were and it is not uncommon to find them running a complete Linux operating system. This would have been regarded as crazy, if not impossible, only a few years ago. Of course, there are very low-cost processors that can't manage to run a full operating system, and these are likely to be with us for some time, but the point is that as hardware evolves and prices fall, Linux in even the simplest devices will become the norm.

What this means is that writing low-level code has to evolve to work with Linux rather than trying to ignore it, or worse struggle against it. Linux, and POSIX systems in general, have many features to make access to hardware and nearly realtime operation easy - and all from user space. The only problem is that a full multi-tasking operating system, complete with security, is a complex beast and finding out how to do things can be difficult. The documentation and many of the "how-tos" on the web aren't aimed at low-level programming, but at end users and applications programmers. What I have tried to do in this book is to collect together all of the different techniques needed to work close to the hardware without having to abandon the OS.

Of course, there are compromises to be made. The OS has to provide security and this often stops you doing something that from your point of view is perfectly safe. The needs of a multitasking OS can also interfere with the timely execution of your code, but given the right scheduling method and core affinity this can be minimized. For these inconveniences you get lots of advantages: a full multi-threaded environment complete with the necessary mechanisms such as locks, high-level access to communications stacks such as TCP/HTTP, interprocess communications such as pipes and shared memory. Finally you get access to powerful graphics, almost for free. You might not have imagined wanting graphics, but now it's at your disposal, it could be worth using, rather than building some custom I/O hardware.

In short this book is about the power of a desktop computer applied to what used to be called embedded programming, physical computing and so on and now often gathered together under the term "Internet of Things", IoT.

The book assumes that you know C to a reasonable standard. If you encounter anything puzzling then either look it up on the web or refer to the companion book: *Fundamental C: Getting Closer To The Machine* ISBN: 978-1871962604.

I'd like to thank Kay Ewbank and Sue Gee for their input in proof-reading the manuscript. With a book of this length there are still likely to be mistakes, hopefully few in number and small in importance, which are entirely mine.

Harry Fairhead
May 2019

This book is part of the I Programmer Library and extracts from it, and its companion volume, can also be found on the website:
www.i-programmer.info

To keep informed about forthcoming titles visit the I/O Press website:
www.iopress.info.

This is also where you will also find errata, update information and can provide feedback to help improve future editions.

Table of Contents

Chapter 1   11
C, IoT, POSIX & Linux

    Why C?..12

    C Standards and Undefined Behavior...........................12

    POSIX and Linux...14

    Toolchains...15

    Types of Linux?..16

    What's Covered..17

    Summary..20

Chapter 2   21
Kernel Mode, User Mode & Syscall

    The Kernel...21

    Multi-tasking - Context Switch....................................22

    Modes and Syscall...23

    Glibc - Wrappers...24

    Your Code In Kernel Mode..26

    Security...27

    Summary..28

Chapter 3   29
Execution, Permissions & Systemd

    Permissions...29

    Running a Program..30

    Automatically Running a Program - systemd...............31

    Systemctl..34

    Journal..36

    Restart and Watch Dog..37

    Periodic Execution..40

    Summary..45

Chapter 4   47

Signals & Exceptions

Signal Basics..47

Dealing with Async..49

Controlling Signals..50

Masking Signals..52

Flags..53

Restarting Syscalls..53

Getting More Signal Info..55

Signals and Threads..55

Sending Signals..56

Waiting for Signals..57

Real-time Signals..57

Signals as IPC...58

Everything is a File - Including Signals...61

Setjmp Non-local Jumps...62

Are Signals Useful?...65

Summary..66

Chapter 5   67

Integer Arithmetic

Binary Integer Addition as Bit Manipulation......................................67

Decimal Arithmetic with BCD...70

BCD Arithmetic..72

Negative Numbers...74

Overflow and Undefined Behavior...76

GCC Overflow Detection...79

DIY Overflow Detection Before it Happens..80

Using Unsigned Arithmetic to Detect Overflow..................................81

Avoiding Overflow by Increased Precision...82

Trapping Signed Overflow..83

Detecting Unsigned Rollover..88

Modular Arithmetic..89

Division by Zero..92

Trapping Division by Zero..93

Summary..97

Chapter 6   **99**
Fixed Point Arithmetic

    Why Fixed Point?..99

    Fixed Point is Integer Arithmetic.......................................100

    Rescaling..102

    Temperature Conversion...104

    Printing Fixed Point...105

    Overflow During a Computation..107

    Avoiding Overflow with 64-bits..110

    Simulating 64-bit Multiply..110

    GCC Fixed Point Extensions...111

    Using a Fixed Point Library..113

    Decimal Fixed Point...117

    Summary...119

Chapter 7   **121**
Floating Point Arithmetic

    Pro and Cons of Floating Point...121

    The Floating Idea..122

    Floating Point Algorithms 123

    IEEE standard – Single & Double.......................................124

    Extended Precision...125

    Special Values – NaN and Inf..127

    Detecting Problems..129

    Mixed Arithmetic – Casting..132

    Floating Point Reconsidered...133

    Summary...136

Chapter 8   **137**
Files

    File Descriptors..139

    A Random Access Example..141

    Descriptors and Streams..142

    fcntl...143

    Sharing Files – Locking...144

    Pipes..149

    A Named Pipe Example..150

    Anonymous Pipes...152

    An Anonymous Pipe Example...153

    File & Directory Operations..154

    ioctl...156

    Summary...157

Chapter 9   **159**
The Pseudo File System
    The Linux Pseudo Directories..159
    Finding a PID by Name..161
    Working with GPIO...163
    Accessing Memory..166
    Memory Mapping Files..167
    Shared Memory...169
    Semaphore Locking..172
    Summary..177

Chapter 10   **179**
Graphics
    Choosing a GUI System..179
    The Framebuffer..180
    Drawing a Line..184
    Bounce..185
    Framebuffer Text PSF 1..188
    Framebuffer Text PSF 2..193
    Windowing Systems - X11...194
    Device, Screen and Window..195
    Graphics Functions...197
    An Example..198
    Color...199
    Events...200
    GTK - a GUI Framework..203
    A First Window...204
    Glade..208
    Graphics Beyond GTK...211
    Summary..212

Chapter 11   **213**
Connecting With Sockets
    Socket Basics..214
    Socket Functions..214
    A Web Client..217
    A WinSock Web Client..220
    Connecting Using a URL 222
    A Server..225
    A WinSock Server..229
    Summary..231

Chapter 12   **233**
Threads
    Why Multi-task?...233
    To Thread or Fork...234
    Pthreads...236
    The Thread Attributes Object..238
    Joinable And Detached Threads...239
    Threads and Scope - Thread Local.....................................241
    Atomic Operations and Locks..243
    Mutex..245
    Condition Variables..248
    First Thread to Finish...249
    Scheduling...252
    Deadline Scheduling...255
    Summary..261

Chapter 13   **263**
Cores, Atomics & Memory Models
    Managing Cores..263
    Affinity..265
    Memory Barrier and Fences...270
    Compiler Reordering and Optimization..............................273
    C11 Atomics..274
    Atomic Structs...279
    C11 Memory Models and Barriers......................................282
    Summary..283

Chapter 14   **285**
Interrupts & Polling
    Interrupts and Poll...285
    An Event Driven Socket Server...287
    GPIO Interrupts and Poll..290
    Complete Listing 292
    Poll on Another Thread...294
    Summary..298

Chapter 15   **299**
Assembler
    Addition...301
    Rotate a Global..303
    Extended Asm..304
    Adding Two Values..306
    Rotate a Variable...308
    The Clobber List..309
    Processor-Specific Constraints...310
    Register Variables..311
    ARM Rotate and Portable Code..312
    Goto Labels...312
    Using the Condition Code Register...313
    Assembler or C..315
    Summary...317

Chapter 1

C, IoT, POSIX & Linux

What is this book about? It is a good question because the subject doesn't really have a good common name, but if you work in the area of using C to write low-level code using small Single Board Computers (SBCs) that run Linux, or if you do any coding in C that interacts with the hardware, then there is a body of knowledge that you will need to know to be effective. Unfortunately there not being a good name for this body of knowledge means that it isn't easy to find a single source. This book gathers together all of these low-level, hardware-oriented, and often hardware-specific, ideas.

As such it is a moderately advanced book. This is not to say that it is difficult, but it does presuppose that you already know how to program and that you know the basic idioms of C. You also need to appreciate C's approach to data as bit patterns that mean different things depending on how you regard them. One minute a bit pattern might correspond to the state of a set of switches, and the next it might be an integer or a character code.

Specifically you are expected to know the basics of the C language, operators and expressions, functions, arrays, strings, structs, pointers, malloc and the use of the bitwise operators. You also need to go a little deeper than this and understand how the low-level code works with the underlying representations of the data at the level of bits. In languages such as Java, Python and so on you don't often question how the data is stored or represented, but for the creation of low-level C code you have to.

You should also be comfortable with hardware ideas such as address, register, stack, heap and the basic idea of a processor. If you don't know any of these or if you encounter something that you don't already know then the Internet is your friend.

You can also find out most of what you need to know from the companion volume to this book: ***Fundamental C: Getting Closer To The Machine*** ISBN: 978-1871962604.

Why C?

The chances are that you are already a C enthusiast, but it is worth making clear what C has to offer in this situation. You could ask if the "small" systems we are discussing aren't really that small, after all they run Linux, why not use a higher-level language? For example, MicroPython, or even Python itself, are popular languages for low-level programming. You can even use Java or C#, which are not generally thought of as being suitable for the task.

Using high-level languages for low-level tasks is indeed possible, but C has one big advantage - it is faster because it is closer to the machine. C can be up to 100 times faster than MicroPython. You might think that this only matters if your project needs the extra speed, but there is another consideration. The slowness of high-level languages means that they cannot work directly with hardware to implement the protocols that they are fast enough to consume. For example, MicroPython is fast enough to read a temperature sensor once every minute, but it isn't fast enough to implement the serial protocol that is used to transfer the data over, say, a 1-wire bus.

As a result high-level languages rely on drivers that have to be installed into the operating system. This introduces dependencies that your project is better off without. The phenomenon of "bit rot" means that sooner or later the driver will change the way that it works, will become unavailable, or will improve its security to the point you cannot use it. A C program can have all of the code it uses incorporated and, with a little care, can have no runtime dependencies and yet it can still be reasonably small.

You don't have to work in this way. If you want to use drivers and dynamically linked libraries you can, but it is usually better not to.

C is a fast "do-it-all" language that can create self-contained programs that mostly just work.

C Standards and Undefined Behavior

One of the characteristics of this sort of low-level programming is that it isn't standards-based, but usually hardware-based. In most cases you will have a specific item of hardware that you are trying to process and the way that the hardware works will be more important than how the C standards tell you that C should work. In many cases where there is variability in the way hardware behaves, the C standard will define it as "implementation-dependent", which is fine as for any real hardware the behavior is well defined Unfortunately the C standards often use the term "undefined behavior" for anything that is machine-dependent or which makes it difficult to optimize C and this is not a good thing.

This seemingly small change in terminology has brought about a completely different way of thinking. If something is machine-dependent then it is OK to use it, but don't expect it to work in the same way on another machine. On the other hand, undefined behavior doesn't become defined behavior just because the machine that you are using does something definite. The implication is that a valid C program should not make use of "undefined behavior". This means that compiler writers and their compilers can make the assumption that a correct program will not contain undefined behavior and can be optimized on this basis. In practice, of course, programs do make use of undefined behavior and usually to good effect. This can result in the compiler "optimizing" your C program so that it no longer works as you intended it.

The best known example of this is that signed integer overflow is undefined behavior and hence should never happen in a correct program. So if you include a test for overflow, the compiler can optimize it away because no correct program ever has signed integer overflow.

This is just one aspect of the crazy approach to undefined behavior. Perhaps the worst is the assumption that if your program contains undefined behavior then the compiler can implement anything it likes - including, according to a famous comment "making demons fly out of the programmer's nose", hence the alternative name for undefined behavior - "nasal demons".

At this point all looks lost, but in practice things aren't this bad. If they were, almost no C program would actually run since most do contain undefined behavior. When you are familiar with the hardware you are using, the implementation is known and the behavior is defined. You might have to switch off some compiler optimizations to get the machine-dependent behavior rather than a nasal demon, but this is always possible. Even so, you need to be on the look out for potential problems and be aware that in such cases you are at war with the compiler and its creators.

This raises the question as to why?

There are two types of programmer using C at the present time. The programmer wanting to write code that works on anything, and the more targeted programmer working with specific hardware. There is a considerable tension between the two as the platform-independent programmer wants C to be an exact standard and considers that any variations between hardware should be eradicated. The problem is that eradication usually means that the standard is modified to make the behavior illegal or undefined. This limits what the programmer targeting a specific machine can do within the standards. In short, programming for a given machine often means that you have to go outside the standards to create a simple program.

This is not to say that you should ignore the standards. There is obviously a big payoff if you can write code that will work anywhere. Knowing what the standards are, and knowing where you go outside them, is the best way of not being locked into using particular hardware. C is fairly platform-independent, until you get to the parts of the program that are platform-specific.

There are a number of important C standards and programs are still written to conform to all of them. The latest standard might be C11, but this doesn't mean that people aren't writing C89 code any more, and there is certainly a lot of existing C89 code out there. C89 is usually referred to as ANSI C as it was the first standard. C99 introduced many modern language conveniences and is a very popular standard for low-level programming. C11 introduced many features to take account of modern processors and the sophisticated way that they can use speculative execution with multiple cores and multi-level caches to speed up programs. Many of the features introduced in C11 were, and still are, controversial, but there are lots of good reasons for using it even on smaller machines with simpler architectures.

There are also a number of different "embedded" C languages, such as Arduino C, and many SBC manufacturers and chip makers have their own dialects of C, complete with their own compilers. These are generally cut down or augmented versions of the language. If you understand C11, these are easy to adapt to and there are too many variations to cover here.

POSIX and Linux

As well as the C standards, there are important C libraries that work with any operating system that conforms to POSIX, the Portable Operating System Interface. Put simply, POSIX is a set of standards that define what a Unix-like system has to support. While Linux isn't Unix, it tends to do things in POSIX-compliant ways. Even Windows, which isn't POSIX compliant, does many things in an almost POSIX way. There is also the Cygwin system which brings POSIX to Windows, or you can use the Windows Subsystem, which is essentially Linux running under Windows.

If you can't find a C standard or C standard library for a facility then the next best thing is a POSIX standard library.

In particular POSIX (all revisions) covers:

> Process Creation and Control
> Signals
>> Floating Point Exceptions
>> Segmentation / Memory Violations
>> Illegal Instructions
>> Bus Errors
>> Timers
>
> File and Directory Operations
> Pipes
> I/O Port Interface and Control
> Process Triggers
> Priority Scheduling
> Real-Time Signals
> Clocks and Timers
> Semaphores
> Message Passing
> Shared Memory
> Asynchronous and Synchronous I/O
> Memory Locking Interface
> Thread Creation, Control, and Cleanup
> Thread Scheduling
> Thread Synchronization
> Signal Handling
> Command Interpreter
> Utility Programs

Occasionally there is something defined by both a C standard and a POSIX standard. The most notable is the threading library, Pthreads. C11 also defines a set of standard threads, but in this case it is often better to use Pthreads, which has been around for a lot longer and is more capable.

Toolchains

A toolchain is the software you need to convert your C program to something that runs. At the bare minimum it consists of a compiler and a text editor. My preferred IDE is NetBeans, but there are other choices including Eclipse, and even using the command line. As already mentioned, many manufacturers also offer IDEs with their compilers and these are generally based on one of the open source IDEs such as Eclipse.

The de facto standard C compiler under POSIX systems is GCC, Gnu Compiler Collection. It has been in use for a long time and it is the base from which many specialist compilers and cross-compilers are derived. Its only disadvantages are its age and the accumulated complexity of so many years. An often-cited alternative is CLang, which is based on a more elegant design and promises faster and more efficient code. In practice there seems to be no decisive advantage in using CLang and, unless you have a good reason, GCC is probably still the best choice.

Beyond CLang and GCC there are a lot of alternative compilers. Probably the best known is Microsoft's C compiler. This works under Visual Studio and does do a good job of compiling C programs, but its main target is C++ and it is usually said that it only supports enough C to make C++ work. However, if you are targeting Windows then it is worth considering. It is also worth knowing that its particular version of C does things slightly differently in many cases and, while these differences are usually small, they can stop a program working. If you are targeting x86 systems then there is Intel's remarkable C compiler, which is tuned to squeeze the last percentage of performance out of the hardware - but at a cost.

Types of Linux?

There are many different cut-down versions of Linux that are intended for use in small realtime systems. In this book only the mainstream Linux distributions, usually Debian, are considered. It used to be the case that for all hardware-based projects a realtime Linux or realtime operating system was necessary. With the increased processing power available this is far less necessary. You can create near-realtime behavior using a standard Linux kernel, and often all that is required is a trimming down of installed packages and a hardening for security. This book isn't about Linux administration or configuration and it is assumed that you will learn how to configure Linux for your needs.

All of the programs in this book have been tested on an x86/64 system running Ubuntu and Cygwin and on a Raspberry Pi 3. The reason for the use of the Raspberry Pi is simply the huge community of users it has gathered around it. There are many "professional" single board machines but none of them has a community of users large enough to address in anything other than a very specialized and targeted book. Other single board computers will come and go, but the Pi has a large enough market to have the inertia needed to keep it around. It has an industrial version and a surprising number of professional users. Don't write it off as a toy.

There is also the fact that ARM devices that are smaller than the Pi generally struggle to run Linux without a great deal of optimization effort. Much of what is true of the Pi is true of other ARM systems and it makes a good example.

What's Covered

So what does this book cover and how do the topics related to one another?

Chapter 2 is an introduction to using system calls and the idea that there is a different execution mode for the operating system versus end user programs. The important glibc library is introduced, along with the idea that you share the machine with other programs.

Chapter 3 is about the problem of actually running your program, including using systemd to run it as a service when the machine first starts. This is essential knowledge before you start to worry about what your program will do.

Chapter 4 explains the way programs interact with signals, the software interrupts generated by the operating system. It is also the first time we meet the "everything is file" idea, which is a recurring theme. As handling signals can be difficult, we also need to find out about non-local jumps. These are C's equivalent of software exceptions and while they are not often used when they are needed nothing else will do.

Chapters 5, 6 and 7 cover the broad subject of arithmetic. Chapter 5 is about integer arithmetic - something that is usually regarded as simple, but when you have to work with it at a low level turns out to be tricky. You need to understand how binary integer arithmetic works. Chapter 6 moves on to introduce the idea of a binary point for representing fractions. It covers fixed point arithmetic, which is often all you need in a limited situation. Chapter 7 explains that floating point arithmetic, so often thought to be the solution to all arithmetic woes, is really a minefield of problems in its own right.

Chapter 8 is about POSIX file handling. It is assumed that you know about standard C's file handling, although there is a short summary. Here we are in the world of file descriptors, which end up describing much more than just files. Files can be used to implement inter-process communication and we look at sharing files and how to implement locking. As an example of how file descriptors go beyond standard files, we also look at pipes and how they can be used to connect processes.

Chapter 9 is dedicated to the grand idea that everything is a file. The pseudo file system turns some very unlikely things into files that you can process as if they were just standard files. You can open them, read them, write to them and close them, but actually what you are working with is nothing like a file, instead it is a piece of hardware. We also look at how files can be loaded into memory and used via memory access, this is a curious round about way of gaining access to the raw hardware.

Chapter 10 is about graphics, which you might find unusual in a book on small systems, but today even small systems have GPUs and graphics comes as standard. It is common to think of adding low-cost output devices such as 7-segment displays to IoT devices, but with low cost HDMI/DVI displays available it becomes cost effective to simply use the built-in graphics hardware. We start from the lowest level with the framebuffer, which is yet another example of everything being a file, then work up to the X11 windowing system and finally to GTK, a complete GUI framework. This chapter cannot make you a graphics expert, but it should provide most of what you need to add displays, and complete user interfaces, to your projects.

Chapter 11 introduces the direct way to the internet. You don't need a web server, you have everything you need in the operating system. Using sockets, yet another example of everything is a file, you can write a web client and server or indeed any sort of client server using your own protocols. This is not only efficient, it can be more secure because, rather than a complete web server, you have something that only does what you want it to.

Chapter 12 returns to core concerns of the low-level programmer with a look at threads. Until recently small machines weren't powerful enough to run multiple processes and the idea of writing multi-threaded programs wasn't an issue. Today things are different and you need to know how to use threads and how to keep them under control. A big part of this chapter is about scheduling, including the relatively new deadline scheduling which makes the need for a custom realtime Linux much less pressing.

Chapter 13 extends the idea of asynchronous code to real parallelism. You can run threads on different cores and manage them yourself. We also look at how C11 provides some advanced ways of dealing with the way modern processors can re-order your instructions and how you can avoid explicit locking using atomic operations.

Chapter 14 returns to a simpler topic - how to implement user mode interrupts. With the help of the poll function and another thread you can implement what looks like an interrupt handler.

Chapter 15 goes beyond C and shows how you can mix it with custom assembler. Your code isn't going to be platform independent but by using inline code you can isolate the dependencies and even let the compiler work out how best to do the job.

Summary

- C is a good language for low level hardware oriented programming. It is fast and can be used to create applications that do not depend on custom drivers.

- C standards are important and keeping to them as much as possible results in a portable program, but hardware dependent behavior makes this difficult if not impossible.

- More problematic is undefined behavior which compiler writers have taken to mean that they can invent any behavior if you make use of it or optimize your program on the assumption that a correct program has no undefined behavior.

- In practice many C programs contain and make use of undefined behavior which is completely defined on a specific system. You can generally turn off aggressive optimization if it makes your program incorrect.

- Undefined behavior results from one faction of C programmers wanting to create a language with no machine dependencies, which is of course impossible if you are concerned with using the raw hardware.

- POSIX is a standard for Unix-like operating systems. If you can't find a C specification for something then the next best thing is often a POSIX standard.

- There are many C compilers and IDEs but GCC is by far the most commonly used. Many machine specific compilers are derived from it.

- There are many real time operating systems, many derived from Linux, but for many applications a standard Linux distribution such as Debian will do the job and has better support.

Chapter 2

Kernel Mode, User Mode & Syscall

Although finding out about the detailed workings of Linux or Unix is unnecessary, it is worth knowing about the general structure of the system. In particular, it is a good idea to know what kernel and user mode are all about and how your programs running in user mode can interact with the kernel using system calls.

The Kernel

The purpose of an operating system is to wrap the hardware, whatever it might be, and present it to user-level software in a uniform way. It also exists to make the hardware seem more sophisticated and easier to use. For example, a disk storage, or any block storage, device generally works at the hardware level in terms of blocks of data. It is the operating system that organizes these blocks into the named files that you are so familiar with. Without the operating system there would be no files or directories. Linux, for example, supports a number of different filing systems with different properties.

The key idea is that an operating system should be a software layer between user programs and the hardware. In a modern design it should also act as a security feature in the sense that it, and only it, should have access to the hardware. That is, user-space programs are prohibited from directly accessing the hardware.

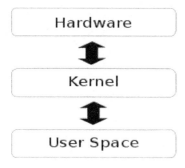

Putting this another way, kernel mode is for trusted software which can do anything. User mode is untrusted and is restricted in the memory and hardware it can access, and how it can interact with the kernel.

It is important to realize that all of the software that you use - the shell, the compiler, text editors, libraries, services and so on all run in user mode. Indeed most of what users think of as making up the operating system runs in user mode, and is no different from any program that you can write.

Multi-tasking - Context Switch

Also notice that there can be many user mode programs loaded and the Kernel will allocate each a share of the processor's time. In the early days there was just one processor which implies that only one program was running at any given time. Today even low-cost SBCs can have two or more cores, which allow more than one user program to run at a time. Even in these cases. the Kernel will mange multiple processes to make it look as if more programs are running than there are cores. The Kernel will allocate a program some time and when that time is up the Kernel interrupts it and stores its state. It then chooses another process to start and allocates it some time to run. The way that the Kernel swaps processes is generally called a "context switch" and, as it is an expensive operation, usually programs are allocated comparatively large units of time. Exactly which program gets to run next is a matter of scheduling, and operating systems generally support more than one scheduling algorithm.

If you are familiar with running code on small embedded processors this will be a strange idea. Your program doesn't get to run 100% of the time. For real-time programs you need to guarantee all sorts of service requirements. For example, if you are generating a signal by toggling a GPIO line, you can't afford to have your program interrupted for any significant time. What a significant time is depends on the application. In a single core system you cannot force a user program to take over the processor 100% of the time simply because the Kernel needs to do some work every now and again. On a multi-core processor the situation isn't so clear cut. You might think at this point that context switching makes Linux a poor choice for any real-time work. This isn't usually true, but you need to keep in mind that there are some difficulties in implementing the most critical applications. See Chapter 12 on scheduling and Chapter 13 on cores.

Modes and Syscall

You might wonder how the kernel can protect itself from modification by user mode programs and how it can stop user mode programs from accessing hardware directly. The answer varies according to the architecture in use but in a modern processor the protection is provided by the hardware. For example the x86 supports four protection "rings" - levels of decreasing privilege. Linux only uses two of these levels - ring 0 for the Kernel and ring 3 for user mode. ARM processors support multiple modes, but again Linux only makes use of user mode and supervisor mode.

In general things are arranged so that a user mode program cannot call code, a function say, that lives in the kernel. This is for reasons of security and stability.

So how does a user mode program communicate its needs to the Kernel?

The answer is that it has to make a system call. Exactly how this is done varies according to the architecture, but it usually involves a software interrupt or something similar.

The basic idea is that at the level of assembly language the parameters to be passed to the Kernel have to be loaded into specific registers. One of the registers holds a number which determines what the system call actually is. To make the call you usually have to use a software interrupt instruction.

For an x86 it is software interrupt `0x80`, i.e. int `0x80`; for ARM it is a SWI (SoftWare Interrupt) instruction, but the number varies according to the exact type. When the software interrupt is issued the hardware changes mode and the user thread starts to execute kernel code. The first thing that happens is that the syscall number is looked up in a table which holds the addresses of the functions which implement each of the actions. These syscall numbers don't change much, if at all, to make sure that code continues to work. However, new syscalls are added, and indeed if you have the time you can add custom syscalls to the kernel.

The actual syscall number, i.e. the number that determines what is to be done, is passed in a particular register. For example x86-64 uses `rax`. Parameters to a `syscall` are usually passed in particular registers - up to seven. These are best thought of as positional, i.e. `arg1` to `arg7` are passed in a specified set of registers - for example for the x86 `arg1` is passed in `rdi`. Return values are similarly passed back in particular registers. In most cases there is s a single return value and an error number.

A syscall is defined by its number and a set of positional parameters. For example, write is syscall 4, i.e. it is fourth in the syscall table, and it has parameters:

1 file descriptor

2 pointer to buffer

3 number of characters

The return value is the number of characters written with -1 being an error indicator.

Glibc - Wrappers

Obviously you cannot make a syscall using C. The reason is that there is no C standard way of invoking a software interrupt or similar. This is completely machine dependent and there are even variations between processors that in principle share the same architecture - x64 and ARM for example. You could code the syscall using embedded assembler, see Chapter 15, but then you would have to change the code for each type of processor you wanted to support.

A much better solution is to use a library of wrapper functions which perform the syscall for you and adjust to the type of processor in use. This is what you have been doing since you first started to create C programs.

The library that most programmers use is glibc and it contains definitions for most of the Linux syscalls and the standard library functions you have been using. There are many header files associated with glibc including stdio.h and stdlib, which are included into most C programs, but there are many more. It is standard practice to add only the header files for the features of glibc you plan to use. One complication is that glibc isn't stored at a standard location and the library is usually called libc6 - the source is called glibc.

The complication with glibc is that it is focused on implementing POSIX and C11 rather than Linux. As a result, while it does wrap most of the Linux syscalls it misses out some that are non-standard. Notice that glibc contains more than just syscalls. For example, printf is defined in glibc and, while this does eventually call the kernel to print things, it does a lot more than just wrap the write syscall.

There are functions in declared in `unistd.h` for most Linux syscalls, but not all. For example, the `write` function which implements `syscall` 4, described in the last section, is declared as:

```
ssize_t write(int fd, const void *buf, size_t count);
```

The actual code that implements this loads the registers for each of the parameters in turn and then uses a software interrupt to transition to kernel mode. For example:

```
const char string[] = "Hello Syscall World \n";
write(1, string, 21);
```

prints the message on `stdout`.

There is a lower level wrapper function which can be used to implement any syscall. This is defined as:

```
long syscall(long number, ...);
```

the first parameter gives the syscall number and the rest of the parameter list consists of however many parameters are required.

For example the `syscall` to `write` given earlier can be written:

```
const char string[] = "Hello Syscall World \n";
syscall(4, 1, string, 21);
```

To make this work you not only need `uinstd.h` but also

```
#define _GNU_SOURCE
```

at the start of the program because `syscall` is not part of POSIX.

It is more usual not to hard code the syscall numbers but to use constants defined in `syscall.h`:

```
#include <syscall.h>
syscall(SYS_write, 1, string, 21);
```

Of course, if there is a wrapper function defined in `glibc` then it is best to use it. The problem is that `glibc` often takes a while to catch up with anything new in Linux and there is a general resistance to include anything that is Linux-specific. In Chapter 12 it is explained that a scheduling option that is unique to Linux has no wrapper in `glibc`. In this case the simplest thing to do is to use `syscall` to create your own wrappers:

```
int sched_setattr(pid_t pid, const struct sched_attr *attr,
                                    unsigned int flags) {
    return syscall(__NR_sched_setattr, pid, attr, flags);
}
int sched_getattr(pid_t pid,struct sched_attr *attr,
                    unsigned int size, unsigned int flags){
    return syscall(__NR_sched_getattr, pid, attr, size, flags);
}
```

Your Code In Kernel Mode

Now that we know how to call kernel mode functions, we can move on to the next question, does your code need to run in kernel mode? If you are used to running code with no operating system, or perhaps a minimal runtime, then you might think that kernel mode is essential. This isn't the case. Moving to kernel mode is a lot more work than coding in user mode. For one thing, you don't have access to the libraries that you are so familiar with, and they don't have easy access to floating point. They do, however, have complete access to all of the hardware; they can respond to interrupts and they have a higher level of execution privilege, but they can still be interrupted. Even a kernel function doesn't have the machine all to itself.

If you still think that kernel code is an attractive proposition you need to know that you can achieve nearly as much in user space with the right techniques, as explained later in this book. My advice is to always start implementing your project in user space and only transition it to kernel mode if there is no other way to meet its requirements.

How do you create kernel mode code?

There are two routes - one hard and one easier. The "hard" way is to add to the kernel by compiling it and including your own syscalls. The problem with this is that you create a non-standard operating system and face the task of maintaining it through subsequent kernel releases.

A simpler way of doing the same job is to write a kernel module. A kernel module is close to what would be called an installable driver in another operating system. A module can be installed by the user via the `insmod` or more commonly the `modprobe` command. You can find out about modules using the `lsmod` command and you can remove a module using the `rmmod` command. Modules are completely general and don't have to be implemented as drivers, but the way that they interact with the kernel is fixed - there has to be an initialization function and a cleanup function. Once you move beyond this you have to learn how to implement the specific type of module you are trying to create – a character device driver, for example. Getting into kernel mode is just the start of the story, you also have to learn how to do what you want within it.

Learning to write kernel modules is a worthwhile, but tough, education and it would fill a book on its own, so for the remainder of this book we concentrate on achieving many of the same results but in user space.

Security

The whole point of kernel mode and user mode is to increase the security of the system. All user programs are suspect, and they are restricted in what they can do and what hardware they can access. Security is an important issue for everyone and it is just as important for the low-level hardware programmer. The IoT is notoriously insecure and there are horror stories of devices being hacked every week. This has resulted in an over-reaction from some system builders who attempt to lock down the hardware as much as possible. This is a reasonable approach to a desktop system, or any system where the user can install new programs. However, for many dedicated devices the code that is installed is trustworthy. That is, if you create a program to operate as a central heating controller, say, then the code you create is by definition trustworthy and should be allowed as much access to the hardware as possible. There is no point in putting up barriers that low-level code is going to have to overcome in any case to get its job done.

In practice, low-level code, with the right approaches, can access nearly all of the memory in a system, including memory-mapped I/O. About the only thing that cannot be achieved is working directly with interrupts and this is a problem if response time is important.

The brings us to the question of what does security mean for a low-level program? The risk only comes from interactions with the outside world. For example, all inputs have to be "sanitized" in the sense that they should not be allowed to cause your program to behave in exploitable ways. That is, inputs should not cause buffer overruns or the execution of other code. It is also important that any source or sink of data is authorized, usually by using a password or, better, a key file. In addition, data that is transferred over public connections should be encrypted. For IoT programs it is particularly important to make sure that upgrade mechanisms are secure using the same techniques.

In short, there is nothing dangerous in your program running as `root` as long as it is your program and remains so.

Summary

- Most operating systems have different levels of execution. In Linux the kernel code can do more or less anything, but user space code is restricted in various ways.

- One of the many services the operating system provides is multi-tasking. It allows multiple user space programs to be loaded into memory and it allocates some processor time to each so as to make it look as if multiple programs are running at the same time.

- You can access the services provided by the operating system by making system calls or sys calls.

- The glibc library allows you to avoid having to implement your own sys calls by providing functions, wrappers, which do the same job.

- You can write your own kernel extensions as installable modules, but this isn't usually necessary and it is more complicated.

- Security is a big problem for the IoT and embedded programs in general. Conventional security often gets between your program and the hardware and does little to improve real security.

- IoT and embedded security is more about checking what inputs are being received by sanitizing the data, identifying its source using passwords or key files and encrypting data being transported.

Chapter 3

Execution, Permissions & Systemd

One of the problems that you have to solve when you are getting near to moving from development to deployment is how to get your program to run. This can be as simple as using the command line, or automatically running the program when the machine starts up. There are lots of different ways of auto-running a program, but increasingly the solution is to use systemd. In this chapter we take a look at the basic idea of an executable and using systemd to control it.

Permissions

Every file in a POSIX system has a set of permissions associated with it. These are implemented as a bit mask which specifies the permissions for the owner, the group and other users. Each has a three-bit field specifying read, write and execute - rwx. If the bit is set then the owner, group or other users can read, write or execute the file. From our point of view, the important permission is execute. If the execute bit isn't set then the program cannot be run by the entity it applies to. You can read each group of three bits as an octal number or you can use the convention that writing a minus sign in the position means that it is zero. So rwxr--r--

means:

```
r w x   r - -   r - -
1 1 1   1 0 0   1 0 0
```

or:

```
744
```

and the owner can read, write and execute the file but a group member or other user can only read the file.

You can use this notation with the chmod command to set a file's permission bits. For example:

```
chmod rwxr--r-- myProgram
```

and you can check the permission bits using:

```
ls -1
```

When a program is run from the command line it executes as if it was the user who started the program. That is, if the user is harry and runs myProgram then myProgram has all of the access rights that harry has, and no more. Notice that the program not only runs with the user's identity, it also runs as if it was a member of the groups that the user is a member of.

You can change this behavior by setting the SUID bit in the permissions. If the SUID bit is set then the program runs with the permissions of the file's owner. In this case, if harry runs myProgram, a file owned by root, say, with its SUID bit set, then it runs with all the access rights of root. To set the SUID bit you can use chmod and instead of using x for the owner execute, use s for sUID. You can also use a fourth octal digit with the SUID bit as the most significant, or you can use s in the symbolic specification of permissions.

For example:

```
chmod rws--r--r myProgram
```

allows myProgram to run with its owner's rights.

You can also use the s notation in the same way to set the group id bit SGID by placing it in the "others" permissions in place of x. This is not as useful, however, unless something like group file quotas are being enforced.

Notice that permissions have different effects on a folder and this discussion applies to files.

Running a Program

If you are using an IDE like NetBeans you may not have tried to run one of your programs from the command line with the Run command doing the job for you. Sooner or later you are going to have to run the compiled program outside of the IDE. This can be slightly more involved than you might expect. In particular, if you are using a remote build server the executable may not be on the machine that the IDE runs on.

There is also the small matter of debug versus release versions. An IDE like NetBeans allows you to set different configurations - usually debug and release. The difference is simply the compiler options chosen. For example, NetBeans uses:

```
-g -Wall -std=c99
```

for debug and:

```
-std=c99
```

for release.

Of course, you can change these. If you do select something more complicated, remember that you have only tested your debug configuration and there could be new bugs due to changes in compiler options.

The executable file is usually stored in a release or debug directory. This may be located deep in your home directory if you are using a remote build server. NetBeans, for example, uploads the code and places the executable in a hidden folder in the user's home directory. You can find its location by reading the output window. To run the program from the command line the simplest thing to do is to copy the file to your home directory.

GCC automatically sets the executable's permissions to rwxr-xr-x, which means any user can run it. If you are new to Linux then you might be surprised that you cannot actually run the program by simply typing its name at the command prompt. That is:

```
myProgram
```

doesn't work. The reason is that, unlike Windows, Linux does not run programs in the current directory by default for security reasons. When you enter the name of an executable, Linux looks for it in all the directories listed in the PATH environment variable and in any directory that you specify as part of the command. You can find the current directories in the PATH using:

```
echo "$PATH"
```

You can add the current directory or any directory to the PATH using something like:

```
PATH=$PATH:/path/to/new/dir; export PATH
```

but this is generally regarded as a bad idea from a security point of view. Instead, to run the program from your current directory use:

```
./myProgram
```

the ./ means use the current directory.

Automatically Running a Program - systemd

Most low-level programs need to run automatically when the system starts. There are quite a few different ways of doing this, but for a modern Linux-based system the best way of doing the job is to use systemd. It is slightly more complicated than some alternatives but it has many additional features. Systemd is often referred to as a replacement for the original Unix System V init and it will read and work with sysvinit configuration files.

You will also find Linux systems that use alternatives to systemd - Upstart, runit, launchd and more. The only commonly encountered alternative running on smaller devices, such as within the mbed operating system, is

BusyBox init, which is much simpler. Anything running full Linux is likely to support systemd.

The basic object in systemd is a unit - something to be run when the system starts. There are a number of different types of unit but in most cases you will be interested in a service unit. A unit is defined by its configuration file, called a unit file. System supplied unit files are generally stored in /lib/systemd/system and any new unit files you create should be added to /etc/systemd/system which take priority over any unit files in the /lib directory with the same name.

A unit file is a description of the program that you want systemd to run and how to do the job. It has the same name as the service you want to run and ends in .system. Typically there are three sections:

[Unit]   contains information not specifically related to the type of the unit, such as the service description.

[Service]   contains information about the specific type of the unit.

[Install]   contains information about the installation of the unit.

Let's suppose you have a compiled C program, myservice, in a home directory /home/pi which simply prints a message every five seconds:

```c
#include <stdio.h>
#include <stdlib.h>
#include <unistd.h>
int main(int argc, char** argv) {
    while (1) {
        printf("Hello systemd world \n");
        fflush(NULL);
        sleep(5);
    };
    return (EXIT_SUCCESS);
}
```

To run this at startup you need to create it a unit file:

```
[Unit]
Description=My Hello Service

[Service]
Type=simple
ExecStart=/home/pi/myservice
Restart=on-failure
RestartSec=10
KillMode=process

[Install]
WantedBy=multi-user.target
```

This should be created in /etc/systemd/system and be called myService.service and you will need root privileges to do this.

Let's look at what the different parts of the unit file do.

The first section just contains a description:

```
[Unit]
Description=My Hello Service
```

Description is used by systemd commands to refer to your service.

The second section defines how your program should be run:

```
[Service]
Type=simple
ExecStart=/home/pi/myservice
Restart=on-failure
RestartSec=10
KillMode=process
```

Type sets the basic behavior of the program. The default is simple which is just a program that can be run from the command line. The ExecStart parameter is the command line instruction that starts your program running. In this case it is just the location of the executable, but in other cases it might start an interpreter and run a script. The Restart parameter tells systemd when to restart your program and RestartSec tells it how long to wait before doing so. Finally KillMode specifies how to stop your program; in this case by killing the process that is running your program.

The final section tells systemd when to start your program running:

```
[Install]
WantedBy=multi-user.target
```

this specifies which other units or targets depend on your program. In this case multi-user.target is used to specify that your program is to be started when the system reaches what used to be called runlevel2, i.e. the system is loaded enough to run multi-user consoles, but not a GUI.

Other runlevel targets are:

Run Level	Target Units	Description
0	runlevel0.target, poweroff.target	Shut down and power off
1	runlevel1.target, rescue.target	Set up a rescue shell
2,3,4	runlevel[234].target, multi-user.target	Set up a non-gfx multi-user shell
5	runlevel5.target, graphical.target	Set up a gfx multi-user shell
6	runlevel6.target, reboot.target	Shut down and reboot the system

It is also worth knowing that systemd is the first program to run after the kernel has been loaded and the file system has been set up. Notice that systemd also supports mount and device units which will perform what you might think were low level configuration after the kernel has loaded.

WantedBy says that the target needs the program started, but nothing will happen if it doesn't start. You can also use Required by to state a hard dependence where the target will shut down if the unit doesn't start.

There are many more options that can be used to specify dependencies and the order that units should be started in or restarted. The unit file listed above is a simple example to get you started on using systemd.

Systemctl

Assuming you have created the program executable in the directory and created the unit file, you can get systemd to notice it by restarting it. Most of your command line interaction with systemd is via the systemctl command.

You can even use it to create or edit a unit file:

```
sudo systemctl edit  myService --full --force
```

This opens the default editor and creates a file called myService.service in /etc/systemd/system. If the unit already exists don't use --force.

If you just want to override a few parameters of an existing unit file you can also use:

```
sudo systemctl edit myService
```

which creates a file called override.conf under a directory at /etc/systemd/system/myService.service.

When you create a unit file systemd only knows about it after a reboot or a manual reload using:

```
sudo systemctl daemon-reload
```

After this systemd knows about your unit file but doesn't do anything with it. If you want it to start automatically then you have to use:

```
sudo systemctl enable myService
```

Following this myService will start at the next reboot. To stop this happening you simply use the same command with disable.

You can also start, stop and restart the unit. Notice that if you change the unit file you also have to use daemon-reload to make systemd reread the unit file. If you change the program executable then restart is enough to reload the code.

To summarize, some useful `systemctl` commands, including some not described in the text, are:

Command	Action
enable	start service on boot
disable	do not start service on boot
start	start service
stop	stop service
restart	restart service
status	show status
list-units --type=service --all	list all active service units
list-units-files --type=service	list all service units
list-unit-files --type=target	list all targets
edit --full --force	edit a service file

Of course to use any of these you add the command to systemctl, i.e.

```
sudo systemctl command
```
and the name of the unit where required.

So assuming that you have the program file in the home directory and the unit file given earlier you can set things up so that it is loaded at boot time using:

```
sudo systemctl daemon-reload
sudo systemctl enable myService
```

and to run it without a reboot:

```
sudo systemctl start myService
```

At this point you might be wondering what permissions a service has? The answer is that by default a service runs as root and has full root permissions. This sounds like a security problem, but only a user with root access can create a unit file or use `systemctl`. If everything is correctly constructed there is little security problem with a service running as root. However, many services run as their own user and in their own group. You can change the default user and groups by adding to the [Service] section:

```
User=username
Group=groupname
```

If your service only needs a subset of root's permissions then setting up a user and group just for it is a good way to allow for customization and sharing of resources.

Journal

To find out the current status of your program you can use the `status` command which also provides a short extract from its log. Although many of the legacy Linux log files are still supported, systemd is supposed to be used by programs to log events. The journal is a central store for all messages logged by the system and all units. It is a binary file and you need to use the `journalctl` command to read it. There are many forms of the command and it is worth finding out how to filter the logs for what you are looking for. To see the log output from `myService` all we need is:

```
sudo journalctl -f -a -umyService
```

The `-f` means show only new log messages and `-a` makes sure that the data that the service has sent to the log is treated as ASCII rather than as a binary blob.

When you see the output you will know exactly where the `printf` has been sending its text.

```
-- Logs begin at Fri 2019-03-22 06:20:23 UTC. --
Mar 23 17:38:57 MyServer myservice[10302]: Hello systemd world
Mar 23 17:39:02 MyServer myservice[10302]: Hello systemd world
Mar 23 17:39:07 MyServer myservice[10302]: Hello systemd world
Mar 23 17:39:12 MyServer myservice[10302]: Hello systemd world
. . .
```

When running as a service, your program's `stdout` and `stderr` are sent to the journal. You can change this using

```
StandardOutput=file:/var/log/logfile
StandardError=file:/var/log/logfileerr
```

This form starts the log file each time the system is rebooted. If you want to keep the log files use `append:` in place of `file:`.

Logs are deleted and recreated on each boot. If you want them to persist you have to configure the journal in detail, including how long you want them kept and how much space can be allocated - consult the documentation.

Restart and Watch Dog

One of the advantages of using systemd is that you can control how your program is automatically monitored and restarted if there is a problem. Our sample unit file has two parameters relating to restarting in the [Service] section:

```
Restart=on-failure
RestartSec=10
```

This means that our program will only be auto-restarted if it exits with a failure code, i.e. any non-zero value. The number of seconds specifies how long systemd will wait before restarting and the default is 100ms. If you want your program to be restarted if it exits for any reason then you can use:

```
Restart=always
```

If you make this change to the example unit file and restart it with the new settings:

```
sudo systemctl daemon-reload
sudo systemctl start myService
```

then a status check will confirm that it is running. You can find the service's process identification number (PID) from the status listing - the number in square brackets:

```
Mar 24 11:08:29 MyServer myservice[11419]: Hello systemd world
```

You can now use this to kill the service:

```
sudo kill 11419
```

and when you check its status you should see something like:

```
● myService.service - My Hello Service
   Loaded: loaded (/etc/systemd/system/myService.service; enabled; vendor
preset: enabled)
   Active: inactive (dead) since Sun 2019-03-24 11:06:14 UTC; 2s ago
  Process: 11419 ExecStart=/home/pi/myservice (code=killed, signal=TERM)
 Main PID: 11419 (code=killed, signal=TERM)
```

If you check the status after 10 seconds you should see the program running again.

It is important to know that systemd gives up restarting your service if it fails to start more than 5 times within a 10 seconds interval. There are two [Unit] options that control this:

```
StartLimitBurst=5
StartLimitIntervalSec=10
```

A simpler way is to use the RestartSec parameter. For example, if you set it to restart after 3 seconds, then you can never reach 5 failed retries within 10 seconds.

Often restart is enough but imagine that your program has a tendency to go into a useless infinite loop. In this case it doesn't end abnormally or normally and it isn't restarted. To protect against running but otherwise ineffective programs, you can set a watchdog.

If you include:

```
WatchdogSec=5
```

in the [Service] section your program has to send a keep-alive-ping every 5 seconds or it will be restarted. To be more precise, if the ping doesn't happen after 5 seconds the program is stopped using a SIGABRT and the program is restarted.

To send a keep-alive-ping you need to use the sd_notify() system call. There are several strings that you can pass which inform systemd of various states or state changes in your program, but if you send "WATCHDOG=1" then this resets the watchdog timer.

To make use of sd_notify you have to make sure that the systemd libraries are installed. On Debian systems you can do this using:

```
sudo apt-get update
sudo apt-get install libsystemd-dev
```

After this you also need to make sure that the compiler can find the header libraries. This is automatic on most systems, but if you are using a remote build machine on NetBeans you need to let it find the system tools again to update its libraries. Select the Services tab and select the Tools Collection of the server you want to update. Finally select Properties and click the Restore Defaults button which rescans the server for the tool chain and the configuration including the header files.

You also have to add the library file so that the linker can find it. Either use NetBeans to add the library file systemd or add -lsystemd to the compiler options.

With these modifications we can change our demonstration service to use a watchdog.

The C program is:

```c
#include <stdio.h>
#include <stdlib.h>
#include <unistd.h>
#include <systemd/sd-daemon.h>

int main(int argc, char** argv) {
    while (1) {
        printf("Hello systemd world \n");
        fflush(NULL);
        sleep(rand()%7+1);
        sd_notify(0, "WATCHDOG=1");
    };
    return (EXIT_SUCCESS);
}
```

Now the program prints to the journal after a random pause between 1 and 7. If we set the timeout to 6 seconds:

```
WatchdogSec=6
```

then there is a one in seven chance of a timeout:

```
[Unit]
Description=My Hello Service

[Service]
Type=simple
ExecStart=/home/pi/myservice
Restart=always
RestartSec=10
KillMode=process
WatchdogSec=6

[Install]
WantedBy=multi-user.target
```

After making these changes you need to do to reload the unit file and the service is:

```
sudo systemctl daemon-reload
sudo systemctl restart  myService
```

You can monitor what is happening using:

```
sudo journalctl -f -a -umyService
```

Sooner or later you will see something like:

```
Mar 24 17:17:36 MyServer myservice[15370]: Hello systemd world
Mar 24 17:17:39 MyServer myservice[15370]: Hello systemd world
Mar 24 17:17:45 MyServer myservice[15370]: Hello systemd world
Mar 24 17:17:51 MyServer systemd[1]: myService.service: Watchdog timeout
(limit 6s)!
Mar 24 17:17:51 MyServer systemd[1]: myService.service: Killing process
15370 (myservice) with signal SIGABRT.
Mar 24 17:17:51 MyServer systemd[1]: myService.service: Main process exited,
code=killed, status=6/ABRT
Mar 24 17:17:51 MyServer systemd[1]: myService.service: Unit entered failed
state.
Mar 24 17:17:51 MyServer systemd[1]: myService.service: Failed with result
'watchdog'.
Mar 24 17:18:01 MyServer systemd[1]: myService.service: Service hold-off
time over, scheduling restart.
Mar 24 17:18:01 MyServer systemd[1]: Stopped My Hello Service.
Mar 24 17:18:01 MyServer systemd[1]: Started My Hello Service.
Mar 24 17:18:01 MyServer myservice[15394]: Hello systemd world
Mar 24 17:18:03 MyServer myservice[15394]: Hello systemd world
```

Notice that after the timeout systemd waits for the restart hold-off of ten seconds before restarting the service.

It is usually a good idea to use sd_notify to send systemd a message that your service has started:

```
sd_notify (0, "READY=1");
```

Periodic Execution

Often you want to run a program at a set interval or date. The usual solution to this is to use cron, which has been part of Unix and Linux for a long time. However, there are a lot of reasons for using systemd to do the same job. Timers in systemd are integrated with units and are sophisticated and flexible. The main disadvantage to using systemd is that you have to create a unit file and a timer file to run a program at a given time. If you are already using systemd, however, then you know how to create a unit file and how to use systemctl to modify how things work.

A timer has two files, usually with the same name. One has the suffix .timer and contains parameters that specify when the program will run, and the other has the suffix .service, which controls how the program runs. You already know how to create a .service file and the only change is that for a timer it doesn't need an [install] as the .timer file controls when the program is run.

A .timer file has to be enabled and started to actually run the program and this is done using the usual systemctl commands. Note that it is the timer you start and it will start the program when appropriate.

The timer can specify either exact dates and times when a program should run, such as the first of the month or at 10:00 every day, or it can specify time spans, such as every 10 minutes. The time spans can be set relative to a number of different clocks" - e.g, time since the timer was activated or time since the last boot. If the machine is suspended these "clocks" are stopped, unlike the calendar clock which continues. If a timer is overdue then usually the timer is triggered immediately. By default a timer is not persistent, but you can make it so and in this case the time of last firing is stored on disk and when the timer is started it will fire immediately if it has missed a triggering.

As a simple example, we can re-implement the hello systemd program so that a systemd timer runs it every five seconds. The program, myService, is:

```
#include <stdio.h>
#include <stdlib.h>
int main(int argc, char** argv) {
    printf("Hello systemd world \n");
    fflush(NULL);
    return (EXIT_SUCCESS);
}
```

The timer file is:

```
[Unit]
Description=Run myService every 5s

[Timer]
OnUnitActiveSec=5s

[Install]
WantedBy=timers.target
```

This specifies that the service should be run every 5 seconds after the timer is started.

The unit file is very simple:

```
[Unit]
Description=My Hello Service

[Service]
Type=simple
ExecStart=/home/pi/myservice
KillMode=process
```

Notice that there are things that you cannot specify in a unit file that is intended to be used with a timer. For example, if you set restart=always then the first instance of the program that the timer creates will be restarted when it finishes.

To make all this work you have to restart systemd:

```
sudo systemctl daemon-reload:
```

and then start the timer:

```
sudo systemctl start  myService.timer
```

After this you can look at the service's journal to see what is happening:

```
sudo journalctl -f -a -umyService
```

which should produce something like:

```
Mar 25 18:43:29 MyServer systemd[1]: Started My Hello Service.
Mar 25 18:43:29 MyServer myservice[20882]: Hello systemd world
Mar 25 18:43:53 MyServer systemd[1]: Started My Hello Service.
Mar 25 18:43:53 MyServer myservice[20906]: Hello systemd world
Mar 25 18:44:30 MyServer systemd[1]: Started My Hello Service.
Mar 25 18:44:30 MyServer myservice[20909]: Hello systemd world
```

Notice that now each time the server sends its message to the log it is running with a different PID, i.e. it is started anew each time. Also notice that the time stamps reveal that it isn't being run every five seconds as requested, but at times typically ranging from 10s to 30s. The reason for this is that the timer is only guaranteed to fire in an interval given by specified time + accuracy. That is, the program won't run before its specified time, but it could be delayed by an amount given by:

```
AccuracySec=accuracy
```

The default is one minute and the purpose of this is to reduce the load on the machine in checking for timeouts. With the default accuracy our program will be run after 5 seconds to 65 seconds. You can also specify a random time to be added to the timer:

```
RandomizedDelaySec=maximum delay
```

You can specify multiple trigger times and you can mix calendar and interval specifications. For example:

```
[Timer]
OnBootSec=15min
OnUnitActiveSec=5m
```

specifies that the program runs 15 minutes after boot and then every 5 minutes after that.

The only thing you now have to master is how to specify when the timer should fire - and there are a lot of options. You can set any of the following time intervals:

OnActiveSec=	time from the activation of the timer
OnBootSec=	time from boot
OnStartupSec=	time from when systemd started
OnUnitActiveSec=	time from last activation of unit
OnUnitInactiveSec=	time from last deactivation of unit

You can use any of the following time units:

- usec, us, μs
- msec, ms
- seconds, second, sec, s
- minutes, minute, min, m
- hours, hour, hr, h
- days, day, d
- weeks, week, w
- months, month, M (defined as 30.44 days)
- years, year, y (defined as 365.25 days)

If you want to set a calendar time and date then you need to use:

OnCalendar=*date and time*

The only problem you have with this is how to specify the date and time as the notation is sophisticated enough to specify some complex dates and times.

For example:

Thu,Fri 2019-*-1,5 11:12:13

specifies 11:12:13 of the first or fifth day of any month of the year 2019, but only if that day is a Thursday or Friday.

The overall form is:

dayOfWeek year-month-day hour:minute:second timezone

The man page explains it well:

> *The weekday specification is optional. If specified, it should consist of one or more English language weekday names, either in the abbreviated (Wed) or non-abbreviated (Wednesday) form (case does not matter), separated by commas. Specifying two weekdays separated by ".." refers to a range of continuous weekdays. "," and ".." may be combined freely.*

> *In the date and time specifications, any component may be specified as "*" in which case any value will match. Alternatively, each component can be specified as a list of values separated by commas. Values may be suffixed with "/" and a repetition value, which indicates that the value itself and the value plus all multiples of the repetition value are matched. Two values separated by ".." may be used to indicate a range of values; ranges may also be followed with "/" and a repetition value.*

> *A date specification may use "~" to indicate the last day(s) in a month. For example, "*-02~03" means "the third last day in February," and "Mon *-05~07/1" means "the last Monday in May."*

> *The seconds component may contain decimal fractions both in the value and the repetition. All fractions are rounded to 6 decimal places.*

> *Either time or date specification may be omitted, in which case the current day and 00:00:00 is implied, respectively. If the second component is not specified, ":00" is assumed.*

> *Timezone can be specified as the literal string "UTC", or the local timezone.*

It should be obvious that you can use the wider `systemctl` commands to list timers and so on.

For example, to list all timers use:

```
systemctl list-timers --all
```

If you are still unconvinced that `systemd` is a good way to automate the running of your programs then you can use `cron` to do periodic execution. It is simply a matter of adding a calendar time specification and the executable as a single line added to the list of cron jobs. The advantage of systemd is that you can arrange a complex set of dependencies, auto executions, auto restarts and periodic execution and it is easy to set up using a C program to write the unit files and give the `systemctl` commands needed.

Summary

- Linux permissions control which users can read, write or execute a file depending on their identity and group membership.

- Compilers generally automatically set the executable they produce to executable, but you still cannot run the program unless you give a path as well as its file name. This is because Linux does not search for programs in the current directory for security reasons. The simplest path is ./ which means "this directory".

- Systemd is rapidly becoming the standard way to run a program on startup.

- It is worth learning to use systemctl to create units needed to run programs. It is also used to install, start, stop and restart programs.

- Systemd maintains a central journal where all services log their status.

- You can specify restart and watchdog functions to make sure that your program is always running.

- Systemd is also a replacement for cron and can be used to run a program at a given time or periodically.

Chapter 4

Signals & Exceptions

Signals are the POSIX way of implementing software interrupts. They are used to inform user-space programs that something has happened and they are also used to terminate a program. Going beyond this they can be generated by user-mode programs to signal to other programs. That is, they can be used as a simple form of inter-process communication (IPC). A signal causes the user program to abandon its normal execution and transfers control to another location. This can be thought of as an exception. There is no exception handling defined within the C language. C has no try-catch type of construct, but there is a standard facility for implementing the same sort of behavior - the longjmp - which deserves to be better known.

Signal Basics

There are a number of system-generated signals, which are mostly the result of hardware interrupts that occur in the kernel, which are converted into signals and delivered to the user-mode program that caused them.

There are a many different signals and variations on the standards. The table below list the most commonly encountered.

Signal	Value	Action	Comment
SIGINT	2	Term	Interrupt from keyboard Ctrl-C
SIGQUIT	3	Core	Quit from keyboard Ctrl-\
SIGABRT	6	Core	Abort signal from the abort function
SIGFPE	8	Core	Floating-point exception
SIGKILL	9	Term	Kill signal
SIGSEGV	11	Core	Invalid memory reference
SIGTERM	15	Term	Termination signal
SIGSTOP	23	Stop	Stop process
SIGCONT	25	Cont	Continue if stopped

The Action column indicates the default action performed in response to the signal. There are four possibilities:

Term = terminate process
Core = terminate and perform a core dump
Stop = stop process
Cont = continue process if stoppe

While these actions are the default behaviors, a process can block a signal, ignore a signal, or handle it with a custom function. A signal that is set to be ignored is lost, but a signal that is blocked remains pending until it is unblocked. If a signal occurs again while it is blocked, only a single instance of the signal is retained.

For obvious reasons SIGKILL and SIGSTOP cannot be ignored, blocked or handled. SIGABRT can be blocked and it can be handled, but it still terminates the process when the handler returns unless you arrange for it not to - see later.

Notice that there are multiple ways terminate a program.

There are two ways to issue a terminate signal to a running process using the kill command line program.

The SIGKILL signal terminates the process immediately and as it cannot be be handled, blocked or ignored it is the signal of last resort. Notice the process gets no chance to do a cleanup operation. You can send SIGKILL to a process using the command:

kill -SIGKILL pid or kill -9 pid

The SIGTERM signal terminates the process but it can be handled, blocked or ignored and so the process has time to clean up and end gracefully. You can send this to a process using the command:

kill -SIGTERM pid or just kill pid

as SIGTERM is the default.

There are two ways to terminate the foreground process using the terminal.

The SIGINT signal terminates the process but it can be handled, blocked or ignored and so the process has time to clean up and end gracefully. You send this signal to the foreground process by pressing Ctrl-C.

The SIGQUIT signal behaves like SIGINT, but with the addition of a core dump. You can send the signal to the foreground process by pressing Ctrl-\.

SIGSTOP and SIGCONT are used by the kernel to start and stop processes. SIGSTOP cannot be handled, blocked or ignored, and SIGCONT is used to restart the process.

Finally, it is worth taking note of the way SIGABRT behaves. This signal is generated by some machine errors or by calling the abort function. It can be handled, but what happens is that first SIGABRT is automatically unblocked. That is, it always interrupts the program without delay. If there is a handler, it gets to run. If there is no handler, the process is terminated. If the handler returns, it is disabled and SIGABRT is sent a second time, so terminating the process. So the handler gets to run, but the process is always aborted. This is not always what you want and how to modify this behavior is described later.

Dealing with Async

It is important that you realize that signals occur asynchronously. Your program can be interrupted at any time by a signal. If you have a handler set then, unless you take steps to block signals, it too can be interrupted. When a handler returns, your program restarts from where it was. The exception to this is if your program was in the middle of a syscall, when what happens depends on the syscall. Either the call fails with an error or the call is restarted.

All of this means that, even if you are writing a single-threaded program, if you are using signals you have to take account of possible race conditions, which action will be carried out first, and asynchronous execution. For example, if you have a global variable that is used by both your program and a signal handler, then you have the same problems that you would have if you were sharing the variable between two threads. If the program is in the middle of updating the shared variable and a signal interrupts it, then its state is not certain and when the handler updates it and returns, the result is probably not what you expected. The situation is even worse if the handler itself can be interrupted by another signal. To stop this happening always block signals within a handler.

Sharing resources between the program and a signal handler is the same as sharing resources between threads, see Chapter 12.

If you don't make use of a handler for any signal, then you can mostly ignore this problem as by default signals bring the process to an end and all you need to worry about is the state of any open resources that you don't get a chance to gracefully close.

You can also ignore the problem if you choose to handle signals using one of the synchronous approaches. In this case, your program isn't interrupted as it simply either waits for a signal or polls to see if there is a signal to process.

Controlling Signals

You can control how a process responds to signals using either the `signal` function or the `sigaction` function. Of the two, `sigaction` is more portable as `signal` has been implemented in slightly different ways across different versions of Linux, but it is more complicated.

The basic form of a `sigaction` call is:

```
sigaction(signum, &action, &oldaction);
```

`signum` is the signal number you want to modify. Both `action` and `oldaction` are `sigaction` structs with `action` specifying the new setting and `oldaction` being used to save the existing action state. You can use `NULL` for either action or old action.

The simplest form of the `sigaction` struct is:

```
struct sigaction {
 void       (*sa_handler)(int);
 sigset_t   sa_mask;
 int        sa_flags;
};
```

The first field is a pointer to the signal handler function which accepts a single int which is set to the signal number. It can also be set to `SIG_DFL` to set the default action or `SIG_IGN` to ignore the signal. The `sa_mask` field is the bitwise OR of a set of constants which indicate which signals are to be blocked while the handler is running. The `sa_flags` field controls how the signal is processed; you can mostly leave this cleared apart perhaps for `SA_RESTART`.

For example, to handle `SIG_TERM` we first need a function to handle the signal:

```
void signalHandler(int sig) {
    printf("SIGTERM\n");
}
```

In principle we shouldn't be using `printf` within a signal handler for the simple reason that the main program has been interrupted and it could be in the middle of a `printf` call, and in principle even this `printf` call could be interrupted and so on. As our main program is going to just use a busy wait we can be reasonably sure that there isn't going to be a problem.

The main program is:

```
int main(int argc, char** argv) {
    struct sigaction psa={0};
    psa.sa_handler = signalHandler;
    sigaction(SIGTERM, &psa, NULL);
    for (;;) {}
    return (EXIT_SUCCESS);
}
```

To make this work we need to include signal.h and in many cases add:

```
#define _POSIX_C_SOURCE  200809L
```

as sigaction is a POSIX standard.

The complete program is:

```
#define _POSIX_C_SOURCE  200809L
#include <stdio.h>
#include <stdlib.h>
#include <signal.h>
#include <unistd.h>
void signalHandler(int sig) {
    printf("SIGTERM\n");
}

int main(int argc, char** argv) {
    struct sigaction psa={0};
    psa.sa_handler = signalHandler;
    sigaction(SIGTERM, &psa, NULL);
    for (;;) {
    }
    return (EXIT_SUCCESS);
}
```

When you compile this you will have to run the program from the command line because there is no easy way to send the SIGTERM signal using an IDE such as NetBeans. You can discover the program's PID using:

```
ps ax
```

and then you can send it the signal using:

```
sudo kill -SIGTERM 32495
```

using whatever the PID is for the running program. Each time you send the signal you will see the message printed as the default action is being overridden by the handler. To terminate the program use:

```
sudo kill -SIGKILL 32495
```

Notice that you don't have to use the other options specified in the struct but they are easy enough to use.

Masking Signals

The mask field is particularly useful because without it your handler is open to being interrupted by another signal. You can block any signal for the duration of the handler, using the appropriate mask, and this can be done using either sigaction or sigprocmask.

The only complication is that the mask is a sigset_t and you shouldn't manipulate its bits directly because the implementation could change. Instead you should use the sigset manipulation functions.

sigemptyset(&sigset);	Clear all bits
sigfillset(&sigset);	Set all bits
sigaddset(&sigset,signum);	Set the bit for signum
sigdelset(&sigset, signum);	Clear the bit for signum
sigismember(&sigset, signum);	Returns 1 if signum is set

As sigaddset and sigdelset change just one bit leaving all the others as they were, you have to initialize the sigset using either sigemptyset or sigfillset. For example, to block all signals while the signal handler is running:

```
sigset_t mask;
sigfillset(&mask);
struct sigaction psa={0};
psa.sa_handler = signalHandler;
psa.sa_mask=mask;
sigaction(SIGTERM, &psa, NULL);
```

To block just one signal you would change the initialization of the sigset to:

```
sigset_t mask;
sigemptyset(&mask);
sigaddset(&mask,SIGTERM);
```

This would block the SIGTERM signal until the handler completed.

You can also use a sigset to block or unblock a signal at any time using the sigprocmask functions:

```
sigprocmask(how, &set, &oldset);
```

where how is one of SIG_BLOCK, SIG_UNBLOCK or SIG_SETMASK,

The first two block or unblock the signals in set without changing other bits and the final one sets or unsets them all according to set.

Notice this works with the current process. If you want to modify the signal mask of a thread use pthread_sigmask. Each thread has its own signal mask.

Flags

The flag field can be used to set the behavior of the signal and handler. It currently accepts the bitwise OR of the following flag constants:

SA_NOCLDSTOP	If signum is SIGCHLD, do not receive notification when child processes stop.
SA_NOCLDWAIT	If signum is SIGCHLD, do not transform children into zombies when they terminate.
SA_NODEFER	Do not prevent the signal from being received from within its own signal handler.
SA_ONSTACK	Call the signal handler on an alternate signal stack provided by signaltstack.
SA_RESETHAND	Restore the signal action to the default upon entry to the signal handler.
SA_RESTART	Make certain system calls restartable across signals.
SA_SIGINFO	The signal handler takes three arguments, not one and sa_sigaction should be set instead of sa_handler.

Noteworthy is SA_RESETHAND which makes sigaction behave more like the original signal in that after a single signal has been handled the default action is restored, i.e. the signal handler is just called once.

Restarting Syscalls

SA_RESTART is a difficult option to know what to do with. If you are within a syscall that can be interrupted by a signal then it isn't obvious what happens when the signal handler returns - resume or return an error code EINT. If the SA_RESTART flag is set then the operation resumes the syscall. You might think that automatically restarting the operation is the best option, but it is much more complicated. What it means exactly depends on the syscall, and not all syscalls can be interrupted - local disk operations, for example, are never interrupted. As you know which syscalls you are using, it is often better to let the EINT error occur and then perform a custom restart of the operation.

The behavior of syscalls is very varied. For example, the sleep function can be interrupted by a signal and if it is then it returns immediately the handler is finished without an error, but the return value gives the number of seconds left.

You can't force a restart using SA_RESTART but you can do it manually. For example:

```c
#define _POSIX_C_SOURCE  200809L
#include <stdio.h>
#include <stdlib.h>
#include <signal.h>
#include <unistd.h>

void signalHandler(int sig) {
    printf("SIGINT\n");
}

int main(int argc, char** argv) {
    sigset_t mask;
    sigfillset(&mask);
    struct sigaction psa = {0};
    psa.sa_handler = signalHandler;
    psa.sa_mask = mask;
    sigaction(SIGINT, &psa, NULL);
    int t = 10;
    do {
        t = sleep(t);
        printf("%d\n", t);
    } while (t != 0);
    return (EXIT_SUCCESS);
}
```

The key part of this is the do-while loop, which keeps restarting the sleep if the returned value isn't zero. You can try this out by running it from the console and typing Ctrl-C to send the SIGINT signal. You will see the remaining time after each signal. Notice that this isn't a good way to get a time delay when signals are involved because of the accumulated error at each interrupt. The best you can say in this case is that the delay will be at least the period specified, but it could be a lot longer.

This example shows how an interrupted syscall can be restarted. In other situations the reasonable way to restart could be different.

Getting More Signal Info

If you set SA_SIGINFO then the handler function accepts three parameters, not just one. You also have to specify the handler using the sa_sigaction field of the sigaction struct which is usually a union with sa_handler. The handler's parameters are:

```
void func(signo,&info,&context);
```

where signo is the signal number and info is a siginfo_t struct which contains a lot of information about the interrupt, however, this varies a lot according to the machine. In most cases, however, the information provided is a lot less than the full definition of the siginfo_t struct and only a few fields exist - usually just si_signo, si_errno and si_code. The behavior of this feature may be standardized, but its implementation varies so much as to make it unreliable if you are trying to write portable code. The context gives the signal context of the receiving thread and is rarely used.

Signals and Threads

Threads are introduced in Chapter 12, but it is important to understand how signals work with a multi-threaded program. Each thread has its own signal mask and so can block signals on a per-thread basis. When first created, a thread inherits the mask of the thread that created it. However, the signal handler, or more generally the signal disposition, is shared among all threads. When a signal occurs, only one of the threads is interrupted. If the signal is due to an error then the thread that caused the problem is interrupted. All other signals are delivered to a thread selected arbitrarily. The only other complication is that instead of using sigprocmask to set the signal mask you have to use pthread_sigmask instead.

The big problem in this situation is that you cannot know which thread is going to be interrupted. A common approach is to set the mask of all but one of the threads to block every signal. The one thread that hasn't blocked the signals is obviously the signal handler and it should just wait for a signal to occur. See later for synchronous ways of dealing with signals.

Sending Signals

Signals are most often thought of as software interrupts that indicate some sort of error has occurred. In fact, any process can use a signal to communicate with another process. It is a matter of opinion how useful this is, but it does have the advantage of being simple.

There are a number of functions which can be used to send a signal to a process.

The function:

```
kill(pid, sig);
```

works in the same way as the kill command. You specify the PID number of the process you want to send the signal `sig` to. If you specify 0 then the signal is sent to every process in the same group as the calling process. If you set it to -1 then the signal is sent to every process that the calling process has permission to send it to. Any other negative PID sends the signal to the process group with that ID. A simpler way of doing this is to use the function:

```
killpg(pgrp,sig);
```

which sends `sig` the process group `pgrp`. If `pgrp` is 0 then `sig` is sent to the calling process's group. Notice you can set the process group of any process you create using C functions or the command line.

Finally, if sig is 0 then no signal is sent, but error checking is performed as if it had been. You can use this to check that a process, or process group, exists. To send a signal, the sender either has to be running as root or as the same user as the receiving process.

The function:

```
raise(sig);
```

is the same as:

```
kill(getpid(),sig);
```

i.e. it sends the signal to the calling program.

The function:

```
sigqueue(pid,sig,value);
```

will send the signal to the process specified by `pid` and `value` will be stored in the `sig_value` field of the `siginfo_t` struct.

You can send a signal directly to a thread using:

```
pthread_kill(thread,sig);
```

This interrupts the specified thread and performs the action common to all the threads.

Waiting for Signals

There are two functions which cause a process to suspend until a signal occurs. The simplest is:

```
pause();
```

and it just pauses the process or thread until a handled or unhandled signal occurs. Slightly more sophisticated is:

```
sigsuspend(&mask)
```

which does the same thing as `pause`, but it sets the signal mask for the duration of the suspension. This means you can use `mask` to temporarily change what signals are allowed.

Notice that `pause` and `sigsuspend` cause a handler to be call asynchronously and the program only continues if the handler returns.

You can also wait for a signal without the help of a handler function.

The process simply waits for the signal and continues when the signal happens i.e. a synchronous signal processing. Another way to think of this is that the process blocks until the signal occurs.

There are three functions that perform a synchronous wait:

```
sigwait(&mask, &sig);
sigwaitinfo(&mask, &info);
sigtimedwait(&mask, &info, &timeout);
```

They work in more or less the same way. The `mask` determines which signals are waited for. For `sigwait` all that is returned when the signal occurs is its signal number. For `sigwaitinfo` and `sigtimedwait` you get a complete `siginfo_t` struct containing all the information about the signal and `sigtimedwait` also specifies a timeout via the `timespec` struct.

There is one subtle point that isn't made very clear in the documentation. The signal that you are waiting for has to be blocked in the calling program and all threads. If it isn't then the result is undefined behavior which in practice generally means that you get default behavior or a handler called.

Real-time Signals

Before going on to an example of using signals to communicate between processes, it is worth explaining real-time signals. All the signals we have been using are standard signals. Signal numbers above 32 refer to real-time signals. They behave in the same way as standard signals, but they have no pre-assigned meaning - they are all user signals. They are used in the same way as standard signals, but they are processed differently by the system:

1. The default action for an unhandled real-time signal is to terminate the receiving process.

2. Multiple instances of real-time signals can be queued. By contrast, if multiple instances of a standard signal are delivered while that signal is currently blocked, then only one instance is queued.

3. Real-time signals are delivered in a guaranteed order. Multiple real-time signals of the same type are delivered in the order they were sent. If different real-time signals are sent to a process, they are delivered starting with the lowest-numbered signal. (i.e. lowest-numbered signals have highest priority.) By contrast, if multiple standard signals are pending for a process, the order in which they are delivered is unspecified.

It is clearly better to use real-time signals for IPC. There is only one small complication. The number of available signals is not fixed. You have to use the macros SIGRTMIN and SIGRTMAX to determine which signal number to use. For example:

```
int SIG= SIGRTMIN +1;
```

These numbers are the same for all processes running on the same system, but vary from system to system.

Signals as IPC

There are many possible ways of using signals to asynchronously or synchronously communicate between processes or threads. The idea is that one process raises a signal and another process either waits for it or handles it. Signals provide a light weight form of Inter Process Communication IPC that is often sufficient for simple situations. For more complex situations you can use shared files, pipes or shared memory all are described later.

One of the biggest problems is discovering the PID of the process you are sending a message to. There are many ways of doing this. The most common is for one process to fork to create a new process and then execute a new process with a known PID, see Chapter 12. The PID is known because you have created the process you want to communicate with and the fork returns it for you to use.

Another alternative is to read the proc pseudo directory to find the name of each PID, see Chapter 9. There is a directory for each PID /proc/pid and within the directory the comm file stores the command line name of the process, cmdline stores the full command line used to start the process.

These pseudo directories and files can be used as if they were real directories and files and hence you can get the information you need - see Chapter 12 for details.

You can also use the same techniques with threads where identification is less of a problem because in most cases you have created them and therefor know their identity.

For simplicity, we ignore the problem of finding the PID and simply use the command line to test.

First write a program that handles a real-time signal:

```c
#define _POSIX_C_SOURCE  200809L
#include <stdio.h>
#include <stdlib.h>
#include <signal.h>
#include <unistd.h>

void signalHandler(int sig) {
    printf("SIGRT\n");
}

int main(int argc, char** argv) {
    int sig = SIGRTMIN + 1;
    sigset_t mask;
    sigemptyset(&mask);
    sigaddset(&mask, sig);

    struct sigaction psa = {0};
    psa.sa_handler = &signalHandler;
    psa.sa_mask = mask;
    sigaction(sig, &psa, NULL);
    for (;;) {
    };
    return (EXIT_SUCCESS);
}
```

This simply uses SIGRTMIN+1 as a signal to be handled and then loops until the handler is called. To test this program you need to run it from a command prompt, then use the:

```
ps ax
```

to find the PID of the process and finally use:

```
sudo kill -SIGRTMIN+1 7174
```

with whatever the PID turned out to be. When the signal is received, the loop is interrupted and the handler is carried out. Notice that you need to block all signals while the handler is running, otherwise it could be interrupted. Recall, of course, that using `printf` is not a safe async function and is used here as a demonstration.

If the receiving process doesn't have anything to do while waiting for a signal then you might as well use `pause` to suspend the execution:

```
sigaction(sig, &psa, NULL);
  pause();
    return (EXIT_SUCCESS);
}
```

With this change to the end of the program, the real-time signal is handled just once and the process is suspended while waiting for it. If you don't need a handler and just want a blocking wait for the signal to occur then you can use a synchronous wait:

```
int main(int argc, char** argv) {
    int sig = SIGRTMIN + 1;
    sigset_t mask;
    sigfillset(&mask);
    sigprocmask(SIG_SETMASK, &mask, NULL);

    sigemptyset(&mask);
    sigaddset(&mask, sig);

    int signo;
    for(;;){
        sigwait(&mask,&signo);
        printf("SIGRT\n");
    }
    return (EXIT_SUCCESS);
}
```

Notice that first the mask is set to all ones and is used to block all signals, then it is modified to select `SIGRTMIN+1` as the only signal that will wake up the process. If you don't block signals the `sigwait` isn't likely to work. Once again, note that we have used `printf`, which in this case is safe to use as there is no asynchronous behavior. To test the program, run it from the command line and then use:

`ps ax`

to find the PID of the process and finally use:

`sudo kill -SIGRTMIN+1 7174`

with whatever the PID turned out to be.

Everything is a File - Including Signals

If you know the Unix/Linux philosophy that everything is representable as a file, see Chapter 9, you might still be surprised that you can treat signals as a file. You can open a file descriptor, see Chapter 8, and then read the signals from the file as they occur. You can use the usual file functions with the file including read, poll, select and close.

To open a file to a set of signals you make use of:

```
int fd=signalfd(-1,&mask,0);
```

where mask defines the set of signals to use. This is Linux-specific and so not portable. The first parameter is optionally an existing signal file descriptor and the effect is to change the signals associated with the file. The final parameter sets options on how the file behaves and it is usually 0.

For this to work the signals being read as a file have to be blocked or the default action or a handler will be called. Once you have the file open you can read it in the usual way and the read blocks until one or more signals are pending, when it returns as many signalfd_siginfo structs as there are signals. The struct signalfd_siginfo contains a lot of information about the signal and you can look it up in the documentation.

So to read a SIGINT as a file you would use:

```
#define _POSIX_C_SOURCE  200809L
#include <stdio.h>
#include <stdlib.h>
#include <signal.h>
#include <unistd.h>
#include <sys/signalfd.h>

int main(int argc, char** argv) {
    sigset_t mask;
    sigfillset(&mask);
    sigprocmask(SIG_SETMASK, &mask, NULL);
    sigemptyset(&mask);
    sigaddset(&mask, SIGINT);

    int count;
    int fd=signalfd(-1,&mask,0);
    struct signalfd_siginfo buffer[10];
    for(;;){
     count= read(fd,&buffer,10*sizeof(struct signalfd_siginfo));
     printf("SIGINT %d\n",count);
    }
    return (EXIT_SUCCESS);
}
```

Notice that we once again use the `mask` to block all signals and then use it to set up `SIGINT` as the signal that the file will capture. Notice that the `read` blocks until a signal occurs and it is a synchronous way to handle signals. As there is no asynchronous behavior it is fine to use `printf`.

Setjmp Non-local Jumps

One of the things that the C language lacks is a try catch statement or any exception handling. What this makes difficult to do in C is try a section of program and abort the execution if it causes an error. However, if you combine signal handling and the `setjmp` function then you can build your own try catch.

The `setjmp` function stores the current state of the program in a buffer and returns a zero.

The program can then carry on as normal until a `longjmp` function call occurs with the same buffer used in `setjmp`. When this happens the stored environment is restored and control is transferred back to the `setjmp` function, but this time it returns the value of the second `longjmp` parameter so that you can use it tell that this is a restart.

That is:

`setjmp(buffer);`

stores `state` in `buffer` and returns 0. After this the program carries on as normal until it meets:

`longjmp(buffer, 1);`

when the environment is restored and control is transferred back to the `setjmp`, which in this case returns 1. Notice that the restored environment wipes out any function calls, i.e. it unwinds the stack. This means that the values of automatic variables in the function that called `setjmp` are unspecified if they are changed between `setjmp` and `longjmp` and not declared as volatile.

There is one more complication. The standards do not specify if the signal state should be stored as part of the environment. Under some operating systems it is, and under others it isn't. Storing and restoring the signal state takes more time and in this case, as we are going to use a `longjmp` to block a signal from its default action, we don't want to store the signal state. The function:

`sigsetjmp(buffer,0);`

will save the environment without the signal state. If the second parameter is non-zero then it will save the signal state.

If you use sigsetjmp then you have to use:

```
siglongjmp(buffer,value);
```

to restart.

For example, if we have a block of code that might fail for some reason we can try it and "unwind" its effects using:

```
#define _POSIX_C_SOURCE  200809L
#include <stdio.h>
#include <stdlib.h>
#include <setjmp.h>
...
static jmp_buf jumpBuffer;
    if (sigsetjmp(jumpBuffer, 0)) {
        code that retries or aborts i.e. catch
    } else {
        code you want to try
        if(exception)siglongjmp(jumpBuffer, 1);
    }
```

where in practice the siglongjmp could be called by any function with the else block that wants to signal an exception.

For example, suppose we have a function that checks for divide by zero and we want to implement a try-catch style execution:

```
#define _POSIX_C_SOURCE  200809L
#include <stdio.h>
#include <stdlib.h>
#include <signal.h>
#include <setjmp.h>

static jmp_buf jumpBuffer;

int myDiv(int a, int b) {
    if (b == 0)siglongjmp(jumpBuffer, 1);
    return a / b;
}

int main(int argc, char** argv) {
    if (sigsetjmp(jumpBuffer, 0)) {
        printf("can't do it\n");
    } else {
        printf("answer %d\n", myDiv(6, 2));
        printf("answer %d\n", myDiv(6, 0));
    }
    printf("program continues\n");
    return (EXIT_SUCCESS);
}
```

Notice that the function myDiv calls the siglongjmp to signal the exception. For this to work the jumpBuffer has to be global and hence accessible to it. The main program simply loads the jumpBuffer and then attempts to do some divisions. The second division is by 0 and so this unwinds the stack and transfers control to the if statement again and the "can't do it" message is printed.

Another approach is to allow the exception raising functions to raise a signal. For example, if we change the myDiv function to:

```
int myDiv(int a, int b) {
    if (b == 0)abort();
    return a / b;
}
```

then as the program stands it would simply perform the default action and terminate.

If we define a handler for SIGABRT then we can use the siglongjmp to return to the program and continue:

```
void signalHandler(int sig) {
    printf("SIGABRT\n");
    siglongjmp(jumpBuffer, 1);
}
```

Setting up the signal handler is the same as always and the complete program is:

```
#define _POSIX_C_SOURCE  200809L
#include <stdio.h>
#include <stdlib.h>
#include <signal.h>
#include <setjmp.h>
#include <signal.h>

static jmp_buf jumpBuffer;

int myDiv(int a, int b) {
    if (b == 0)abort();
    return a / b;
}

void signalHandler(int sig) {
    printf("SIGABRT\n");
    siglongjmp(jumpBuffer, 1);
}
```

```c
int main(int argc, char** argv) {
    sigset_t mask;
    sigfillset(&mask);
    struct sigaction psa = {0};
    psa.sa_handler = signalHandler;
    psa.sa_mask = mask;
    sigaction(SIGABRT, &psa, NULL);

    if (sigsetjmp(jumpBuffer, 0)) {
        printf("can't do it\n");
    } else {
        printf("answer %d\n", myDiv(6, 2));
        printf("answer %d\n", myDiv(6, 0));
    }
    printf("program continues\n");
    return (EXIT_SUCCESS);
}
```

Of course, if the signal is generated automatically by the error, e.g. a SIGABRT, it can be raised if there is a signed overflow - see Chapter 5 - and in this case we just need the handler.

Are Signals Useful?

Opinion is divided on the use of signals. They are generally said to be too primitive to be of much use. However, for a small system a signal can be the easiest way to inform processes and threads that something has happened. As long as you keep in mind that asynchronous signal handling is dangerous in terms of race conditions, and the need to block signals in signal handlers, then it is safe enough. Also, don't make use of any asynchronous unsafe function calls. The ones you can use are listed in the documentation. There is also the issue of restarting syscalls if they are interrupted by a signal and this can be complicated.

Of course, if you handle signals in a synchronous way then you can use any system calls you like and arrange for them not to be interrupted by signals. There is a great deal to be said for using signalfd to read signals like a file.

Summary

- Signals are system-generated software interrupts and their default behavior is to terminate the program that receives them.

- You can write signal handlers that are called asynchronously when the signal occurs.

- The asynchronous nature of signals means you have to protect against interruptions and restarts. In particular, make sure you block signals when in a signal handler.

- Syscalls are a particular problem in that a signal can occur while they are executing. It is possible to automatically restart an interrupted syscall, but it is usually better to test manually for a signal interruption and control the restart.

- Your program can send a signal to another process and a process can wait for a signal.

- Sending and waiting on a signal can be used as a simple inter-process communication method.

- Signals can be treated synchronously using a file to access them.

- Sometime you need setjmp to implement a non-local jump to successfully handle a signal. This can be used to implement a try-catch style of programming.

Chapter 5

Integer Arithmetic

Arithmetic is the forgotten task. We just expect machines to evaluate whatever expression we write and we expect it to get it right – or right enough not to cause a problem. Part of the reason for this unreasonable assumption is the availability and success of floating point arithmetic. However, even floating point arithmetic can give you results that are closer to random numbers than a valid answer if you don't take care.

This chapter isn't about floating point arithmetic – for that see Chapter 7. Smaller computers often don't have a hardware floating point unit and if you want to use floating point you have to use a software implementation which is slow. In most cases a better option is to use integer or fixed-point arithmetic which is more appropriate for embedded processors and special digital signal processors, for example.

In this chapter we look at the basics of integer arithmetic and the next tackles its extension to fixed-point arithmetic.

It is assumed that you know the basics of binary numbers, the bitwise operators and how to use hexadecimal. If you are in any doubt about these topics see: ***Fundamental C: Getting Closer To The Machine*** (ISBN: 978-1871962604)

Binary Integer Addition as Bit Manipulation

Computer arithmetic is almost universally done in binary. It hasn't always been this way and even today decimal representations are sometimes important, see the next section on Binary Coded Decimal, BCD.

Binary integer addition is something we generally take for granted – the hardware just does it, but it can be implemented using bitwise logic and shifts, and it is instructive to do so.

Addition of two bits generates a Result bit and a Carry bit:

```
A + B = R   C
0   0   0   0
0   1   1   0
1   0   1   0
1   1   0   1
```

You can see that the result is an XOR and the carry is simply an AND.

This is called a half adder because it doesn't deal with the problem of taking account of anything that might have been generated by an earlier pair of bits being added.

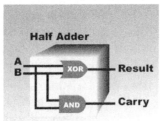

A half adder takes two bits and adds them to give a result and a carry

To create a full adder all we need to do is combine two half adders so that the first adds the two bits to produce a result and a carry and the second adds the result and the carry to produce a final result and a final carry. *A full adder takes two bits and the carry from the previous addition and produces a result and a carry*

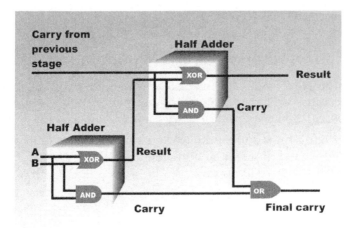

Can we do the same job in C without using the add operator?

A half adder is easy as it is just two logical operations. If a and b are ints then:

r=a^b;

is the set of result bits and:

c=a&b;

is the set of carry bits when a and b are "half added".

For example, for a=0101 and b=0111:

r= 0101 ^ 0111 = 0010

and:

c= 0101 & 0111 = 0101

If you do the addition you will see that these are the result and carry bits of half adding each pair of bits without worrying about any earlier carry bits. Each of the carry bits has to be added to the result but to the next higher-order bit. In other words, we need to add the carry to the result shifted one bit to the left:

a+b=r+c<<1

or:

a+b= a^b + a&b<<1

This is the fundamental formula for addition but notice that it doesn't get rid of the addition operator! To do this we have to write it in terms of the logical operators.

That is, to add the result and the shifted carry we have to use:

r1=r^(c<<1);
c1=r & c;

You can now see what the problem is – there might be another carry bit in c1 that has to be added to the result.

The fact of the matter is that addition is an iteration of two logical operations and a shift, and this fact is hidden from us by its implementation in hardware. In hardware, the carry bits propagate through the full adder and it is the propagation time that is the hardware's equivalent of the iteration.

So, to compute an addition, a+b, without using the addition operator, we need to use:

```
int ans = a;
int c = b;
int temp=0;
while (c > 0) {
    temp = (ans^c);
    c = (ans & c) << 1;
    ans=temp;
}
```

The loop ends when there is no carry and if the most significant bit of the carry is set at any point then an overflow has occurred.

It is worth noting that the term overflow is perhaps not the correct one. The C90 standard states that integer addition cannot overflow, it simply rolls over. That is, if a is the maximum value that can be represented, a+1 is 0. This is the wrong answer, but it isn't necessarily an error, as we shall see.

Decimal Arithmetic with BCD

Although decimal hardware is rare, there are lots of reason to want to work in decimal in software. For example, binary often doesn't give results that are the same as a human would get doing manual arithmetic. For example, if an expression results in 0.1 in decimal this isn't exactly representable in fixed point binary. However, for integer arithmetic binary gives the same result as decimal arithmetic.

A more common reason for needing decimal in small systems is that sensors and displays often make use of it. For example, a sensor might naturally return some decimal digits to represent a temperature, or a numeric display might need to be fed decimal values. You can avoid decimal arithmetic by always converting to binary and then back to decimal as needed but in many cases it is simpler to stay with the representation the device provides. It is also instructive to see that in C and in low-level programming in general all we have are bit patterns and how you interpret them is up to you.

Binary Coded Decimal is very simple. The bit patterns 0000 to 1001 are used to code 0 to 9. These bit patterns can be stored one per byte or, packed as BCD, as two digits per byte. Four bits are often referred to as a nibble and so we use one nibble to store a digit. Notice that you are not using the full range of the nibble and often the unused values represent symbols such as plus or minus.

To convert a binary value to BCD all you have to do is extract the decimal digits. For example, starting with:

```
int myVal = 123;
```

you can get the least significant digit by taking the remainder on division by 10:

```
myBCD1 = myVal % 10;
```

The remainder of 123 after division by 10 is 3 and so myBCD1 now contains 3. All we now have to do is repeat after removing the least significant digit:

```
myVal = myVal / 10;
myBCD1 += (myVal % 10) << 4;
```

The shift by 4 bits is to move the digit into the next nibble. The next digit is extracted in the same way, but this time is shifted 8 bits to move it to the next nibble:

```
myVal = myVal / 10;
myBCD1 += (myVal % 10) << 8;
```

Now you have seen how this works, it is easy to convert it into a loop that will convert any positive binary value to BCD:

```
int s = 0;
int myBCD1=0;
while (myVal > 0) {
    myBCD1 += (myVal % 10) << s;
    s += 4;
    myVal = myVal / 10;
}
printf("%x\n", myBCD1);
```

It is worth remembering that to convert BCD to an ASCII char you simply have to add 0011 to the start of each nibble. You also have to unpack each nibble into a byte. One way to do this is to shift right and use a mask:

```
char myASCII[5] = {0};
int i=0;
while (myBCD1 > 0) {
    myASCII[3-i] = (myBCD1 & 0x0F) | 0x30;
    myBCD1 >>= 4;
    i++;
}
printf("%s\n", myASCII);
```

To convert to binary you simply proceed as you would with a decimal number, but in this case extracting nibbles for each digit.

```
myVal=0;
int p=1;
while (myBCD1 > 0) {
    myVal += (myBCD1 & 0x0F)*p;
    myBCD1 >>= 4;
    p=p*10;
}
printf("%d\n", myVal);
```

BCD Arithmetic

Now we come to the difficult topic of how to perform BCD arithmetic. If you have a lot of arithmetic to do then the best solution is to convert to binary, do the arithmetic and then convert back. This has the advantage that you know how to work with binary and the disadvantage that, if it involves division, you might not get the same answer as a human.

In many cases, however, the arithmetic that you want to do is very simple. One way of doing BCD arithmetic is to unpack the nibbles into an array and then add nibbles one by one. The problem with this is that you have to take care of the decimal carries. For example, 9+1 gives you a nibble that isn't a decimal digit i.e. 10 or 1010 in binary or A in hex. To correct this you have to subtract 10 from this nibble and add one to the next nibble so performing a carry. That is, if you add the nibbles together you have to scan for values that are greater than 9 and from each you subtract 10 and add a carry to the next nibble. Notice that as 9+9 is 18 decimal or 0001 0010 you can even overflow 4 bits and so each nibble should be stored in its own byte.

Consider for a moment addition of just two BCD digits each one stored in a byte. For example:

```
   9  +    9  =   18
0x09  + 0x09  = 0x12
```

At this point you need to subtract 10 and carry 1 onto the next nibble. However, if you look, the addition has already put a 1 into the next nibble, it is only the original nibble that is wrong. The reason is that the carry 1 into the next highest nibble has actually carried 16 not 10 from the lower nibble - remember this is implemented as binary. To get the correct BCD we have to return 6 to the lower nibble.

```
   9  +    9  =   18
0x09  +  0x09  = 0x12 + 0x06 = 0x18
```

If you have implemented BCD arithmetic before, you might have wondered where the mysterious "6" comes from.

```
int result = myBCD1 + myBCD2;
if(result>9)result=result+6;
```

You can extend this method so that you can add multiple digits and then correct the result to BCD, but it isn't straightforward as you have to detect the binary carry between the nibbles and add 6 to the lower nibble whenever it has occurred.

If we have two packed BCD values in four byte unsigned ints then we can simply add them together:

```
unsigned int myBCD1 = 0x90000;
unsigned int myBCD2 = 0x90000;
int result = myBCD1 + myBCD2;
```

but the result will be incorrect in any nibble that generated a carry to the next nibble. We need to find out where the carries occur. This we can do because we already know that exclusive or (XOR) is addition without taking the carries into account. So:

```
(myBCD1 ^ myBCD2)
```

is the addition without carry. If we XOR this with the sum that did include a carry there will only be bits set where they differ, i.e bits that result from a carry:

```
(myBCD1 ^ myBCD2)^result
```

This gives a one at every bit that was generated by a carry, but we are only interested in carries from one nibble to the next and these can only be positioned at the first bit of the nibble. To pick just these out we have to use a mask:

```
int carry = (myBCD1 ^ myBCD2)^result & 0x011111110;
```

notice that the first nibble cannot have received a carry.

Now we have a carry which has a one in the first bit of any nibble that received a carry from the adjacent nibble. We need to create a mask with a 6 in each position that generated a carry and this we can do using a shift and OR:

```
int sixmask = (carry >> 2) | (carry >> 3);
```

Finally we can add the sixes into the result to correct it:

```
result += sixmask;
```

Notice that you cannot allow a carry in the final nibble - the result is an overflow.

You can extend this bit manipulation technique to long long types if you need more digits. You can also make it work for subtraction by using ten's complement, see the next section.

Negative Numbers

You can see that there are a variety of ways of representing numbers as bit patterns. The next question is, how do we represent negative numbers in integer types?

If you know about computer arithmetic then you will be familiar with the most common way of doing the job – two's-complement representation - but it is worth looking at the problem again.

The simplest way is to use a sign magnitude system, which is what we use when doing pencil and paper arithmetic. In this case we have a sign bit, the most significant bit, that is 0 for positive values and 1 for negative values. The usual arithmetic hardware in a processor doesn't know anything about sign bits and just treats the representation as if it was a normal positive number. For example, 0011 is 3 in four-bit sign magnitude and 1011 is -3.

Notice that if you just do integer arithmetic with sign magnitude, the sign doesn't take care of itself, i.e. 3+(-3) = 0011+1011 = 1110 i.e -6, which is "the wrong answer".

There is nothing wrong with this representation, but to make it work the computer hardware would have to be extended to include a subtractor circuit as well as an adder. That is, the computer would have to be built to do subtraction like you do with pencil and paper. Adding a whole extra arithmetic hardware module isn't particularly practical and there is a much easier way to do the job. We just need to find something that acts like a negative number and add it.

Working in four bits to make the example easier - what can you add to 0001 to get zero? If you can find a value that you can add to 1 to get zero then this value behaves like -1. At first it seems impossible, but when you remember that integer arithmetic in C rolls over you can see that adding the largest representable value to 1 gives zero. That is, in four bits:

0001+1111 = 0000

Notice that this only works if integer overflow results in a rollover. Also notice that it only works if the result is restricted to four bits.

So, if you represent -1 by 1111, which is 15 in decimal, we can do subtraction using standard arithmetic with rollover. Notice that 15 is 2^4-1. Similarly:

-2 is 1110 = 2^4-2 = 14

-3 is 1101 = 2^4-3 = 13

..

In general $-x$ is 2^4-x

If you are working with n bits then $-x$ is:

2^n-x

This is called two's-complement representation.

Two's-complement also divides the positive range into positive and negative sub-ranges.

For example in four bits:

0000 to 0111 0 to 7   positive 0 to 7

1000 to 1111 8 to 15 negative -8 to -1

Notice that the sub-ranges are not quite even, i.e. the positive only goes up to 7 but the negative represents -8. The reason is that 0 is included in the positive range – another example of programmers counting from zero.

You can also see that two's-complement still allows you to regard the most significant bit as a sign bit, even though we didn't set out to design things this way. However, you can no longer treat the other bits as the magnitude of the number.

It is also important to know that to increase the precision of a two's-complement value you have to extend the sign bit. For example, 1 in four bits is 0001 and in five bits it is 00001, but -1 in four bits is 1111 and in five bits it is 11111.

While two's-complement is the most common way to work with negative numbers, you will also encounter one's-complement representation. This is similar to two's-complement but instead of subtracting from 2^n you use 2^n-1.

For example, in one's-complement -1 in four bits is:

$(2^n-1)-1 = 1111-1 = 1110 = 13$.

Notice that $1 = 0001$ and $-1 = 1110$. This isn't an accident and the one's-complement of any value is simply its bitwise NOT:

$(2^n-1)-x = \sim x$

and this is one of the advantages of the system.

That is, in one's-complement $-x=\sim x$.

There are various minor problems with one's-complement. For example, as in the case of signed magnitude, there are two zeros, 0000 and 1111. The biggest problem is the need to implement end around carry. For one's-complement arithmetic to work correctly you need to add any final carry bit to the least significant bit, whereas in two's-complement any final carry is simply lost.

For these reasons one's-complement isn't often used today. However, you can use it to compute a two's-complement value:

$2^n - x = (2^n - 1) - x + 1 = \sim x + 1$

That is, to find a two's complement value, find the one's-complement and add one.

A question that might arise at this early stage is, do two's-complement numbers work for multiplication and division?

As multiplication is repeated addition and division is repeated subtraction, two's-complement just works for them, with the proviso that the result can be represented in the number of bits used. However, as the result of multiplying two n-bit numbers can be as large as MAX_INT^2, you need 2n bits to represent the result.

For example:

$-2 * 7 = 1110 * 0111 = 0010 = +2$

Here the multiplication has rolled over and only the last four bits have been retained. If you want to do the calculation correctly in say 8 bits you need to sign-extend the values, i.e.:

$11111110 * 00000111 = 11110010 = -14$

The idea of a complement extends to other bases. For example, in base 10 we have both 10's and 9's-complement and again 10's-complement is generally preferred. For example, if you are working with just two digits what do you have to add to 01 to get zero? The answer, remembering roll-over at 99, is 99. That is:

$01 + 99 = 00$

and 99 is the 10's-complement of 01.

In general the 10's-complement of x with d digits is $10^d - x$.

It is usually easier to compute the 9's complement and add one:

$99 - 01 = 98$ and $98 + 1$ is 99, the 10's-complement of 01.

You can use 10's-complement to implement subtraction in BCD arithmetic.

Overflow and Undefined Behavior

Overflow is what happens when you take the largest value that can be represented in a variable and add one to it.

For unsigned values there is no problem or ambiguity according to the standards. What happens with most hardware full adders is that the computation proceeds as if nothing was wrong and the most significant bit is discarded. This results in a "rollover" and this is what the C standard says should happen.

Notice that there are other possible behaviors. One is that the hardware could detect the overflow and generate an interrupt or trap. Alternatively the hardware could implement saturation arithmetic, where rollover doesn't occur, but the largest representable integer is the result. Notice that many digital signal processors use saturation arithmetic.

The C library limits.h contains a set of constants that you can use to find what the largest value is for any type:

```
#include <limits.h>
```

For example, UINT_MAX is the largest value you can store in an unsigned int, thus:

```
printf("%d \n", UINT_MAX +1);
```

is valid C and should always print 0 with no hint of undefined behavior.

This makes it sound as if overflow/rollover detection for unsigned integers is a solved problem – it isn't. There are times when you need to know that a rollover has occurred. Unsigned ints might not cause undefined behavior, but they can still cause problems. We return to the subject at the end of this chapter after looking at the seemingly more complicated problem of signed integer overflow.

The situation with respect to signed overflow is quite different. Signed integer overflow is specified as undefined behavior and in some optimization modes some compilers assume it can never happen and hence they optimize away any use made of it.

This difference is often attributed to the fact that there are different ways to represent signed values, but as already pointed out differences in behavior are also possible for unsigned ints, e.g. saturation in place of rollover.

Notice that rollover occurs naturally in two's-complement arithmetic – it has to if the negative values are to act as negative values. As already explained, using 4-bit two's-complement 1 is 0001 and -1 is 1111 and adding them together gives 0000, the correct answer, but only if rollover is allowed to happen without it being an error of any sort.

This brings us to the question of what exactly is a signed overflow?

In two's-complement arithmetic, overflow is when the sign changes incorrectly. For example, INT_MAX+1 and INT_MIN-1 will produce an overflow.

If you try:

```
printf("%d %d\n", INT_MAX +1,INT_MIN-1);
```

then in principle you are invoking undefined behavior and the compiler is free to generate any code it cares to. In practice this only happens if you select an aggressive optimization option – but it does happen. For example, you can test for overflow after the fact using something like:

```
int x=INT_MAX;
if(x+1<x){
     printf("Overflow");
}
```

Using GCC with the -O2 option you will discover that you don't see the Overflow message! The reason is that the compiler has assumed that signed overflow does not occur because the program does not engage in undefined behavior and so it has removed the if statement as its body can never be executed.

Many C programs assume that signed arithmetic will always roll over with behavior given by two's-complement arithmetic. Without a way of turning off this undefined behavior most of the C programs ever written would fail to compile or give the wrong result.

Most compilers will let you control how signed arithmetic is treated. For example GCC supports two options:

```
-fwrapv
```

which enforces wrapping at all times and:

```
-ftrapv
```

which generates a SIGABRT under Linux as explained in Chapter 4.

If you compile the previous example using the -fwrapv option you will find that you do see the overflow warning and the result is what you would expect from a rollover.

It is important to know that most compilers will allow a signed rollover by default and, if there is nothing to optimize, then your program is likely to work much as you would expect. For example, even without the -fwrapv option set the program:

```
printf("%d, %d \n", INT_MAX+1,INT_MIN-1);
```

works as you would expect from a rollover, that is INT_MAX+1 is INT_MIN and INT_MIN-1 is INT_MAX.

In most cases, however, it is safer to set the -fwrapv or equivalent option to ensure that there are no optimizations.

This all raises the question of how you detect signed overflow?

GCC Overflow Detection

There are libraries and other facilities that will solve the problem for you. Obviously what is available depends on the machine you are targeting and the compiler you are using. For example, GCC has built-ins to test for overflow – lookup __builtin_add_overflow, __builtin_mul_overflow and related functions. Built-ins are like extensions to the C language provided by the compiler; there are no libraries to install, you simply use the functions as described in the compiler's manual.

For example:

```
int a=1;
int b=2;
int result;
__builtin_add_overflow(a, b, &result);
```

adds a to b and stores the answer in result. The function returns true if there has been an overflow and you can simply test for this.

Similarly, there are functions for multiplication. For example:

```
int a=1;
int b=2;
int result;
__builtin_mul_overflow(a, b, &result);
```

computes the product of a and b and stores the answer in result. As before, the function returns true if there has been an overflow and you can simply test for this.

The documentation says that this is implemented as an infinite precision operation that cannot overflow and then a test is performed to see it the answer causes an overflow when stored in result. This sounds as if it would be expensive in time, but the documentation also says that it makes use of hardware overflow detection, which in some instances might make the speed acceptable. For example, in the case of the Raspberry Pi 3, the add function call is virtually the same speed as a raw addition but 0.7 times faster than an add together with the if statements to check for overflow. Similarly, the multiply function call is more than twice as slow as a raw unchecked multiplication, but six times faster than multiplication with the if statements needed to check for overflow. See later for more information on efficiency.

If you are using GCC with a machine for which the built-in functions have been optimized, they are well worth using. However, not everyone uses GCC and there is no guarantee that the built-in functions have been implemented efficiently on the hardware you are using. There are also other considerations which make it useful to know how to implement your own overflow checks.

DIY Overflow Detection Before it Happens

One method of detecting a signed overflow was demonstrated in an earlier example where adding one made the result decrease because of overflow. In general, if you add a positive then you expect the result to increase and if you add a negative you expect it to decrease. In fact, you can only generate a signed overflow when adding values that have the same sign. The rule is that when you add values with the same sign the result has to have the same sign.

A naive test would be something like:

```
int a=INT_MIN;
int b=-10;
int result=a+b;
if(a>0 && b>0 && result<0)printf("Overflow \n");
if(a<0 && b<0 && result>0)printf("Overflow \n");
```

Of course, as a test for overflow this doesn't avoid undefined behavior, which was triggered when we did a+b. To avoid undefined behavior we have to test for overflow before we perform the operation that causes the overflow. In other words, to protect against undefined behavior you have to test for overflow before you do the arithmetic that might produce it. This can be done with a slight rearrangement of the test:

```
if (a > 0 && b > 0 && a>INT_MAX-b)printf("Overflow \n");
if (a < 0 && b < 0 && a<INT_MIN-b)printf("Overflow \n");
```

You can see that the final term in the test is a way of testing for a+b>INT_MAX or a+b<INT_MIN without actually having to work out a+b.

You can make this slightly more efficient by dropping the initial test on a:

```
if (b > 0 && a>INT_MAX-b)printf("Overflow \n");
if (b < 0 && a<INT_MIN-b)printf("Overflow \n");
```

The reason is that in the first case a>INT_MAX-b can only be true if a>0 and in the second a<INT_MIN-b if a<0. Even though this is more efficient, you are still having to calculate two sum operations and four comparisons – a lot of overhead for a single sum.

Notice that for subtraction, e.g. a-b, you simply use -b in the tests:

```
if (b < 0 && a>INT_MAX+b)printf("Overflow \n");
if (b > 0 && a<INT_MIN+b)printf("Overflow \n");
```

For multiplication there are a range of methods, most of which involve using higher precision arithmetic. A simple method that works for a*b is:

```
if (a > INT_MAX / b) printf("Overflow \n");
if (a < INT_MIN / b) printf("Overflow \n");
```

which is simply a rearrangement of a*b>INT_MAX and a*b<INT_MIN.
Notice that this only works if b>0. If b<0 you need to use:

```
if (a < INT_MAX / b) printf("Overflow \n");
if (a > INT_MIN / b) printf("Overflow \n");
```

which means that to protect against overflow you need:

```
if (b > 0) {
    if (a > (INT_MAX / b)) printf("Overflow 1\n");
    if (a < (INT_MIN / b)) printf("Overflow 2\n");
};
if (b < 0) {
    if (a < (INT_MAX / b)) printf("Overflow 1\n");
    if (a > (INT_MIN / b)) printf("Overflow 2\n");
};
```

The disadvantage is that division is usually more expensive in terms of clock cycles than multiplication and you have two divisions and at least three comparisons for a single multiply.

Also notice that INT_MIN*-1 can result in an overflow, even though it isn't out of range, and you might need to test:

```
if ((a == -1) && (b == INT_MIN))printf("Overflow \n");
if ((b == -1) && (a == INT_MIN))printf("Overflow \n");
```

Finally, when it comes to division, there is little to do as overflow is only possible for INT_MIN/-1, but you do have to remember to avoid division by zero.

Using Unsigned Arithmetic to Detect Overflow

There is a little-known alternative to detecting overflow before it happens. Unsigned arithmetic never overflows - it always rolls over and never exhibits undefined behavior. As two's-complement arithmetic is identical to unsigned arithmetic – we simply interpret the bit patterns differently – an alternative is to perform the arithmetic unsigned and then test for overflow using unsigned tests.

For example:

```
unsigned int temp= (unsigned) a + (unsigned)b;
if(a>0 && b>0 && temp>INT_MAX) printf("Overflow \n");
if(a<0 && b<0 && temp<=INT_MAX) printf("Overflow \n");
result=(signed int)temp;
```

In this case we cast a and b to unsigned integers. While this is always possible, it depends on the representation used for negative values. The addition is done as if the numbers are positive and if rollover occurs it is ignored. Next we test for overflow in the usual way. If a and b are positive then the result has to be positive and hence less than or equal to INT_MAX. If a and b are negative then the result has to be negative and hence greater than INT_MAX.

If you don't follow why negative implies greater than INT_MAX then go back and read up on two's-complement, but the key is that the range of positive values representable in two's-complement is 0 to INT_MAX.

You can use the same technique to implement and check for overflow in other situations.

Avoiding Overflow by Increased Precision

If you want to work only with 32-bit integers then one way of dealing with overflow is to do the arithmetic using a representation that cannot overflow.

If you add one n-bit number to another the largest and smallest possible results are 2*MAX and 2*MIN respectively, which means the result can always be represented in n+1 bits. Similarly, if you multiply one n-bit number by another the largest is MAX*MAX and the smallest is MIN*MIN and the result can always be represented in 2n bits.

What this means is that if you want to do 32-bit arithmetic you can avoid overflow problems by doing it in a 64-bit representation. That is, if the machine you are using supports long long then you can do the arithmetic in 64 bits and use the result to work out if it is representable in 32 bits, hence detecting 32-bit overflow without risking undefined behavior and with only one additional test.

For example, to multiply a and b:

```
long long temp=(long long) a * (long long) b;
if(temp>INT_MAX || temp<INT_MIN){
    printf("Overflow \n");
}else{
    result=(int)temp;
};
```

A similar approach works for addition and for any other operation that always gives a result representable in 64 bits. Notice that while squaring is fine, cubing can overflow 64 bits. This approach has a number of advantages. On machines that support 64 bits it has the potential to be fast and, perhaps more importantly, it is very simple and understandable. However, you have to remember to perform the overflow check after every operation and essentially reduce the values to 32 bits.

For example, if you want to compute a*b*c then the simple-minded approach:

```
long long temp=(long long) a * (long long) b * (long long) c;
```

can overflow.

You have to do the job in two steps:

```
long long temp=(long long) a * (long long) b;
if(temp>INT_MAX || temp<INT_MIN){
   printf("Overflow \n");
}else{
   temp=temp * (long long) c;
   if(temp>INT_MAX || temp<INT_MIN){
      printf("Overflow \n");
   }else{
      result=(int)temp;
   };
};
```

Notice that there is no need to reduce the intermediate result back to 32 bits as all that matters is that it is representable in 32 bits.

Trapping Signed Overflow

The tests described above are often too time-consuming for machines with limited resources. There is an alternative that is probably the best way to deal with the signed overflow problem if it is available – and it usually is. Most, if not all, hardware has the ability to detect signed overflow in hardware. The logic is fairly simple in that it compares the sign bits of the two operands and the result and sets an overflow flag in the status register. If you were writing in assembler than you would simply check the overflow flag, but C doesn't provide a standard way of accessing the status register. ARM, for example, has a C bit for unsigned overflow and a V bit for signed overflow and these can be tested using the cs, cc, vs and vc instructions. If you want to use status flags you have no choice but to write some assembler, see Chapter 15.

Some systems and compilers provide a non-standard way of reading the status register of the machine, but an alternative is to trigger a software interrupt, or trap, when overflow occurs. This is what GCC does if you use the -ftrapv compiler option, generating a SIGABRT signal, see Chapter 4, under Linux and Windows.

What this means is that you can check for overflow within your program almost for free. All you have to do is define a signal handler function:

```
void signalHandler(int sig) {
  printf("Overflow detected\n");
}
```

You also need to include `signal.h`:

```
#include <signal.h>
```

To ensure that your handler is called when the overflow occurs, you need to register the handler with the system and mask all signals in the usual way. For example:

```
#define _POSIX_C_SOURCE  200809L
#include <stdio.h>
#include <stdlib.h>
#include <signal.h>
#include <limits.h>

void signalHandler(int sig) {
    printf("Overflow detected\n");
}

int main(int argc, char** argv) {
    sigset_t mask;
    sigfillset(&mask);
    struct sigaction psa = {0};
    psa.sa_handler = signalHandler;
    psa.sa_mask = mask;
    sigaction(SIGABRT, &psa, NULL);
    int a = 1;
    int b = INT_MAX;
    printf("%d \n", a + b);
    return (EXIT_SUCCESS);
}
```

Of course, you also have to remember to compile this with the `-ftrapv` option. If you do then, under Linux, you will see:

```
Overflow detected
RUN FAILED (exit value -1, total time: 94ms)
```

Notice that the signal is raised if overflow occurs within any expression. This means you don't have to break an expression down into small steps and test for overflow after each operation. This in itself is a simplification worth the effort of using `-ftrapv`.

There is a problem in that you cannot modify the default behavior of SIGABRT. When you return from the signal handler, your program is terminated in response to the abort signal, even if you have defined a handler. There is also the problem of identifying the reason for the abort – was it an overflow or did something else send the signal? Even if you can pin down the cause to an overflow, you still don't know which expression in your program caused the overflow.

In this form the -ftrapv is useful for testing and debugging your program, but it isn't of any use in arranging for your program to handle an overflow that occurs in use. The SIGABRT signal always aborts your program and gives it no chance to fix the problem.

It is possible to override the default behavior of SIGABRT but you have to use setjmp and longjmp - see Chapter 4. The reason is that SIGABRT is different from other signals in that it always fires twice. The first time you can intercept it with a handler, but when the handler returns the SIGABRT disables it and fires the SIGABRT a second time, which of course terminates the process. To stop this happening we need a siglongjmp to restore the program state without any pending signals.

First we need the includes and the buffer we are going to use to store the environment:

```c
#define _POSIX_C_SOURCE  200809L
#include <stdio.h>
#include <stdlib.h>
#include <signal.h>
#include <limits.h>
#include <setjmp.h>

static jmp_buf jumpBuffer;
```

We still need a signal handler, but this is going perform a siglongjmp back to the point in the program just before the expression that caused the overflow:

```c
void signalHandler(int sig) {
    printf("Overflow detected\n");
    siglongjmp(jumpBuffer, 1);
}
```

The main program sets up the variables involved in the expression and the mask for the handler:

```
int main(int argc, char** argv) {
    sigset_t mask;
    sigfillset(&mask);
    struct sigaction psa = {0};
    psa.sa_handler = signalHandler;
    psa.sa_mask = mask;

    int a = 1;
    int b = INT_MAX;
```

Then we use an if statement to implement a try-catch block:

```
    if (sigsetjmp(jumpBuffer, 0)) {
        printf("Overflow \n");
        printf("%d \n", a);
    } else {
        sigaction(SIGABRT, &psa, NULL);
        int result = a + b;
        printf("%d \n", result);
    }
    return (EXIT_SUCCESS);
}
```

The first time the sigsetjmp function is executed, it stores the environment in jumpBuffer and returns 0 so the else clause is executed, and we set the signal handler and proceed to do the calculation we want to check.

As soon as the expression a+b is executed, an overflow occurs which calls the signal handler which performs a siglongjmp back to the start of the if where the sigsetjmp function returns a value of 1 and now the true clause is executed giving us a chance to handle the error.

Notice that the second time the if is executed it has access to all of the variables it would normally have access to. It is possible to allow the signal handler to modify and create variables, but it is much safer not to – if not done correctly it can result in undefined behavior. Let the code in the if statement in the main program do the work and just use the signal handler as a way of getting back to the point in the program where the trouble occurred.

There is an overhead in using this approach as the environment has to be saved. However, this is usually very low, around a 5% slowdown on Raspberry Pi 3 and on Windows. As the environment only has to be saved once for each block of expressions you are protecting, this is a much lower overhead than having to test each operation that makes up the expression.

The complete program is:

```
#define _POSIX_C_SOURCE  200809L
#include <stdio.h>
#include <stdlib.h>
#include <signal.h>
#include <limits.h>
#include <setjmp.h>

static jmp_buf jumpBuffer;

void signalHandler(int sig) {
    printf("Overflow detected\n");
    siglongjmp(jumpBuffer, 1);
}

int main(int argc, char** argv) {
    sigset_t mask;
    sigfillset(&mask);
    struct sigaction psa = {0};
    psa.sa_handler = signalHandler;
    psa.sa_mask = mask;


    int a = 1;
    int b = INT_MAX;
    if (sigsetjmp(jumpBuffer, 0)) {
        printf("Overflow \n");
        printf("%d \n", a);
    } else {
        sigaction(SIGABRT, &psa, NULL);
        int result = a + b;
        printf("%d \n", result);
    }
    return (EXIT_SUCCESS);
}
```

If you can make use of this approach, it is probably the best way to handle the signed overflow problem. Notice that you have to put any arithmetic you want to check in an if statement of the sort used above and you should disable the signal handler when you don't want to make use of it.

Detecting Unsigned Rollover

The problem of detecting unsigned rollover is just as important in some applications as signed overflow detection. As already discussed, unsigned arithmetic rolls over at a value of 2^n, where n is the number of bits. Another and more technical way of saying this is that all unsigned arithmetic is performed mod 2^n and modular arithmetic is the subject of the next section.

It is often said that unsigned arithmetic is inherently safer in that it avoids undefined behavior, but it can still provide the wrong answer. Detecting rollover is important and especially so when it becomes more likely when we use fixed point arithmetic – see the next chapter.

So how do we test for rollover?

Most of the techniques we have encountered for signed arithmetic work for unsigned but with some important differences.

The first is that as unsigned arithmetic cannot result in undefined behavior we can check for rollover after the computation, but it is still much easier to check before the computation.

For example to check for rollover on addition we can use:

```
unsigned int a = 1;
unsigned int b = UINT_MAX;
if (a>UINT_MAX-b)printf("Overflow \n");
unsigned int result=a+b;
```

as a and b are both positive the sum has to be larger than either.

To test for rollover on multiplication we can use:

```
if (b!=0 && a > UINT_MAX / b) printf("Overflow \n");
```

If you are using GCC then you can also use the built-in functions.

For example, to check for rollover on addition you would use:

```
if (__builtin_add_overflow(a, b, &result)) printf("Overflow \n");
```

and for multiplication:

```
if (__builtin_mul_overflow(a, b, &result)) printf("Overflow \n");
```

If the machine supports a larger precision unsigned integer, then you can also use the approach of using more bits than are needed and check for rollover.

For example:

```
unsigned int a=2;
unsigned int b=UINT_MAX;
unsigned int result;

unsigned long long temp=(unsigned long long) a *
                             (unsigned long long) b;
if(temp>UINT_MAX){
    printf("Overflow \n");
}else{
    result=(int)temp;
};
```

What you cannot do easily is check for rollover using the carry flag to trap the event. That is, there is no unsigned equivalent of the -ftrapv flag for the GCC compiler. This is a pity because unsigned rollover does normally set the carry flag and this could be used to automatically detect rollover. C doesn't support a standard way to access the carry flag but you can always use inline assembler to do the job.

Modular Arithmetic

In the previous section it was stated that unsigned integer arithmetic is performed mod 2^n where n is the number of bits. In fact modular arithmetic is more generally important and deserves to be better understood.

If you are not familiar with modular arithmetic then all you need to know is that arithmetic mod n is like working with a clock face with n markings starting at 0 and you count 0,1,2,..n-1 and then rollover to 0 again.

You can convert any number to its mod equivalent by counting up to it on the clock face until you have advanced enough to reach a final value. Another way to get the mod equivalent of a number is to notice that it is just the remainder after dividing by n.

In C you can compute the remainder after dividing by n using the mod operator %.

For example:

7%3

is 1 because 7/3 is 2 remainder 1.

You can see that the mod operator is closely related to the integer division operator.

That is:

```
7 = (7/2)*2+7%2
```

as 7/2 is 3 and 3*2 is 6 plus 7%2 the remainder on dividing by 2 gives a total of 7 and in general:

```
a = (a/b)*b+a%b
```

In non-integer arithmetic you would expect (a/b)*b to be exactly a, but in integer arithmetic you have to remember to add the remainder.

Looking at this another way, a/b gives you the number of rollovers when a is represented modulo b and a % b gives you the value shown on the clock face.

Integer division comes in useful whenever you are trying to chop something up into a number of parts and the mod operator is useful when you need to know what is left over after chopping something up into a number of parts.

For example, how many pages is 20000 lines of text taken 66 lines to a page?

Answer 20000/66=303 whole pages plus one with 20000%66 lines on the last page.

Notice that a number mod b can be considered to have an additive inverse. For example:

```
(3+4) % 7 = 0
```

and so in mod 7 you can regard 4 as the additive inverse of 3 and vice versa. If you wanted to, you could regard 4 as being a representation of -3 in mod 7 arithmetic.

Now you can see that unsigned arithmetic is mod 2^n and signed two's-complement arithmetic is mod 2^n arithmetic with the additive inverses of the first half of the range regarded as negative numbers. Of course, all of this works for multiplication and division because they are just repeated addition and subtraction. Notice that if you want to work in mod 2^n where n isn't one of the sizes of variable available to you, then you could make use of a mask to reduce the precision to n bits. For example, if you want to use arithmetic mod 2^8 you could use unsigned char:

```
unsigned char a=42;
unsigned char b=205;
unsigned char result=a+b;
```

gives you $(42+205)\%2^8$ as its result.

Alternatively you could use:

```
unsigned int a=42;
unsigned int b=205;
unsigned int c=(a+b) & 0xFF;
```

as reducing the result to eight bits ensures that the result is mod 2^8.

On a binary machine working mod to a power of 2 comes naturally, but for decimal machines arithmetic modulo 10 has some uses. For example, how can you get the second decimal digit of a value?

If a = 123456 notice that:

```
a/100 = 1234
a%100 = 56
```

you can see that $a/10^n$ is a shift right by n decimal places and $a\%10^n$ is a decimal n-place mask which returns the least significant n digits. We can complete the set of operators by noting that $a*10^n$ is a left shift by n digits and $a-a\%10^n$ is decimal n-place mask which removes the least significant n digits. Putting this together gives:

```
(a%100)/10=56/10=5
```

or:

```
(a/10)%10=5
```

and in general to extract the dth decimal digit you can use:

```
(a%10^d)/10^{d-1}
```

or:

```
(a/10^{d-1})%10
```

remembering that $10^0 = 1$.

If you think that this looks a lot like bit manipulation but in base ten, then there is some truth in the idea. Integer division and modular arithmetic are often used in this way. Notice, however, that we are still working in binary. That is, in the example a = 5 and this is the bit pattern 101.

You can use this sort of technique to convert binary values in other representations such as Binary Coded Decimal (BCD) to a string, see earlier in the chapter. For example, to convert a = 5 to a char you would simply cast it to a char after OR-ing it with 0x30 to give the ASCII code for the digit 5:

```
unsigned int a=5;
char digit=(char)(0x30 |a);
printf("%c",digit);
```

This is how, with optimizations, printf and sprintf convert a binary value to a decimal string representation.

Of course, if you want all of the digits of a value you would implement the digit extraction as an iteration:

```
unsigned int a = 123456789;
unsigned int temp = a;
char digits[25];
unsigned int i = 0;
while (temp != 0) {
    digits[i] =(char)(0x30 | temp % 10);
    temp = temp / 10;
    i++;
};
digits[i]=0;
printf("%s", digits);
```

Working with binary as decimal digits is particularly useful if you want to implement decimal fixed point arithmetic – see the next chapter.

Division by Zero

You may know that in mathematics division by zero is undefined. This is true in the C language for integers, but not for floating point numbers. That is, both a/0 and a%0, which has an implied division by zero, are undefined behavior and hence should be avoided.

Avoiding division by zero is very easy – simply test before the division:

```
if(b!=0) result=a/b;
```

or:

```
if(b!=0) result =a%b;
```

More problematic is what to do when you have a divide by zero. Many programmers believe that there are sensible choices for a/0 – this isn't the case. For example, the argument that as a/b gets bigger as b gets smaller leads to a logical choice of infinity, or at least INT_MAX, as the result when b=0. This may have some validity when evaluating some functions using floating point, but in general it isn't true. In particular, for integers there are no fractional values to approach zero in the limit. The point is a/b is undefined when b is zero because it makes no logical sense within the framework of integer arithmetic. If you give a/0 a value, x say, then you can deduce that x*0 = a, which is nonsense. Put simply, there is no x which multiplies zero to give a non-zero value – hence there is no division by zero.

In nearly all cases, an attempt to divide by zero in integer division is the result of some error earlier in the program. In the case of floating point calculation, you can get a legitimate division by zero due to a value becoming too small to be represented – underflow. In this case, substituting a very big value for the result has some theoretical, if not practical, validity.

92

Trapping Division by Zero

Is there anyway to trap a division by zero?

The answer to this question is usually yes, but it is a non-standard operation. For C, division by zero is undefined behavior and so should never happen in a properly formed program. However, most machines implement a hardware or software interrupt for any attempt to divide by zero. The reason is simply that the hardware that does division generally can't cope with division by zero and so generates an interrupt. The problem is that how this interrupt is handled depends on the machine and the operating system and very rarely the language in use. For example, although division by zero is undefined behavior on an x86 machine, or an ARM machine, running Linux, the result is usually a runtime error.

You can attempt to trap the error. Under Linux an integer divide by zero generates a SIGFPE signal, which can be handled in the usual way. Notice that SIGFPE is a signal for a floating point error, but while integer divide by zero triggers it, floating point divide by zero doesn't.

For example:

```
#define _POSIX_C_SOURCE  200809L
#include <stdio.h>
#include <stdlib.h>
#include <signal.h>

void signalHandler(int sig) {
    printf("signalHandler\n");
}

int main(int argc, char** argv) {
    sigset_t mask;
    sigfillset(&mask);
    struct sigaction psa = {0};
    psa.sa_handler = signalHandler;
    psa.sa_mask = mask;
    sigaction(SIGFPE, &psa, NULL);

    int a = 1;
    int b = 0;
    int result = a / b;
    printf("result= %d \n", result);
    return (EXIT_SUCCESS);
}
```

Under Linux running on ARM the program prints signalHandler and then 0, i.e. divide by zero sets the result to zero. Under Linux on x86 returning from the handler fires the signal again and the program never stops printing signalHandler. Under Windows it simply ends in a runtime error. The differences between Linux on ARM and x86 are due to hardware differences. On the Windows machine it is also the fault of the operating system.

To handle the signal properly under Linux running on any hardware you need to implement a try-catch using setlongjmp as in the case of overflow trapping described earlier:

```
#define _POSIX_C_SOURCE  200809L
#include <stdio.h>
#include <stdlib.h>
#include <signal.h>
#include <limits.h>
#include <setjmp.h>
static jmp_buf jumpBuffer;

void signalHandler(int sig) {
    printf("signalHandler\n");
    siglongjmp(jumpBuffer, 1);
}

int main(int argc, char** argv) {
    int a = 1;
    int b = 0;
    int result;
    sigset_t mask;
    sigfillset(&mask);
    struct sigaction psa = {0};
    psa.sa_handler = signalHandler;
    psa.sa_mask = mask;
    sigaction(SIGFPE, &psa, NULL);
    if (sigsetjmp(jumpBuffer, 0)) {
        printf("Divide by zero \n");
    } else {
        result = a / b;
        printf("%d \n", result);
    }
    printf("result= %d \n", result);
    return (EXIT_SUCCESS);
}
```

Now the signal is handled correctly on both ARM and x86 under Linux. It also works on x86 under Windows, but you need to change sigsetjmp and siglongjmp to setjmp and longjmp. You would still need to verify it worked on the particular hardware you were using as there are many variations on how divide by zero is handled.

Notice that SIGFPE can be triggered for more than just divide by zero. To make it work correctly you need to use the three-parameter form of the signal handler and examine si_code in the returned structure to see what error actually caused the problem. This is FPE_INTDIV for divide by zero. For example:

```c
#define _POSIX_C_SOURCE  200809L
#include <stdio.h>
#include <stdlib.h>
#include <signal.h>
#include <limits.h>
#include <setjmp.h>
static jmp_buf jumpBuffer;

void signalHandler(int sig, siginfo_t *info, void *ucontext) {
    printf("signalHandler\n");
    printf("%d\n", info->si_code==FPE_INTDIV);
    siglongjmp(jumpBuffer, 1);

}

int main(int argc, char** argv) {
    int a = 1;
    int b = 0;
    int result;
    sigset_t mask;
    sigfillset(&mask);
    struct sigaction psa = {0};
    psa.sa_mask = mask;
    psa.sa_flags = SA_SIGINFO;
    psa.sa_sigaction = signalHandler;
    sigaction(SIGFPE, &psa, NULL);
    if (sigsetjmp(jumpBuffer, 0)) {
        printf("Divide by zero \n");
    } else {
        result = a / b;
        printf("%d \n", result);
    }
    printf("result= %d \n", result);
    return (EXIT_SUCCESS);
}
```

In most cases you will see zero printed as, despite what the standard says, si_code often contains a negative number, indicating a signal generated from a process rather than the kernel, i.e. it doesn't give the cause of the SIGFPE.

Overall the state of runtime detection of overflow or divide by zero errors is a mess. Some excuse the situation by saying that in C signed overflow, or division by zero, is undefined behavior and therefore should be detected at compile time and not left to a runtime error. This is, of course, nonsense. Even if C was the only language to use these POSIX features, they should still be implemented correctly and, even if you regard a runtime error as undefined behavior, we should still be allowed to write code to handle it in a reasonable way.

Summary

- Integer arithmetic is achieved using a full adder. When implemented in software, integer addition is iterative.

- Binary is not the only possible representation - Binary Coded Decimal is also common.

- Implementing BCD arithmetic is surprising difficult to do efficiently.

- There are different ways of representing negative numbers. Sign magnitude is common, but two's-complement is preferable as it takes care of the sign automatically.

- What happens when arithmetic results in a value that cannot be represented is a difficult topic. For unsigned arithmetic the standard defines that it should result in a rollover. For signed arithmetic overflow is undefined behavior.

- Detecting overflow before it happens is an important task and there are many ways of doing the job. There are built-in functions in GCC, but if you don't want to, or can't, use them it is possible to test for overflow using conditionals.

- To avoid problems with undefined behavior, you can always implement signed arithmetic using unsigned operators, or you can increase the precision so that overflow cannot occur.

- In many cases the operating system will provide a software interrupt, or trap, that you can use to detect and handle signed overflow. In most cases you will also need to use some advanced C to implement a try-catch construct.

- Although most of the problems are centered on signed overflow, it can be important to detect unsigned overflow.

- Modular arithmetic is, in fact, what all integer arithmetic is. Integer division and the mod or remainder operator are very useful in general programming.

- Detecting division by zero should be easy, but it is often difficult to detect it in a way that allows you to handle it in software.

Chapter 6

Fixed Point Arithmetic

Integer arithmetic is usually supposed to be good for some things but not for others – which need floating point arithmetic. In fact, for small machines, integer arithmetic might be all you need. In this chapter we look at how to implement fixed point arithmetic, which is just integer arithmetic with a scale factor.

Why Fixed Point?

If you are accustomed to using big computers and modern languages such as Java or Python, you will hardly give a second thought to multiplying or dividing two numbers. The most commonly used format for numeric values is floating point arithmetic and, despite its problems, it is usually the best to use. The problems are to do with accuracy and how rounding errors accumulate. However, for small machines and low-level programming floating point is a problem for another reason – it can be slow. What is more many small machines, the Arduino Uno for example, don't have floating point hardware and when this is the case you have to resort to a software emulation. The nature of this software emulation depends on the CPU in question, but there are a number of standard floating point libraries.

A modern CPU has a floating point unit (FPU) also referred to as a math coprocessor, that is almost as fast as its integer arithmetic unit. This wasn't always true and it means that you can no longer assume that fixed point is faster than floating point. Before you make a commitment to using fixed point on a machine that has a modern FPU, you need to benchmark the standard operations of arithmetic. For example on the Raspberry Pi 3, a floating point multiplication is only 30% slower than an integer multiplication. When working with a CPU that implements floating point in a similar time to integer operations, it is unlikely that fixed point will perform better as it has additional steps.

Often, however, external devices deliver their data in a form that is closer to fixed point than anything else. In these cases it is often easier to work in fixed point rather than convert to floating point and perhaps back again.

What all this means is that for much arithmetic you don't need floating point as fixed point will do the job very well. In most cases you don't need a fixed point library, if you need one then the chances are it will be the machine architecture that you are working with that pushes you to a specific choice. Otherwise use libfixmath, which is described later.

Fixed Point is Integer Arithmetic

Fixed point arithmetic is just scaled integer arithmetic. For example, suppose you need to work with values in the range zero to a hundred to two decimal places – a temperature say. You can easily represent such a value as an integer by multiplying by a hundred. That is, a temperature of 57.89C would be represented by:

```
57.89*100 = 5789
```

You can see that we are using four decimal digits with the lower two dedicated to representing the fractional part of the value.

Things are a little more complicated than this sounds because of the way arithmetic operations affect the scale factor and indeed the need to remember to include the scale factor at all. Essentially we have removed the need to worry about fractional parts of values by converting everything to an integer.

In the above example we have been using a decimal scale factor, but as we know that a shift is almost the same as multiply or dividing by multiples of 2 and is very fast, it is more efficient, if slightly more difficult conceptually, to use a power of two as a scale factor.

Each left shift multiplies by two and adds another bit to the representation of the fractional part of the value:

Fraction Bits	Scale Factor	Precision
1	2	0.5
2	4	0.25
3	8	0.125
4	16	0.0625
5	32	0.03125
6	64	0.015625
7	128	0.0078125
8	256	0.00390625
9	1024	0.0009765625
10	2048	0.00048828125

The usual rule of thumb is that for one decimal place you need at least four fraction bits and for two decimal places at least seven, preferably eight.

Of course if you are using n bits for the fractional part of the value you only have 32 − n bits, assuming a 32-bit int, to represent the value. The table below shows the largest value that can be represented in a 32-bit int with the number of bits used to represent the factional part.

Fraction Bits	Unsigned	Signed
1	2147483648	1073741824
2	1073741824	536870912
3	536870912	268435456
4	268435456	134217728
5	134217728	67108864
6	67108864	33554432
7	33554432	16777216
8	16777216	8388608
9	8388608	4194304
10	4194304	2097152

You can see that with 32-bit integers there is a good range of values at reasonable accuracy.

If you select n bits for the fractional part then you can think of the binary point as being at position n. There is no standard notation for fixed point format, but Qm.n, which means m bits for the non-fractional part and n used for the fractional part, is common. For example Q16.16 would be a 32-bit int with 16 fractional bits.

When you enter data you need to scale it so that the binary point is at position n. As you do calculations it is possible that the position of the binary point will change. To avoid this you have to rescale to keep the binary point fixed, hence *fixed* point arithmetic.

Notice that you could even position the binary point to the right of the value so working with a scaling that allows for very large numbers to be represented. For example, if the binary point is at bit -1 then the scale factor is ½ and a value of x actually represents 2x. This is the binary analog of our usual exponent notation, i.e. the value is $x*2^s$ where s is the position of the binary point, which can be negative as well as positive.

Rescaling

Let's consider the way the four operations of arithmetic behave under fixed point with the binary point at position s.

Suppose we have two variables containing variables a and b with the binary point at bit s, then:

a+b;

and:

a-b;

Both have the binary point at bit s as:

$a*2^s+b*2^s = (a+b)*2^s$

and:

$a*2^s-b*2^s = (a-b)*2^s$

Things are not so simple for multiplication:

a*b

is the same as:

$a*2^s*b*2^s = (a*b)*2^{2s}$

and hence a*b has the binary point at bit 2s. To keep the binary point at s you have to rescale by 2^s. That is, you implement a*b as:

$a*b/2^s$

or:

a*b>>s

That is, to multiply two fixed-point binary numbers you need to perform an s-bit shift right to restore the binary point to its fixed position.

Notice that you are throwing away s fractional bits by truncation. In some cases rounding is needed to keep all of the precision possible.

There are many different ways of rounding, but rounding up is easy to implement. All you have to do is take the lower s bits that are about to be thrown away and, if they are greater than ½ of the new lowest-order bit, add one to the low-order bit. You don't need to use a conditional to do this. Simply take the fractional bits about to be discarded, shift left by one bit and add to the value then truncate. That is, if s is 8:

```
value = value+((0xFF & value)<<1);
value>> =8;
```

is a rounded result.

Notice that it is possible for the multiplication to overflow, even if in principle the result could be represented – more on this later.

Division has the same problem as multiplication in that it moves the binary point, but in the other direction.

That is:

a/b

is the same as:

a*2^s/(b*2^s) = (a/b)

and the binary point has been shifted to the far left. In this case we have to perform a scaling to return the binary point to the same position.

(a*b)*2^s

or:

(a/b)<<s;

Notice that as the result has no fractional bits, a simple rescaling after the division will have all zeros as the fractional part. The fractional part of the division has been lost during the implicit shift right that occurs during division. We can avoid the loss of precision by performing the scaling before the division:

a*2^s/b

which gives an answer with the binary point at s and preserves the fractional part of the result.

That is, implement:

a/b

as:

(a<<s)/b;

and not as:

(a/b)<<s;

Notice that, despite this being a division which makes the result smaller you can still generate an overflow by the shift left.

This is nearly all there is to know about fixed point arithmetic. Other functions such as square, square root and so on have to analyzed in the same way and their results have to be scaled to bring the binary point back to the same position.

Temperature Conversion

Let's look at an example. Consider the problem of a temperature measuring sensor returning a fixed point value in Celsius and we need to convert it to Fahrenheit. The usual formula is to multiple by 9, divide by 5 and then add 32 and for the sake of a fixed point demonstration let's do exactly this using two digits precision with the binary point at bit 8, i.e. using a scale factor of 2^8.

Our first problem is how to get some example values into the program. Suppose the temperature is 43.25C, how do we convert this decimal value into fixed point? We can implement the scale factor by a shift of the integer part, but this doesn't work for the fractional part. However, the compiler will evaluate a floating point expression for you and assign it as an integer value. So we can get the fixed point value into temp using:

```
int temp = 43.25*(1<<8);
```

For the sake of a more interesting example, we can store the 5, 9 and 32 in variables in the same fixed point format.

```
int nine = 9.00*(1<<8);
int five = 5.00*(1<<8);
int constant = 32.00*(1<<8);
```

Now we can proceed to the fixed point calculations broken out one instruction at a time to make things clear. First we multiply by nine and scale the result to bring the binary point back to its original position:

```
temp = temp*nine >>8;
```

next we can divide by five, this time scaling temp to ensure we get a fractional part in the answer:

```
temp = (temp<<8)/five;
```

Finally we add the constant and, of course, no scaling is needed:

```
temp = temp+constant;
```

Of course, in practice, as the 9, the 5 and the 32 are constants, we wouldn't normally have scaled them before use and so the correctly scaled fixed-point calculation would be written:

```
temp = temp*9/5+(32<<8);
```

As 9/5 is 1.8 exactly in decimal you might think that a better way to do the calculation is to simply multiply by 1.8 and cut out the costly integer division.

You can do this quite easily:

```
int fact = 1.8*(1<<8);
int temp = 43.25*(1<<8);
int temp = (temp*fact >>8)+(32<<8);
```

and it works, but it isn't accurate as the previous method. This is puzzling as 9/5 is exactly 1.80, which can be represented to two decimal places using a scale factor of 8, but this doesn't take into account that in binary 1.8 is not exactly representable. If you work it out you will find that 1.8 is:

```
1.1100110011001100…
```

To get the same precision as the multiply by 9 divide by 5 method, you need to go to a scale factor of 2^{10}. Notice that if you go to 2^{16}, i.e. Q16.16, with a signed int, then the calculation overflows.

Arithmetic can be tricky.

Printing Fixed Point

Finally, how do we print a fixed point value as a decimal?

This is more difficult than you might imagine and is often implemented incorrectly. You can get the integer part of the result simply by shifting:

```
temp>>8
```

and this can be printed as if it was just an integer, which is exactly what it is. You can also isolate the bits of the fractional part using a mask:

```
temp&0xFF
```

and at this point the temptation is to print this as if it was an int:

```
printf("%d.%d \n",temp>>8,temp&0xFF);
```

but it isn't and this doesn't work.

The reason is that the bit pattern is weighted by inverse powers of 2 and the bit pattern doesn't correspond to the usual decimal values.

A simple example will illustrate the problem and give us the solution. Consider a fixed point value with the fractional part bit pattern:

```
10000000
```

which, if just treated as a decimal value, 128, gives a decimal fraction of:

```
.128
```

which is obviously wrong.

With the binary point inserted, the fractional part corresponds to:

`0.10000000`

and this is 0.5 in decimal, not 0.128.

The fractional part of the fixed point represents a value in the range 0 to less than 1, but as an unsigned binary integer it represents a range from 0 to 2^s. We can use this to obtain a decimal representation. For example, for the binary fraction:

`0.10000000`

the integer representation is:

`10000000`

which is 128, and this corresponds to the decimal fraction:

`128/2⁸ = 128/256 = 1/2 = 0.5`

Of course, we can't do the division to get 0.5 because we only have integer arithmetic, but if we multiply by 1000, a power of ten sufficient to give an integer, then we can do the entire calculation using integer arithmetic:

`1000*128/2⁸ = 1000*128/256 = 500`

which when printed with a decimal point in front is:

`0.500`

You can see that the power of ten gives you the corresponding number of decimal places.

Thus, if f is the fractional part converted to an integer, then $1000*f/2^s$ is the decimal representation of the fraction.

To print the temperature we use:

```
printf("%d.%d \n",temp>>8,(temp&0xFF)*1000/(1<<8));
```

This works with obvious adjustments for any scale factor and any number of decimal places.

It is important to note that the multiplication has to be performed before the division and this introduces the possibility of overflow. The rule is that the number of decimal places, d, has to satisfy:

$d*2^s<2^{32}$ or $d<2^{32-s}$

for a 32-bit int.

For example, if s is 16:

$d<2^{32-16}<2^{16}<65536$

the largest value of d that avoids an overflow is 10,000. If s is 8 then d can be as large as 10,000,000.

Overflow During a Computation

Notice that there is a possibility of an overflow due to the need to scale when you multiply or divide, even if the result could fit into the n-bit fixed-point format. That is, as fixed-point values are just scaled integers, there is the possibility of simple integer overflow and you can detect and handle this is in the usual way. However, for fixed point computations there is an additional overflow danger due to the scaling needed to keep the binary point at the same location. This can cause overflow during the computation, even if the final result is within the range of the format.

In multiplication you generate 2s fractional bits in the answer and then truncate to s restoring the fixed point format you started with. For example, suppose s is 8 then a and b have 8 fractional bits then a*b has 16 fractional bits and after s right shifts it has 8 fractional bits. The additional s fractional bits can cause the value to overflow during the computation, even though the final result is representable in that format after rescaling.

Our temperature recording problem would work very well with 16 bits out of 32 dedicated to the fractional part. This would allow for a maximum integer part of plus or minus 32,768, more than enough to represent plus or minus 100 degrees.

On the other hand if you start off with a temperature a of 50.42 and multiply by b which is set to 2 we have, in fixed point:

a*b

which is equivalent to:

$50.42 * 2^{16} * 2 * 2^{16} = 50.42 * 2^{33}$

This cannot be represented in 32 bits thus the calculation overflows, even though after scaling the actual result:

(a*b)>>16
$50.42 * 23^{17}$

fits easily into 32 bits.

If you multiply two fixed point Q16.16 numbers then the intermediate result always has 32 fractional bits, which means you lose the non-fractional part of the result in an overflow. Clearly this isn't useful. In general there is nothing you can do about this unless you are happy to lose precision or move to a higher precision, say 64 bits, where you can avoid the overflow by applying the rescaling before the multiplication.

For example, 16 fractional bits gives you a precision of 0.00001525878906 and if you perform the full 16-bit rescaling before the multiplication then you lose all of the fractional part and compute for example:

```
(a>>16)*b
```

which is equivalent to:

$$50*2^{17}$$

You have a result without overflow, but it has no fractional part.

A better way of doing the job is to distribute the rescaling between both values.

For example:

```
(a>>8)*(b>>8)
```

In this case both values are roughly accurate to two decimal places and the calculation is equivalent to:

$$50.42 * 2^8 * 2 * 2^8 = 50.42 * 2^{16}$$

which gives a correctly scaled result without overflow, but only accurate to 2 decimal places, even though the fixed point format suggests accuracy to better than 4 places.

In other words, by performing the rescaling before the multiplication you can distribute the precision between the values and obtain a lower precision result without overflow.

Sometimes this technique can give results that are fully accurate in the fixed-point format in use. If one of the two values can be represented exactly in a lower precision, then the multiplication can be done with no loss of precision. For example, if you want to multiply by b=2 exactly then use:

```
a*(b>>16)
```

The result is accurate to full 16-bit precision.

Of course, if you want to multiply by 2 then you would just use:

```
a<<2
```

and get an exact result faster. However, the principle holds for any value that can be represented exactly at a lower precision.

One small warning - the value has to be exactly representable as a binary fraction not a decimal fraction. For example, in the case of the conversion from Celsius to Fahrenheit, the multiplicative factor is 9/5, or 1.8 exactly. Unfortunately 1.8 is a recurring binary fraction and isn't representable exactly in any number of fractional bits.

However, the b=1.75 is exactly representable in just two fractional bits i.e. 1.11 and you can compute a*b using:

```
a*(b>>14) >>2
```

with no loss of precision.

If you would like to try this out first set up two values with 16-bit precision:

```
int f = 1.75*(1<<16);
int t = 50.515625*(1<<16);
```

Notice that both values are exactly represented using just four fractional bits. Variable f is set to:

```
0001c000
```

and t is set to:

```
00328400
```

Both can afford to lose 8 bits without losing precision.

The standard way of multiplying these values:

```
c = (t*f)>>16;
```

gives:

```
0.4023
```

which is incorrect due to overflow. Moving the rescaling to t:

```
c = (t>>16)*f;
```

results in:

```
87.5000
```

and this is close to the calculator result of 88.40234375 as the calculation performed is 50*1.75.

As the two values are accurate to two decimal places, scaling both by 2^{8}:

```
c = (t>>8)*(f>>8);
```

results in the correct answer:

```
88.4023
```

You can avoid overflow in division in the same way by trading magnitude for precision. That is, if:

```
(a<<s)/b;
```

results in an overflow, move some of the rescaling to after the division. For example, if there are 8 fractional bits you could use:

```
((a<<4)/b)<<4
```

Once again you have lost precision, but at least you have an answer.

Avoiding Overflow with 64-bits

Another approach to the problem, one which is the preferred solution in many cases, is to use twice the number of bits during the calculation. This guarantees that you don't get an overflow due to scaling. For example, using Q16.16, and displaying only the integer part of the result:

```
int a = 1.23*(1<<16);
int b = 4.56*(1<<16);
int result = (a*b)>>16;
printf("result = %d \n", result>>16);
```

prints -1 due to the inevitable overflow.

Using 64-bit integers solves the problem:

```
int a = 1.23*(1<<16);
int b = 4.56*(1<<16);
int result = (int)((((long long)a)*((long long)b))>>16);
printf("result = %d \n", result>>16);
```

You can simplify the expression by using a temporary long long variable rather than casting and by relying on the promotion rules for arithmetic to avoid some of the casts. This is an approach used by some fixed point libraries, but it obviously depends on having access to reasonably fast 64-bit arithmetic in hardware.

Simulating 64-bit Multiply

If you don't have a 64-bit integer to work with, you can always simulate one, even though this slow things down a little. The idea is to represent each of the values in the multiplication by a pair of 32-bit integers. The trick is to put the integer part into one of the pair and the fractional part in the other. This means you are multiplying two pairs of 16-bit values which cannot overflow in 32 bits.

If the high and low 16 bits of a and b are stored in al, ah, bl and bh we have:

$$a*2^s*b*2^s/2^s \quad = (ah*2^s+al)*(bh*2^s+bl)/2^s$$
$$= (ah*bh*2^s*2^s+al*bh*2^s+ah*bl*2^s+al*bl)/2^s$$
$$= ah*bh*2^s+al*bh+ah*bl+al*bl/2^s$$

Converting this to C:

```
int ah,al,bh,bl;
ah = a>>16;
al = a&0xFFFF;
bh = b>>16;
bl = b&0xFFFF;
result = ((ah*bh)<<16)+ah*bl+al*bh+((al*bl)>>16);
```

This gives you the full precision as if the multiplication had been performed using 64-bit integers. The cost is that now a single multiplication takes four operations.

GCC Fixed Point Extensions

The situation with regard to fixed point libraries is fragmented. What libraries you can actually expect to use depends very much on the machine you are targeting. There is also the issue of do you need a full implementation of a library?

Many programs do only simple and isolated calculations and in this case the DIY approach is usually sufficient. If you need to do more complex calculations then you may need to find implementations of functions such as sin, cos and square root. Even in this case it may be better to use off-the-shelf functions rather than an entire library. The reason is that there is no single well-supported fixed point library for all platforms and if you adopt a library then your app is dependent on future support for that library.

You may be surprised that there is no support for fixed point in the C standards. There was, and is, a draft proposal (ISO draft 18037), but nothing has come of it and it is currently dormant. However, GCC has implemented some of its recommendations as built-in functions, types and operators, but at the moment this is only supported on one target – ARM. If you try to make use of these built-ins on any other architecture, you will see the message:

error: fixed-point types not supported for this target

As a result the GCC built-ins are only useful for specific targets.

Notice that manufacturers often provide compilers based on GCC that include their own propriety extensions to C, including fixed point support.

Another problem with the GCC fixed point built-ins is that they are under-documented and hence seem complex. However, once you know what has been provided it is fairly simple.

GCC fixed point provides types for fixed point with overflow and with saturation, i.e. when the maximum or minimum value is reached the computation carries on using that value. There are two general types, accum which has an integer and fractional part, and fract which only has a fractional part, i.e. is in the range 0 to 1 or -1 to 1. The types vary in size depending on machine architecture, but typically the fracts are:

short fract	signed byte Q0.7
unsigned short fract	byte Q0.8
fract	Signed 16-bit word Q0.15
unsigned fract	16-bit word Q0.16
long fract	Signed 32-bit word Q0.31
unsigned long fract	32-bit word Q0.32
long long fract	Signed 64-bit word Q0.63

Notice that for signed types the most significant bit is the sign bit.

111

The accums are:

short accum	Signed 16-bit word Q0.15
unsigned short accum	16-bit word Q8.8
accum	Signed 32-bit word Q16.15
unsigned accum	32-bit word Q16.16
long accum	Signed 64-bit word Q32.31
unsigned long accum	64-bit word Q32.32
long long accum	Signed 128-bit word Q64.63
unsigned long long accum	128-bit word Q64.64

The accum types are twice the size of the corresponding fract types.

You can also add sat to the start of the declaration if you want saturated arithmetic to be used.

There are also built-in functions that let you perform fixed-point arithmetic on the new types, but these are usually not needed because the compiler implements the fixed-point versions of all of the usual arithmetic operators.

For example:

```
accum a = 1.23k;
accum b = 4.56k;
accum result = a*b;
printf("%d.%d \n",result>>15,
                ((int)(result<<15)&0x7FFF)*1000/(1<<15));
```

If you want to use the alias's accum for the built-in names _Accum and similar, you need to include:

```
#include <stdfix.h>
```

Notice that casting an accum to int automatically performs a truncation of the fractional part. Thus, if result is 5.123 (int)result is 5. So for the printf conversion to work we have to shift result 15 places left. The bitwise logical operators are not redefined to work with fixed point types and so you need to convert to int. Also notice the use of k to indicate a fixed-point literal of type accum.

If you try this out you should find that it gives you the correct answer. It will also give you the correct answer if the intermediate calculation overflows in the number of bits available. GCC does the calculation using twice the number of bits as the result needs.

There are also lots of built-in functions for doing comparisons and type conversions. Consult the documentation for more information. Also notice that the support for fixed point is very basic and there are no trigonometric or any other functions available.

It is worth saying that in tests using the Raspberry Pi 3, the GCC fixed point built-ins are slower by a factor of 10 for division than hardware floating point and you need to test to see if there is any advantage in using it for any particular hardware.

Using a Fixed Point Library

There are a number of fixed point libraries and, despite having poor documentation and no current project activity libfixmath is commonly used. It only supports Q16.16 and works best if the platform supports 64-bit arithmetic, but it does work with 32-bit integers. Perhaps more importantly, it has trigonometric functions and the exponential function implemented in fixed-point.

The first problem we have is getting the library and installing it. You can currently find the source on both Google Code and GitHub – search for libfixmath. If you obtain it from GitHub you don't need to clone the repository, simply download a zip. To make use of it as a library you need to unzip the file and copy the libfixmath directory to a location where you are going to make use of the library.

You can copy it to one of the standard folders:

```
/usr/local/include/
/usr/include/
```

for header files (.h) and:

```
/usr/local/lib/
/usr/lib/
```

for the actual library files (.o), but there are advantages in setting it up as a NetBeans project so that you can easily modify it if needs be.

The library as provided is simply a set of source files. To create the compiled files that are needed to use the library you have to compile it. All you have to do is run make as there is a MakeFile in the folder which will build the library. To do this from the command line make sure that GCC and make can be run from the command line without having to provide a full path. Once you have successfully built the library you will find additional object files with extension .o in the folder.

A much more flexible way to use the library is to use NetBeans to import it as a C project with existing sources. To do this it is easier to copy the libfixmath folder from the zip to the NetBeansProjects folder and then use this as the basis for the new project. NetBeans will notice that there is a make file and to build the project. All you have to do is select the Clean and Build option. This will compile all of the object files needed to use the library. If you are using a remote build make sure to do a clean build to the target so that other projects to that target can make use of the library.

To actually make use of the library all you have to do is start a new NetBeans project and add:

```
#include "../libfixmath/fixmath.h"
```

Assuming that the header files are in the libfixmath folder within the NetBeanProjects folder, this includes all of the header files needed to use the library. If you have stored the folder in another location then you will have to adjust the path.

As well as putting the include file into the project, you also have to tell the compiler where the library's object files are so that they can be linked into the final code. To do this you need to use a command line option to specify the location of the library's archive file (with extension .a). If you look in the libfixmath folder you will find that the make file created libfixmath.a for you.

In NetBeans you can specify the library file by simply right clicking on the project and selecting properties.

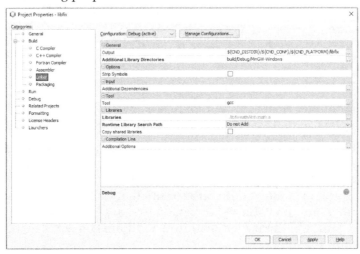

In the dialog box that appears select Linker and then Libraries.

114

Finally select Add Library File and navigate to the correct folder and select `libfixmath.a`.

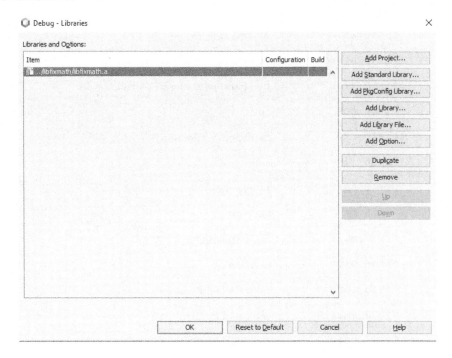

Now you can use the functions in the library within the project. If you make changes to the library's source then all you have to do is rebuild the library before you recompile the project that uses it.

Another alternative is to simply copy and paste the functions you want to use into your project. This is a good approach when you only want a limited range of arithmetic operations.

If you are working with the command line you have to add:

`../libfixmath/libfixmath,a`

to the use of GCC.

Now you can start using the functions that the library provides.

The main functions are:

`fix16_acos`	inverse cosine
`fix16_asin`	inverse sine
`fix16_atan`	one-parameter inverse tangent
`fix16_atan2`	two-parameter inverse tangent
`fix16_cos`	cosine
`fix16_exp`	exponential function
`fix16_sin`	sine
`fix16_sqrt`	square root
`fix16_tan`	tangent
`fix16_mul`	multiplication
`fix16_div`	division
`fix16_sadd`	saturated addition
`fix16_smul`	saturated multiplication
`fix16_sdiv`	saturated division

There are also some conversion functions:

`fix16_to_dbl`	Convert Q16.16 to a double
`fix16_to_float`	Convert Q16.16 to a float
`fix16_to_int`	Convert Q16.16 to an integer
`fix16_from_dbl`	Convert double to a Q16.16
`fix16_from_float`	Convert float to a Q16.16
`fix16_from_int`	Convert integer to a Q16.16

Notice that there is also a new type, `fix16_t`, but this is just an alias for `int32_t`. Also notice that you don't need functions for addition and subtraction as these correspond to the usual operators. There are also some useful Q16.16 constants such as `fix16_pi`, `fix16_e` and `fix16_one`.

For example:

```
fix16_t a = fix16_from_float(12.34);
fix16_t b = fix16_from_float(5.678);
fix16_t result;
result = fix16_mul(a, b);
char buf[25];
fix16_to_str(result, buf, 3);
printf("%s \n", buf);
```

On an x86 and on a Raspberry Pi 3, fixed point multiplication takes twice as long as floating point and division is slower by a factor of four. Clearly on both of these floating point is to be preferred unless there is some other reason than speed, but this is not going to be the case for all processors.

Decimal Fixed Point

So far we have used powers of two as scaling factors because the multiplication and division can be implemented as fast shifts. There are advantages to using fixed point based on powers of ten as the precision is exactly specified as a number of decimal digits. The way that this all works is exactly the same as for binary fixed point, only now we have to use multiplication and division.

For example, suppose we choose 10^3 as the scale factor then every value has three digits after the decimal point. Notice that everything is still in binary, it is just the scale factor which has changed.

```
int a = 1.234*1000;
int b = 2.0*1000;
int  result = a*b/1000;
```

In this case the result is 2.468 accurate to three decimal places. This is about a factor of two slower than integer multiplication and a factor of 1.5 slower than using a power of two and a shift.

Everything works in the same way as before, with the exception of how you arrange to print the fixed point value. In this case you have to divide by the scale factor to retrieve the integer part and find the mod by the scale factor to retrieve the fractional part:

```
printf("%d.%d \n", result/1000,result%1000);
```

The largest values you can represent are INT_MAX/10^5 and INT_MIN/10^5 and you can get overflow during multiplication, even if the final result can be represented. Notice that using a scale factor of 10^3 is roughly between using 2^9 and 2^{10}.

Decimal scale factors are often natural choices because external devices often supply their data as an integer part and a decimal fraction part scaled to be an integer.

Of course, the ultimate decimal fixed point is to use BCD and this is no different from what we have looked at so far, apart from the need to implement the arithmetic operations and scaling.

Some Speed Comparisons

Using a Raspberry Pi 3 the relative speeds of each of the possible approaches to doing arithmetic are (time for int a*b scaled to 1):

Operation	Time
Int a*b	1
Fixed 10	2.0
Fixed 2	1.3
Float a*b	1.4
libfixmath	2.3

Both the binary and the decimal fixed point were implemented without moving to 64-bit arithmetic which is what libfixmath implements and this, plus the function calls, accounts for the difference.

And for division:

Operation	Time
Int a/b	1
Fixed 10	3.5
Fixed 2	3.2
Float a/b	1.2
libfixmath	18.1

Summary

● Fixed-point arithmetic is just scaled integer arithmetic and is therefore simple and fast. However, modern floating point hardware can often match its speed.

● You have to select the total number of bits and the number of bits to use as the binary fraction.

● Fixed-point multiplication and division require rescaling to bring the binary point back to the original location.

● Printing a fixed-point value is easy for the integer part, but the fractional part needs more care.

● Because of the way the scaling works, fixed-point calculations can overflow, even though the final result can be represented in the given format. This can be avoided by working with more bits or by applying the rescaling during the calculation with the subsequent loss of precision.

● There is no standard library for fixed point computation. GCC has some built-in functions, but these only work with specific hardware. An alternative that works with all hardware is libfixmath.

● As well as using binary scaling in fixed point, you can also use decimal scaling. This is slower, but sometimes it is more direct.

● It is worth remembering the fixed point doesn't always have a speed advantage over hardware-implemented floating point. Always benchmark before making a choice.

Chapter 7
Floating Point Arithmetic

Fixed point may be simple, but it is very limited in the range of numbers it can represent. If a calculation involves big scale changes, i.e. with results very much smaller or bigger than the initial set of numbers, then it fails due to under- or over-flow unless you are paying a great deal of attention to the fine detail. A better scheme if you want trouble free calculations is to use a floating point representation.

Pro and Cons of Floating Point

Floating point is easy to use. You feed it the numeric values and the expression and simply expect it to get the right answer. You can usually forget about overflow and other problems and just rely on the FPU to get on with it. This is one of the many things that programmers believe about floating point and it is mostly wrong. Floating point is flexible and easy to use, but unless you know what you are doing you can get almost random values back from a calculation.

Not so long ago floating point was the exception rather than the rule for small machines. Even processors that had floating point hardware were often rendered unusable because of lack of software support. For example, Linux for the Raspberry Pi, Raspbian, took some years before making floating point available. In particular, floating point on ARM processors was a mess of confusing different types of hardware. Today there are still some processors that don't implement floating point hardware to save cost and power, including the Arduino Uno and most of the PIC range of processors.

Another big change is that today's FPUs are fast. Only a few years ago, floating point hardware incurred a significant overhead in communicating with the CPU, making floating point much slower than integer arithmetic and the default practice was to use fixed point wherever speed was important. Today, FPUs are much better integrated with the CPU and they are optimized. In most cases, you can expect a speed penalty of only 20 to 30%. What this means is that if you have to use as few as two integer operations to implement an alternative to floating point then it runs slower.

If you have a modern FPU then use it.

In this chapter we look at some of the aspects of floating point that are important to the general programmer. The whole subject is very big and leads into issues of numerical analysis and exactly how to do a computation. Here the aim is to make you aware of some of the subtle problems that you can encounter with floating point – it's stranger than you might imagine.

In particular, unless your calculation is with moderate values and only a few decimal points of accuracy are important, you can't simply supply an arithmetic expression and just expect it to give you the right answer. Floating point arithmetic can go very wrong unless you understand it – and even then it can still go wrong.

Computers working with numbers is a complete field of study in its own right - numerical analysis - and there is no way that a single chapter can even touch on the subject. What this chapter is about is the way floating point works and some of the problems that arise in simple computations.

The Floating Idea

Floating point allows the precision and magnitude of the representation to change as the computation proceeds. You can do the same thing with fixed point by varying the position of the binary point to accommodate the result and this can be considered a primitive form of floating point. Of course, as you move the fixed point you lose precision to gain an increase in magnitude. So it is with floating point, but there are generally many more bits allocated to the problem.

In floating point the binary point is allowed to move during the calculation, i.e. the binary point "floats", but extra bits have to be allocated to keep track of where it is.

The advantage of this approach is clear if you consider multiplying a value such as 123.4 by 1000. If the hardware (decimal in this case) can only hold four digits then the result is an overflow error. That is:

 123.4 * 1000 = 123400

truncates to 3400, which is clearly not the right answer.

If the hardware uses the floating point approach it can simply record the shift in the decimal point four places to the right. You can think of this as a way of allowing a much larger range of numbers to be represented, but with a fixed number of digits' precision. Notice that the number of digits of precision remains the same, but the percentage accuracy changes.

A floating point number is represented by two parts – an exponent and a fractional part. The fractional part is just a fixed-point representation of the number – usually with the fractional point to the immediate left of the first bit, making its value less than 1. The exponent is a scale factor which determines the true magnitude of the number.

In decimal we are used to this scheme as scientific notation, standard form or exponential notation. For example, Avogadro's number is usually written as 6.02252×10^{23} and the 23 is the exponent and the 6.02252 is the fractional part – notice that in standard form the fractional part is always less than 10 and more than 1. In binary floating point representation it is usual for the fractional part to be normalized to be just less than 1.

Binary floating point is just the binary equivalent of decimal standard form. The exponent is the power of two by which you have to multiply the fraction to get the true magnitude. At this point you might want to write floating point off as trivial, but there are some subtleties. For example, when the fractional part is zero what should the exponent be set to?

Clearly there is more than one representation for zero. By convention, the exponent is made as negative as it can be, i.e. as small as possible in the representation of zero. If two's-complement were used this would result in a zero that didn't have all its bits set to zero and this is to be avoided for obvious reasons. To achieve this a small change is needed to use a biased, rather than two's-complement exponent, i.e. by adding the largest negative value to it. For example, if the exponent is six bits in size, the two's-complement notation range is −32 to +31.

If instead of two's-complement, a simple biased representation is used then we have to subtract 32 from the exponent to get the signed value. In this case an exponent of 0 represents −32, 32 represents 0, and 63 represents 31. The same range is covered, but now the representation of zero has all bits set to 0 and it corresponds to $0x2^{-32}$, i.e. zero with the most negative exponent possible.

Floating Point Algorithms

Algorithms for working with floating point numbers are complex and very easy to get wrong. For example, consider the algorithm for adding two floating point numbers. You can't simply add the fractional parts because the numbers could be very different in size. The first task is to shift the fraction with the smallest exponent to the right to make the two exponents equal. When this has been done the fractional parts can be added in the usual way and the result can then be normalized so that the fraction is just less than 1.

This sounds innocent enough, but consider what happens when you try to add 1×2^{-8} to 1×2^8 using an eight-bit fractional part. Both numbers are represented in floating point as 0.1, but with exponents of 2^{-7} and 2^9 respectively. When you try to add these two values the first has to be shifted to the right nine times, with the result that the single non-zero bit finally falls off the end and the result is zero in the standard precision. So when you think you are adding a small value to 1×2^8 you are in fact adding zero. This contradicts all your expectations. You are adding a small positive quantity to another value and hence that value should increase – only it doesn't. This may not be much of a problem, but try the following:

```c
int main(int argc, char** argv) {
    float v = 0.999999F;
    do {
        v = v + 0.0000001F;
    } while (v < 1);
    return (EXIT_SUCCESS);
}
```

This program does complete the loop, but if you add one more 0 before the 1 in the quantity added to v, the loop never ends. Notice that because of the use of IEEE standard floating point this behavior is almost machine-independent.

Floating point arithmetic can be dangerous!

Be aware that adding or subtracting values of very different sizes can be the same as adding or subtracting zero.

IEEE standard – Single & Double

To try to make it safer, there is a standard for floating point arithmetic, the IEEE standard, which is used by nearly all floating point hardware, including all flavors of Intel-derived hardware since the Pentium was introduced. It applies to the ARM range of processors and most DSPs (digital signal processors) that have floating point.

Single precision IEEE numbers, floats in C, are 32 bits long and use one sign bit, an 8-bit exponent with a bias of 127, and a 23-bit fraction with the first bit a 1 by default. This gives 24 bits, or 7.22 decimal digits, of precision. You should now see why the loop listed above fails to operate at exactly seven zeros before the 1.

Double precision IEEE numbers, doubles in C, are 64 bits long and have one sign bit, and an 11-bit exponent with a bias of 1023. This provides nearly 16 decimal digits of precision.

There are other IEEE standard formats for floating point, but these two are the ones you are most likely to encounter.

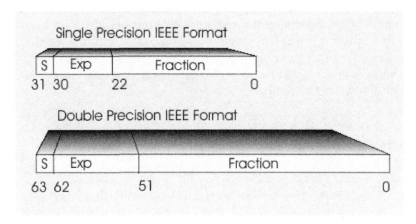

IEEE standard floating point formats used inside nearly every modern machine.

If you need to choose between single and double precision, it is worth knowing that, for a modern FPU, double precision floating point addition and multiplication take about the same time as single precision floating point, but double precision division is often slower by a factor of 1.5 or more.

The other issue is that, whereas single precision takes four bytes, double requires eight bytes.

Extended Precision

Now we come to a complicated matter – extended precision. The IEEE standard allows for two extended precision formats, single extended and double extended, which are intended to be more accurate than their counterparts. While single extended has to have more than 42 bits and double extended has to have more than 78 bits, the exact size and precision of the two formats depends on the implementation. For example, Intel FPUs generally support 80-bit double extended format, whereas ARM's have a 79-bit format.

The main purpose of extended precision is to allow intermediate calculations to be performed at the higher precision and then rounded back to single or double. That is, when a floating point expression is evaluated, the actual arithmetic may be done at a higher precision. When the result is stored it is rounded back to the originally specified precision.

What this means in practice is that the results that you get, even using IEEE floating point, can vary according to the architecture you are running the program on and the way that computation is implemented. If a computation can be completed in floating point registers without being stored in memory, then it will be performed at full extended precision. If it has to be stored in memory, then it will be rounded to the precision you are using. This can result in some strange behavior, depending on whether the value is in reduced or extended precision.

For example:

```
double a,b[2];
 computations that determine a
b[0] = a;
if(b[0] == a) ?
```

If the calculations that determine a were all done using the extended precision, because the value could always be held in a register, then at the point of the assignment, a is in extended precision. When it is assigned to the array, a can no longer be held in a register, so the extended precision is rounded to a double and hence the two values might now be different, resulting in the equality condition being false.

The C99 standard made an attempt at regularizing the way C and floating point worked. In particular, it introduced the long double type, which is supposed to be double extended, i.e. 80-bits on Intel machines. However, even with C99 what the compiler actually does varies. GCC on Intel machines running under Windows, MinGW, works until you try to use printf when it reverts to double when you use the format specifier %Lf for long double. C99 also introduced the FLT_EVAL_METHOD in float.h to indicate how arithmetic was being performed. If its value is 0 then arithmetic is performed in the precision you specify. If its value is 1 then at least double precision is used. If it is 2 then long double is used. In all cases the result is converted to the precision you specify by rounding.

The important point is that working with extended precision gives a result that is at least as accurate as the precision you think you are working with, and in some cases more accurate. For this reason, FLT_EVAL_METHOD == 2 is supposed to be the default for x86 hardware. However, using GCC revealed that while it is true under Windows, both Linux on x86 and on ARM reported: FLT_EVAL_METHOD == 0.

The float.h header file also contains definitions of useful constants such as FLT_MAX and DBL_MAX.

As well as extended precision, there is also the issue of denormalized numbers. This is an extension of the usual representation that can allow values much smaller than the smallest normalized number. The idea is that once you reach the smallest exponent, the fractional part of the value no longer needs to be normalized so that it starts with a leading one. This allows smaller values to be represented, but with an increasing loss of precision as the value approaches zero – hence the alternative name gradual underflow. In most cases you can ignore denormalized numbers, but you might want to check that the result that you have computed hasn't lost precision – see FE_INEXACT later.

Special Values – NaN and Inf

Now we come to another controversial and much misunderstood aspect of IEEE floating point arithmetic – the special values NaN (Not a Number) and inf (infinity). These two special values are represented by bit patterns that cannot occur in normal floating point.

The NaN and inf special values are related and this is often not understood. The operations that can produce NaN are:

Operation	NaN produced by
+	inf+ -inf and equivalent subtractions
×	0 x inf and equivalent
/	0/0 or inf/inf
%	x%0, inf %y
√	√x if x<0

inf is the result of an operation that produces an overflow. For example, FLT_MAX *2 evaluates to inf and -FLT_MAX *2 gives -inf.

At this point you are probably thinking that this isn't a good idea. When something like NaN or inf occurs in an expression then the system should generate an error and the program should either handle the error or terminate. The intention of the IEEE standard is to allow a complex expression to continue to be evaluated and produce a reasonable result.

It is easy to see how NaN and inf are generated, but how do they allow the expression evaluation to continue. The situation with NaN is very simple - the whole expression evaluates to NaN which you can test for. For example:

```
float w;
w = 0.0/0.0;
printf("%f \n",w);
```

prints -nan.

The problem with testing for NaN is that there is no machine- or compiler-independent way of doing the job. This is because the representation of NaN is not specified and there can be more than one. For example, a single precision float representation of NaN is:

s111 1111 1xxx xxxx xxxx xxxx xxxx xxxx

where s is the sign bit and the x sequence is non-zero and can be used to encode additional information, the payload, which is usually ignored.

If the bits are 0 then this is a representation of a signed infinity.

That is:

```
inf = 0x7F800000;
```

and the first value that can be used as NaN is:

```
nan = 0x7F800001;
```

As NaN is not ordered, one test that always works is x == x, which is false only if x is NaN. The GCC recommended way of testing is to use the isnan function. For example:

```
w = 0.0/0.0;
printf("%d \n",isnan(w));
printf("%d \n",w == w);
```

prints 1 and 0 respectively.

More of a problem is inf. This is a value that allows an expression to continue to be evaluated and in some cases it can disappear to produce a final expression that looks as if nothing has gone wrong.

For example:

```
float w = 3/(1.0/0.0);
printf("%f \n",w);
```

If you were asked what the above expression printed, most likely you would guess that it was an error as you would properly regard the 1.0/0.0 is either undefined or infinity. In fact using IEEE floating point the result is 0.0.

If you rewrite the expression as:

```
float w = 3*0.0/1;
```

then the answer `0.0` isn't so unexpected.

To be clear, in math division by zero using integers, rationals, reals or complex numbers is undefined and there is no room for argument. Given `a/0` there is no number of any sort that multiplies 0 to give a.

However, programming isn't math and we are free to use a pragmatic interpretation of division by zero and many other operations. The idea is that we assume continuity of operations and assign a value to expressions such as `a/0`, the value in the limit of `a/b`, as b is reduced to 0. Clearly in this case the result gets bigger and bigger as b gets smaller and smaller. Hence we are being reasonable when we assign infinity to `a/0`. Notice that if a is negative then we have -inf. However, as IEEE floating point has a `+0` and a `-0`, we also have `a/-0` is `-inf` if a is positive and `+inf` if a is negative.

In this case the sign of the zero is taken as indicating the side that the limit is taken from, `+0` implies a positive value getting smaller and `-0` is a negative quantity getting smaller.

What this means is if you change the last example to:

```
w = 3/(1.0/-0.0);
```

then you will see `-0.0` printed.

Things can go wrong as the limit isn't defined in all cases. Consider `inf/inf` and `0/0`. In both cases the answer depends on how the limit is reached and you can produce any answer you like by a careful choice. In these cases the result is `NaN`.

You can think of IEEE floating point as being arithmetic with limiting arguments used to produce unique results for otherwise undefined operations and `NaN` where there is no such unique result.

Finally, while positive and negative zero determine the "side" the limit is taken, it is still true that `+0 == -0` However, as `+inf! = -inf`, `x == y` does not imply `1/x == 1/y` as it fails for `+0` and `-0`.

Detecting Problems

You can see that IEEE floating point has been designed to carry on with the calculation and return a result as close to the correct result as is reasonable. However, in many cases this is not acceptable and any arithmetic irregularity needs to be handled. The bad news is that there is no portable way of doing this. Only C99 defines functions that allow you to check for problems in floating point and if you can't use C99 then you have to fall back on compiler and machine specifics. While all floating point hardware has a status register that has flags for each type of floating point error, there is no standard way to access this except under C99.

However, there is also a GNU library that implements the C99 floating point functions and this can be used with GCC with any version of C. Of course, exactly what works depends on the hardware.

There are five types of exception defined in `fenv.h`:

FE_INEXACT	inexact arithmetic
FE_DIVBYZERO	divide by zero
FE_UNDERFLOW	The underflow exception.
FE_OVERFLOW	The overflow exception.
FE_INVALID	The invalid exception.

These are used to create a bit mask by ORing them together to indicate what exceptions you are interested in.

There is also:

FE_ALL_EXCEPT

which is the bitwise OR of all of them.

The key to using the facility is a set of functions that will read, set and clear the floating point status register. The two most important are:

int feclearexcept (int excepts) - clear flags
int fetestexcept (int excepts) – tests flags for set

For example, to detect just a divide by zero exception:

```
feclearexcept(FE_ALL_EXCEPT);
float w = (1 / 0.0);
int raised = fetestexcept(FE_DIVBYZERO);
if(raised) printf("divide by zero");
```

For this to work you have to include:

```
#include <fenv.h>
```

and you have to link against the GNU math library, which means you need to add `libm.a` to the libraries.

You can check for any error using:

```
feclearexcept(FE_ALL_EXCEPT);
float w = 0.0/0.0;
if(fetestexcept(FE_DIVBYZERO))     printf(" FE_DIVBYZERO");
if(fetestexcept(FE_INEXACT))       printf(" FE_INEXACT");
if(fetestexcept(FE_INVALID))       printf(" FE_INVALID");
if(fetestexcept(FE_OVERFLOW))      printf(" FE_OVERFLOW");
if(fetestexcept(FE_UNDERFLOW))     printf(" FE_UNDERFLOW");
if(fetestexcept(FE_ALL_EXCEPT)==0) printf(" none");
```

For many small machines there is often no choice but to examine the hardware directly to determine the state of the floating point hardware.

It is also possible to raise a signal, using the feenableexcept function, when a floating point error occurs, but this is very dependent on operating system and hardware. For example, this program works under Linux on x86, but not under MinGW or ARM Linux:

```c
#pragma STDC FENV_ACCESS on
#define _POSIX_C_SOURCE   200809L
#define _GNU_SOURCE
#include <stdio.h>
#include <stdlib.h>
#include <signal.h>
#include <math.h>
#include <float.h>
#include <fenv.h>
void signalHandler(int sig, siginfo_t *info, void *ucontext) {
    printf("Floating Point exception %d\n", sig);
    printf("%d\n", info->si_code);
}

int main(int argc, char** argv) {
    sigset_t mask;
    sigfillset(&mask);
    struct sigaction psa = {0};
    psa.sa_mask = mask;
    psa.sa_sigaction = &signalHandler;
    psa.sa_flags = SA_SIGINFO;
    sigaction(SIGFPE, &psa, NULL);

    feenableexcept(FE_INVALID |
                     FE_DIVBYZERO |
                       FE_OVERFLOW |
                         FE_UNDERFLOW);
    feenableexcept(FE_DIVBYZERO);
    printf("flags %d\n" , feenableexcept (FE_DIVBYZERO));

    float w = 1.0 / 0.0;

    printf("%f \n", w);

    return (EXIT_SUCCESS);
}
```

Mixed Arithmetic – Casting

C allows you to mix integer and floating point. In this case it is important to know that the integers are always converted to floating and the final result is a float or a double. For a complete understanding you also need to know about the usual arithmetic conversions, which are covered in **Fundamental C: Getting Closer To The Machine** (ISBN: 978-1871962604)

For example:

```
float a = 1.234;
float result = 2 * a;
printf("%f \n", result);
```

prints 2.468000. It is even better to use 2.0 or 2f to indicate a float literal. You can use l or L to indicate a double literal. However, you need to be careful about exactly when the conversion to float or double occurs. For example, changing the calculation to:

```
float result = 1/2 * a;
```

gives the result zero because the division is done first and the 1 and 2 are integers and hence the result is zero.

You can avoid this problem by an explicit cast:

```
float result = (float)1/(float)2 * a;
```

or just:

```
float result = (float)1/2 * a;
```

Now the division has to be floating point division.

In the case of literals another solution is to explicitly give the type of the literal:

```
float result = 1.0/2.0 * a;
```

or:

```
float result = 1f/2f * a;
```

Leaving an integer product or division in an otherwise floating point expression is a very common error and one that often goes undetected for a long time. This means it is important to check some examples of the arithmetic you have implemented.

When you cast a float or a double to an integer or vice versa the usual C approach of trying to preserve the value in the new representation is applied. Casting any integer type to a float simply gives the corresponding floating value. That is (float) 2 is 2.0. Notice that this involves a change in the bit pattern and, unlike casting between integer types, this is not just a reinterpretation of the bit pattern, but instead is proper active type conversion and as such is less efficient than integer to integer casting.

When you cast a float or double to integer then the value is truncated, i.e. the fractional part is simply lost. If you cast to an integer type that is too small to hold the integer that results from truncation then the result is undefined. If you want to avoid undefined behavior then you should always check that the result of the cast will fit into the destination variable. You can always check before casting using the predefined constants that give the maximum value. For example, assuming f is positive:

```
int i;
if(f<=INTMAX) i=f
```

There are many areas of floating point behavior that haven't been discussed in detail here. For example the GCC compiler supports additional floating point types and hardware often has vector floating point units which can work with multiple values at a time. Most of these facilities are non-standard and very specific to the machine and/or the compiler in use and are best avoided unless you are targeting a known and fixed environment.

Floating Point Reconsidered

This is by no means all you need to know about floating point arithmetic. What really matters is that you don't take it for granted that you will get the right answer when you make use of it. It should now be obvious why:

```
float a = 0.1f;
float total;
for(int i = 0;i<1000;i++){
    total = total+a;
}
printf("%.7f\n", total);
printf("%d\n",total == 100.0);
```

prints 99.9990463 and 0, 0.1. isn't exactly representable as a binary fraction it is 0.0001100110011.. This is the reason for the usual advice of "don't test floating point numbers for equality". However, in this case it is more general in that the same problem arises with the corresponding fixed point value. That is, it is more to do with binary fractions than it is to do with floating point representation.

If you think that such a small error could never make a difference, consider the error in the Patriot missile system. The system used an integer timing register which was incremented at intervals of 0.1 seconds. However, the integers were converted to decimal numbers by multiplying by the binary approximation of 0.1. After 100 hours, an error of approximately 0.3433 seconds was present in the conversion. As a result, an Iraqi Scud missile could not be accurately targeted and was allowed to detonate on a barracks, killing 28 people.

The recommended way of testing for equality between floating point values is to use something like:

```
if(fabsf((total - 100.0))/100.0 <=FLT_EPSILON))...
```

`FLT_EPSILON` is a macro that gives you the accuracy of a float. There are other useful constants defined in `float.h`. The idea is that if two numbers differ by less than the accuracy of the representation then they can be considered equal. Of course in practice numbers computed in different ways accumulate errors that are larger than the representational error. In the case of the example above with `a = 0.1`, the two numbers are very much further apart than `FLT_EPSILON` due to the inability to represent 0.1 in binary. In practice is usual to include a factor that summarizes the errors in the computation something like:

```
if(fabsf((total - 100.0))/100.0 <=K*FLT_EPSILON))...
```

To get our example to test equal, `K` has to be `80` or more. However, a small change and `K` has to be bigger. Run the loop a thousand times and compare the result to `1000` and `K` has to be even bigger.

The point is that there is no single way of setting a reasonable interval that works for a range of computations. You have to analyze the computation to find out what it is safe to regard as being equal. This leads us into the realm of numerical analysis.

If you applying any formula then it is always worth checking what the best way to compute it is. It is rare that the form given in a textbook is the best way to compute a quantity. For example, the mean is traditionally computed using:

```
float total;
int n = 1000000;
for (int i = 0; i < n; i++) {
    total = total + (float)i;
}
total = total/(float)n;
printf("%f\n",total);
```

This forms a total and then divides by the number of items. The problem with this is that the total gets very big and we lose precision by adding comparatively small values to it. If you try it, you will discover that instead of `500000.00` the result is `499940.375000`.

Using the alternative iterative method, which keeps the size of the running estimate down:

```
total = 0;
for (int i = 0; i < n; i++) {
    total = total + ((float)i-total)/(i+1);
}
printf("%f\n",total);
```

gives a result of 499999.500000 which is only wrong by 0.5.

There are even better methods of computing the mean - see Kahan Summation and Pairwise Summation.

In many cases you can't avoid a detailed analysis of a calculation but it helps to have an idea of why things go wrong when you are using floating point. Imagine that you are working with three significant digits. For addition everything is fine as long as the exponents allow the digits to interact. For example consider:

$$1.23 \times 10^2 + 4.67 \times 10^3$$

written out like this:

```
  123 +
4670
4793
```

Normalizing this gives 4.79×10^3 and you can see that, ignoring rounding etc, only two digits of each value "overlapped" in the sum. If the exponents differ by 4 then none of digits are involved in the sum. For example $1.23 \times 10^2 + 4.67 \times 10^6 =$

```
    123 +
4670000
4670123
```

and after normalizing the result we have 4.67×10^6. Clearly for addition and subtraction if you are working with floating point numbers with a precision of d then the accuracy of adding and subtracting goes down as the difference between the exponents approaches d. This is the sense in which you need to be careful about floating point arithmetic involving large and small numbers.

There are no similar problems with multiplication and division, apart from the accumulation of errors if operations are performed in succession.

Finally, if possible always use double or larger floating point types. Whereas float has 7 decimal digits of precision, double has 15 digits and this provides useful latitude.

Summary

- Floating point arithmetic is so easy to use that we simply expect an arithmetic expression to be worked out correctly – this isn't true.

- Modern floating point hardware is almost as fast as integer operations and using double precision values doesn't have an overhead, except for division.

- Floating point arithmetic can give very wrong answers if the two operands differ by a large amount. The necessary normalization can reduce non-zero quantities to zero and the loss of precision can make results close to random.

- A confusing factor is the use of extended precision during a calculation to minimize this loss of precision. This always gives a result that is as accurate, or more accurate, than if extended precision wasn't used, but it can result in quantities that are supposed to be equal not testing as equal.

- Standard floating point has two special values, NaN, not a number, and inf, infinity. The rules that govern how these are used in an expression are reasonable, but not foolproof. You can get a very wrong answer without even knowing that a special value is involved.

- There are some standard ways of detecting special values and problems with floating point, but only in C99 and later. In practice, the results vary according to architecture.

- You can cast integer to float and float to integer types. Everything works as you would expect, but casting to an integer type that is too small to hold the integer part of a float is undefined behavior.

- Implementing floating point calculations is difficult an in many cases you need to find out how other people have tackled the problem. There are often optimized ways of computing the formulae you find in text books.

Chapter 8

Files

There is a standard C approach to files, but there is also a POSIX standard that is implemented in Linux/Unix and in many ways this is more general than the C file functions. The reason is that once you move beyond files stored on disks, suddenly it is the POSIX approach to files that becomes the natural one to use. Of course, the C file handling functions are mapped onto the native file functions of the operating system and in the case of the POSIX system these are based on the use of a file descriptor. In most cases, however, you are better off using the standard C file functions as they are robust, easy to use and buffered.

In any particular implementation these functions are mapped to the file system calls that the operating system provides. The file pointer returned by fopen and used by the other file handling functions is actually a pointer to a structure that defines the file. However, this structure is supposed to be opaque in the sense that you are not supposed to make use of its internal structure, which may vary according to the operating system.

What all this means is that the C standard library file handling is a uniform wrapper around the varying file handling facilities provided by the operating system. If you can avoid using anything else your programs will have the advantage of being portable.

In this chapter it is assumed that you know the basics of file handling and, in particular, are familiar with the C standard file functions.

A brief summary of the C file functions is given in the table below:

Function	

`FILE *fptr=fopen("filename","mode");`	Open a file. Mode determines how the file is opened and is any of:
	 `r` open for read
	 `w` open for write
	 `a` open for append
	 `r+` open for reading and writing
	 `w+` open for reading and writing
	       if the file exists it is overwritten
	 `a+` open for reading and appending
	       if the file doesn't exist it is created

`fclose(fptr);`	Close file
`fprintf(fptr,"format string",` `            list of variables);`	Works like printf but sends chars to file
`fscanf(fptr,"format string",` `                &variable);`	Works like scanf but reads chars from file
`fputs(string,fptr);`	Works like puts but sends string to file
`fgets(string,length,fptr);`	Works like gets but reads string from file
`fread(ptrToBuffer, size,` `            number, fptr);`	Read number*size chars from file
`fwrite(ptrToBuffer,size,` `            number,fptr);`	Write number*size chars from file
`fputc(charAsint,fptr);` `putc(charAsint, fptr);`	Write a single character to a file
`fgetc(fptr);` `getc(fptr);`	Read a single character from a file
`ungetc(charAsint,fptr);`	Undo a character read
`fflush(fptr);`	flush the file buffer
`rewind(fptr);`	Return file pointer to start of file
`fseek(fptr,offset,whence);`	Move file pointer to whence+offset
`ftell(fptr);`	Position of file pointer.
`feof(fptr);`	Test for end of file

File Descriptors

There are many occasions when you need to call functions that are provided by the operating system and if the call involves a file then it will generally need to be passed something that corresponds to the native way that the operating system works with files. While there is no overall standard for this, for Linux and other Unix-like operating systems we rely on POSIX.

A POSIX-conforming operating system uses a file descriptor rather than a file pointer. A file descriptor is a simple int that is an index into an internal operating system table of open files. Each process has its own table and each such table references a globally held table of files.

By default there are three predefined file descriptors:

```
STDIN_FILENO
STDOUT_FILENO
STDERR
```

which under Linux/Unix correspond to 0,1 and 2.

What all of this means is that most programs running under Linux, or any POSIX operating system, sooner or later have to abandon the C standard way of working with files. This is both good and bad news. The bad news is, of course, that this is not as portable. The good news is that it is a lower-level way of working with files that makes it possible to do more, in particular they are not buffered. The final piece of good news is that the POSIX functions, defined in unistd.h and fcntl.h are very similar to the C standard library files.

The open function, defined in fcntl.h:

```
open(filename,flags, mode);
```

opens the file and returns an int, the file descriptor. The flags and mode parameters control how the file is to be opened and file permissions to be set when the file is created. The flags are formed by the bitwise OR of one of:

```
O_RDONLY        open for reading only
O_WRONLY        open for writing only
O_RDWR open for reading and writing.
```

with any of the following optional arguments:

```
O_APPEND        append on each write
O_CREAT         create file if it does not exist
O_TRUNC         truncate size to 0.
```

If you are creating a file you also have to supply the mode parameter. This is simply the Linux permissions code and, as this is usually presented to the end user in octal, you can also use octal. There are also a set of predefined macros that can be ORed together to set the permission you require. For example S_IRUSR sets the user read bit.

The actual permissions that result are complicated by the fact that the process has a default permissions mask - umask. The effective permissions are given by mode & ~umask which means that the bits in umask that are set are unset in the result i.e. umask blocks the setting of some permissions.

For example, to obtain a file descriptor fd:

```
int fd=open("filename",O_RDWR |O_CREAT, 0644);
```

opens a file for read and write and creates it if it doesn't exist with permissions 0644, which is owner read/write and the rest read only.

You can open the same file with a file descriptor more than once and these may have read/write positions and status flags. You can set the default permissions using the umask function.

As with C file handling, any file you open has to be closed using:

```
close(fd);
```

File descriptor files have block read and block write commands:

```
read(fd, ptrToBuffer, numbytes);
```

and:

```
write(fd, ptrToBuffer, numbytes);
```

These are similar to fread and fwrite but simpler as it is up to you to work out how many bytes to read and write.

All of these functions return -1 if there is an error, and read and write return the number of bytes transferred. Notice that file descriptors do not support text format mode and it is up to you to code or convert raw data into the bytes that represent it.

Also notice that a call to read or write might return before all of the bytes you specified have been transferred. For example, the call to read or write might be interrupted by a signal. It is up to you check and restart the read or write if you want all of the data you requested.

There is also a file positioning function:

```
lseek(fd,offset,whence);
```

If whence is SEEK_SET then offset is from the start of the file, if it is SEEK_CUR it is from the current location and if it is SEEK_END it is from the end of the file. The function returns -1 if the seek failed and the offset from the start of the file if it worked.

This means that lseek can be used to return the current position:

```
off_t currentPos=lseek(fd,0,SEEK_CUR);
```

where off_t is the type defined to hold an offset. If you position beyond the end of the file and write data then the gap is filled by zero bytes until real data is written to the location.

You can probably see how to make use of the open, read, write and lseek functions to do the same job as the file pointer functions of the C standard. An extra facility is provided by the dup and dup2 functions. These allow you to duplicate a file descriptor so that you can make use of the file in more than one way at a time. For example, you could duplicate a file descriptor and maintain two different reading positions. The difference between the two functions is how the file descriptor is determined:

```
int fd2 = dup(fd);
```

returns the next free integer file descriptor and sets it to reference the same file as fd and:

```
dup2(fd,fd2);
```

sets the existing fd2 to reference the same file as fd. You should be able to see that these file functions can be used in a very similar way to the file pointer functions.

A Random Access Example

For example, to implement a random access record program you would first have to write some records to the file:

```
#include <stdio.h>
#include <stdlib.h>
#include <string.h>
#include <fcntl.h>
#include <unistd.h>
struct person {
    char name[25];
    int age;
};

int main(int argc, char** argv) {
    struct person me;
    strcpy(me.name, "Harry");
    me.age = 18;
    int fd = open("myFile.bin",O_RDWR |O_CREAT, 0644);
    for (int i = 0; i < 10; i++) {
        write(fd,&me, sizeof (struct person));
        me.age++;
    };
```

You can see that the only difference from using C file functions in writing out ten records is that the open function has to specify the permissions and the write doesn't specify the number of records, just the size of the record.

To now read the fifth record you would use:

```
int record = 5;
lseek(fd, record * sizeof (struct person), SEEK_SET);
struct person me2;
read(fd,&me2, sizeof (struct person));
printf("%s  %d", me2.name, me2.age);
```

No flushing is needed as buffers aren't used, or if they are they are transparent to the program. You can use the same techniques to read a record, modify it and write it back to the file. If you write beyond the end of file then the file is extended with zeros to fill in the gap.

Descriptors and Streams

Descriptors are the POSIX low-level file functions and on a POSIX system the file pointer or stream functions are built on top of these. This means that on a POSIX system when you use the C standard fopen to open a file a file descriptor is created behind the scenes.

If you want to work with a file using that file descriptor you can.

The function:

```
int fd=fileno(fptr);
```

returns the file descriptor corresponding to the file that the file pointer references. Once you have the file descriptor you can use read, write, lseek and any other function that works with a file descriptor.

In the same way as a stream is associated with a file descriptor, you can open a stream given a file descriptor. The function:

```
FILE *fptr=fdopen(fd, "mode")
```

where mode is any of the usual file stream opening modes e.g. w for write. Notice that the mode has to match the mode of the already open file descriptor and you can't use b as file descriptors are always binary. The key point is that the stream isn't actually opened at this point because it has already been opened as a file descriptor.

Finally, this ability to switch between file descriptors and file pointers is only possible on POSIX systems and isn't a part of the C standard.

fcntl

The fcntl i.e. file descriptor control function provides a way of working with a file descriptor to find out the status of the file and to modify the way it is used. It is very similar to the ioctl function, see later, but it is specifically targeted at devices that have a file descriptor.

The general form of the function is:

```
int fcntl(fd, cmd, ... );
```

where fd is a file descriptor, cmd is an int specifying what you want the function to do and there is often a third parameter according to the cmd.

For example:

```
newFd=fcntl(fd,F_DUPFD,10);
```

this does the same job as dup but you can specify the lowest file descriptor to be used i.e. 10 in this case.

A common use for fcntl is to read and set descriptor and file flags. The difference is that descriptor flags are set on the descriptor and file flags are shared between all descriptors referencing the same file. There are four status commands:

F_GETFD - get file descriptor flags
F_SETFD - set file descriptor flags
F_GETFL - get file flags
F_SETFL - set file flags.

At the moment there is only one file descriptor flag FC_CLOEXEC which if set closes the file after any exec functions. The default is for files to stay open after the exec.

The file status flags are:

O_APPEND   - set append mode
O_NONBLOCK   - no delay
O_DSYNC   - synchronize data
O_SYNC   - synchronize data and the file
O_TEMP   - temporary file I/O
O_CACHE   - cache data.

and the access modes are:

O_RDONLY   - Open for reading only
O_WRONLY   - Open for writing only
O_RDWR   - Open for reading and writing.

You can read all of the flags using F_GETFL and you can set all but the access modes using F_SETFL.

For example, to read the status flags and unset the O_APPEND flag:

```
#include <stdio.h>
#include <stdlib.h>
#include <fcntl.h>
#include <unistd.h>

int main(int argc, char** argv) {
    int fd = open("/tmp/fd.txt", O_RDWR | O_CREAT | O_TRUNC |
                                 O_APPEND, 0644);

    int flag = fcntl(fd, F_GETFL);
    printf("%x\n", flag);
    printf("%d\n", flag & O_APPEND);

    fcntl(fd, F_SETFL, flag&~O_APPEND);
    flag = fcntl(fd, F_GETFL);
    printf("%x\n", flag);
    printf("%d\n", flag & O_APPEND);
    return (EXIT_SUCCESS);
}
```

Notice that if you want to leave the other status bits unaltered you have to read them and then use bit manipulation to modify just the bits you want to change.

Sharing Files – Locking

Files, or more generally streams, are sometimes used as a communication channel between different processes, different programs and even different machines. The idea is that a file can be read and written by more than one agent. If files are shared then there is the problem of simultaneous update. The solution is to use a lock to restrict who can access it while it is being changed or read.

There are usually two types of lock - a reader lock and a writer lock. A reader lock allows other readers to lock the same area of the file but blocks a writer lock from changing the file while it is being read. A writer lock stops any reader lock being acquired while that portion of the file is being changed. Notice that while a read lock allows sharing the file with other processes, it blocks any changes while it is held. In all cases a lock should be held for the shortest possible time.

There are locking functions provided by POSIX but they aren't reliable and a much better portable solution is to use general resource locking mechanisms, see Chapter 12. A more reliable solution is provided by Linux but it goes beyond the POSIX standard.

You will also encounter the idea of a lock file. This is just a dummy file that is tested for to determine if another process has the file open already.

There are four well established file locking facilities under Linux-based - BSD locks, POSIX `lockf` function, POSIX record locks and Open file descriptor locks. BSD locks are less capable than POSIX record locks and the `lockf` function is just a repackaging of the POSIX record lock to make it slightly easier to use at the expense of some features. The file description lock is a Linux-only feature and it is basically a modification of the POSIX record lock - so it makes sense to start with this.

All of the file locking mentioned so far is "advisory" in the sense that it only works if processes call the appropriate locking functions before accessing a file. Linux does support mandatory locking which stops all access to a file but this, at the time of writing, is not reliable and best avoided.

Locks are only allowed on files and not on directories and you cannot lock a file that is available to any user. All locks are removed when the process exits.

The POSIX record lock supports locking a byte range within a file, reader and writer locks and it guarantees that a lock is acquired in an atomic way - see Chapter 13.

Acquiring a lock is a matter of using the `fcntl` function with the commands:

F_SETLK   - acquire or release lock non-blocking, returns -1 if not acquired
F_SETLKW - as F_SETLK but blocking, returns -1 if a signal interrupts it
F_GETLK   - test to see if there is a lock of the type specified.

Each of these uses an `flock` struct to determine the details of the lock:

```
struct flock {
    l_type;     /* Type of lock: F_RDLCK,  F_WRLCK, F_UNLCK */
    l_whence;   /* How to interpret l_start:
                             SEEK_SET, SEEK_CUR, SEEK_END */
    l_start;    /* Starting offset for lock */
    l_len;      /* Number of bytes to lock */
    l_pid;      /* PID of process blocking our lock
                        (set by F_GETLK and F_OFD_GETLK) */
};
```

Obviously to hold a read lock the file must be open for reading, for a write lock open for writing, and for both open for read/write. A process can hold multiple overlapping locks. In general, a reader or a writer process would lock the logical equivalent of a record, usually implemented as a struct to make sure that no other changes can be made to the record while it is being read or written.

Here is a simple example of a write process which repeatedly writes two different bit patterns 0x55555555 and 0xaaaaaaaa to part of a file:

```c
#include <stdio.h>
#include <stdlib.h>
#include <fcntl.h>
#include <unistd.h>

int main(int argc, char** argv) {
    struct flock lockwrite={0};

    lockwrite.l_type = F_WRLCK;
    lockwrite.l_whence = SEEK_SET;
    lockwrite.l_start = 10;
    lockwrite.l_len = 4;

    int value = 0x55555555;

    int fd = open("/tmp/fd.txt", O_RDWR, 0600);
    for (;;) {

        lseek(fd, 10, SEEK_SET);

        lockwrite.l_type = F_WRLCK;
        fcntl(fd, F_SETLKW, &lockwrite);

        value=~value;
        write(fd, &value, 4);

        lockwrite.l_type = F_UNLCK;
        fcntl(fd, F_SETLK, &lockwrite);
    }
    close(fd);
    return (EXIT_SUCCESS);
}
```

Notice that the program seeks to byte 10, gets a write lock, writes a 4-byte bit pattern and then releases the lock. The call to fcntl is blocking, so if any other process has the same four bytes locked the process will wait.

To test this we need a simple reader which follows the same general pattern as the writer:

```c
#include <stdio.h>
#include <stdlib.h>
#include <fcntl.h>
#include <unistd.h>

int main(int argc, char** argv) {
    struct flock lockread={0};
    lockread.l_type = F_RDLCK;
    lockread.l_whence = SEEK_SET;
    lockread.l_start = 10;
    lockread.l_len = 4;

    int value=0;

    int fd = open("/tmp/fd.txt", O_RDWR , 0600);
    for (;;) {
        lseek(fd, 10, SEEK_SET);

        lockread.l_type = F_RDLCK;
        fcntl(fd, F_SETLKW, &lockread);

        read(fd, &value, 4);
        lockread.l_type = F_UNLCK;
        fcntl(fd, F_SETLK, &lockread);

        if((value!=0x55555555) && (value!=~0x55555555)){
            printf("%x\n", value);
        }
        fflush(stdout);
    }
    close(fd);
}
```

In this case the process attempts to gain a read lock and then reads the value from the same four bytes that the writer process writes to. The call to fcntl is blocking, so if the read lock cannot be acquired the process waits. After reading the value we test to make sure that it is one of the two possible values that the writer process writes to the file.

If you compile both programs and run them you will see no errors printed. The reason is that the reading program cannot read the four bytes while the writing programming is updating the value and the writing program cannot write to the four bytes while the reading program is reading a value.

This use of locks may sound unnecessary, but if you remove the call to fcntl to acquire the lock in the writing program you will soon see that it is very necessary.

You will see values such as:

```
555aaaaa
555555aa
aaaa5555
555555aa
aaaa5555
```

These result when the writing program is in the middle of changing the value while the reading program is in the middle of reading the value.

Notice that the locks are per process and any threads within the process share the same set of locks. This also means that if a process closes a file then all of its locks are released, even if it still has other file descriptors open on the same file. In particular, if a library function opens and then closes the same file then all the locks are lost.

The fact that all the threads in a process share the same set of locks imposes some restrictions on what you can achieve. For example, if a single thread acts as the writer program, then with a other threads acting as readers, everything works. Either the process has a read lock or it has a write lock and only the writer or one of the reader thread can access the file. Where things go wrong is if two threads try to write to the same area of the file. In this case the process will have a write lock on the region and both threads will attempt to write at the same time. Put simply, you cannot stop multiple threads modifying the same region of the file at the same time.

If you need to use locks with threads and you want to protect your program from a loss of locks if a file is closed, you need to use open file description locks. This is a Linux-only facility; to use it you simply change the commands used in the fcntl call:

F_OFD_SETLK   - acquire or release lock non-blocking
F_OFD_SETLKW - as F_OFD_SETLK but blocking, returns -1 if interrupted
F_OFD_GETLK   - test to see if there is a lock of the type specified.

Pipes

The previous example uses a file as a way of sending data between two processes. In most cases a better way to do the same job is to use a named pipe. This is also another example of how a file descriptor can apply to things other than standard files.

A named pipe, or FIFO, behaves like a file that can be opened, written to, and read by any process that cares to open it. The reason is it called a FIFO is that it operates like a First In First Out stack. The writing program can write bytes to it and they are stored until a reading program starts to read in the order that the bytes were written. You can think of the writing program pushing bytes into the pipe and the reading program taking them out at the other end.

There is a subtlety, however. When a process writes to a named pipe the call blocks until a process has opened the pipe for read. Notice that the process doesn't actually have to perform the read to unblock the write call, it is enough that it is ready to read to move the pipe on. In the same way, an attempt to read from a pipe will block until there is some data to read.

To create a named pipe you first use the `mkfifo` function:

```
mkfifo(filename,permissions);
```

where `filename` is the name of the pipe and it is a full path including directories, and `permission` is the usual file access permissions. Notice that the `mkfifo` really does behave as if it is inserting a file into the filing system in that the directories have to exist, the file has to not exist as a standard file, and the process has to have permission to create a file.

Once the named pipe has been created it can be used just like a standard file - it can be opened and you can use `read` and `write` to work with it. However, you can only open a named pipe for `read` or for `write`. If you want two-way communication you need to use two named pipes. It is possible to use C file handling, i.e. streams, with a named pipe, but as these are buffered it is easier to use file descriptors. It is also worth knowing that there can be multiple readers and writers of a named pipe.

You can see the file that corresponds to the pipe in the directory list and it is indicated as a pipe file by a `p` next to its permissions. The pipe file remains available until you explicitly remove it. Notice that although the named pipe looks like a standard file, the operating system makes use of memory to store the data passing through it, hence it is faster.

A Named Pipe Example

For example, a named pipe version of the previous file writer is:

```c
#include <stdio.h>
#include <stdlib.h>
#include <unistd.h>
#include <fcntl.h>
#include <sys/stat.h>

int main(int argc, char** argv) {
    int value = 0x55555555;
    mkfifo("/tmp/myfifo", 0666);
    int fd = open("/tmp/myfifo", O_WRONLY);
    for (;;) {
        value = ~value;
        write(fd, &value, 4);
        printf("W%X", value);
        fflush(stdout);
        sleep(1);
    }
    return (EXIT_SUCCESS);
}
```

Notice the file has to be opened for writing. If you run this program you will see nothing printed until the reading program opens the pipe:

```c
#include <stdio.h>
#include <stdlib.h>
#include <sys/stat.h>
#include <unistd.h>
#include <fcntl.h>

int main(int argc, char** argv) {
    int value;
    int fd = open("/tmp/myfifo", O_RDONLY);
    for (;;) {
        read(fd, &value, 4);
        if ((value != 0x55555555) && (value != ~0x55555555)){
            printf("%x\n", value);
        }
        printf("R%X", value);
        fflush(stdout);
        sleep(1);
    }
    return (EXIT_SUCCESS);
}
```

Notice that the reader doesn't have to create the named pipe using `mkfifo` as the pipe is available to other processes as soon as it is created and remains available until it is explicitly deleted. Things go wrong if the pipe file hasn't been added to the file system as the reading program will then try to treat the file as a standard file. In most cases it is a good idea to use `mkfifo`, even if you know the pipe file already exists.

The final subtlety is that the writing process will block until a reader connects, but after this, if the reader closes the pipe or terminates, the writer will not block but fail with a runtime error. In fact, a `SIGPIPE` signal is generated and you can handle it if you want the writer to detect the closing of the pipe. That is, if you want to handle the closing of the pipe by the reader you need to change the writer's main program to:

```
int main(int argc, char** argv) {
    int value = 0x55555555;

    struct sigaction psa={0};
    psa.sa_handler = signalHandler;
    sigaction(SIGPIPE, &psa, NULL);

    mkfifo("/tmp/myfifo", 0666);
    int fd = open("/tmp/myfifo", O_WRONLY);
    for (;;) {
        value = ~value;
        if(write(fd, &value, 4)<0){
            close(fd);
            fd = open("/tmp/myfifo", O_WRONLY);
        }
        printf("W%X", value);
        fflush(stdout);
        sleep(1);
    }
    return (EXIT_SUCCESS);
}
```

The handling of the signal is standard, see Chapter 4, but notice that when the handler returns you have to check that the write returned an error to close and re-open the pipe. This way the pipe is ready to be connected to by another reader. A reader can detect a pipe closed by the writer by testing for zero bytes returned by `read` - which normally blocks until data is available.

Notice that you can open named pipes in non-blocking mode, simply use `O_NONBLOCK` in the `open` function. In this case both `read` and `write` return at once and they return an error if the other end of the pipe isn't open.

All of this works just as well with threads as with separate processes. You could easily convert the reader and writer code into a single process with two threads.

You might be wondering why no locks are needed when using a named pipe as they were in the case of a real file? The answer is that writing to a pipe is an atomic operation, that is it cannot be interrupted, as long as the amount of data is less than PIPE_BUF defined in linux/limits.h (currently 4096 bytes). If you keep writes to less than this size there is no need to lock.

Anonymous Pipes

As well as named pipes there are anonymous pipes, usually just referred to as a pipe, which only have file descriptors but otherwise work in the same way as named pipes. To create an anonymous pipe all you have to do is call the pipe function with a two-element array to receive two file descriptors:

```
int fd[2];
pipe(fd);
```

When pipe returns it has stored a read file descriptor in fd[0] and a write descriptor in fd[1]. These can be used immediately to read and write to the pipe - you don't need to open any files.

The only question is how does the reading and writing process get the file descriptors? The answer is that they have to be related - one has to be a child process of the other and hence it inherits open file descriptors. The usual way to implement pipes between processes is to first create the pipe and then use fork to create a child process. For more information on fork see Chapter 12. There are other ways of passing a file descriptor to another process. You could use shared memory or a shared file.

Anonymous pipes also work with threads and in this case there is no need to worry about passing file descriptors as threads share file descriptors. However in most cases it is simpler to allow threads to share global data structures than to make use of an anonymous pipe for interthread communication.

An Anonymous Pipe Example

A simple implementation of the reader/writer example using pipes is:

```c
#include <stdio.h>
#include <unistd.h>
#include <sys/types.h>
int main(int argc, char** argv) {
    int value1 = 0x55555555;
    int value2;
    int fd[2];
    pipe(fd);

    if (fork() == 0) {
        close(fd[0]);
        for (;;) {
            value1 = ~value1;
            write(fd[1], &value1, 4);
            printf("W%X", value1);
            fflush(stdout);
            sleep(1);
        }
    } else {
        close(fd[1]);
        for (;;) {
            read(fd[0], &value2, 4);
            if ((value2 != 0x55555555) && (value2 != ~0x55555555)) {
                printf("%x\n", value2);
            }
            printf("R%X", value2);
            fflush(stdout);
            sleep(1);
        }
    }
    return (EXIT_SUCCESS);
}
```

In this case we simply call pipe to get a read and a write descriptor. The fork creates a new process which is a complete copy of the program. The child code "knows" which one it is as fork returns 0 for it and not for the parent process. In this way the child process executes the if clause, i.e. the writer, and the parent executes the else clause, i.e. the reader.

This code omits all error checking and you need to take into account the need to deal with the possibility that the pipe or the fork might fail and that the reader or writer might close the pipe so stalling the other process.

Notice that both named and anonymous pipes can be used with processes or threads. In the case of anonymous pipes you would work in exactly the same way as for the fork example, but in this case sharing the same copy of the file descriptor array.

It is also worth mentioning that pipes are used to connect command line operations using the pipe symbol |. In this case stdout is connected using a pipe to stdin. The easiest way to use this mechanism in a program is to use the popen and pclose command. However, this isn't much used in low-level or systems programming.

File & Directory Operations

Reading and writing files are fairly standard operations, but operating systems provide many other ways to manipulate files including permissions, passwords and so on. These are not so easy to standardize. C includes a small number of additional functions that manipulate files, including:

remove(*filename*);	Removes file - usually deletes it.
rename(*oldfilename*,*newfilename*);	Renames file - details are system dependent
tmpfile();	Returns a file pointer to temporary file open in wb+. File is removed when closed.
tmpnam(&*string*);	Stores a temporary file name in string.
mkdir(path,mode)	Make a directory
getcwd(&path)	Get current working directory

You can also read a directory and work with it as if it was a standard file, which of course it almost is.

To open a directory you use:

```
DIR * dir=opendir (dirname)
```

which returns a directory stream for the directory at the end of the path in the string dirname.

Once open you can read the director using:

```
struct dirent *direntry= readdir(dir);
```

which returns a `dirent` struct which details a single file in the directory and typically has the following fields:

```
struct dirent {
    ino_t           d_ino;       /* Inode number */
    off_t           d_off;       /* Location in stream */
    unsigned short d_reclen;     /* Length of this record */
    unsigned char  d_type;       /* Type of file; not supported
                                            by all filesystem types */
    char            d_name[256]; /* Null-terminated filename */
};
```

POSIX only defines d_name and d_ino. The order of the files and the length of file names is also not fixed.

To move position within a directory stream you can use:

```
rewinddir(dir);
long position=telldir(dir);
```

which returns the current position and:

```
seekdir(dir,position);
```

which moves the current location to `position`. Notice that you can only use a value of `position` that has been returned by `telldir`. Finally, you can close a directory stream using:

```
closedir(dir);
```

As a simple example let's read the home directory on a Raspberry Pi:

```
#define _POSIX_C_SOURCE  200809L
#include <stdio.h>
#include <stdlib.h>
#include <dirent.h>
#include <sys/types.h>
int main(int argc, char** argv) {
    struct dirent *direntry;
    DIR *dir = opendir("/home/pi");
    while ((direntry = readdir(dir)) != NULL) {
        printf("%s \n", direntry->d_name);
    }
    closedir(dir);
    return (EXIT_SUCCESS);
}
```

There are many other file and directory handling functions but these are the most commonly useful.

ioctl

The `ioctl` function is the most common reason for needing to work with file descriptors. The function is used to provide a direct access to device drivers. The big problem is that `ioctl` calls are implemented by third party device drivers and are often poorly documented.

A general `ioctl` call takes the form:

```
ioctl(fd,request, optional void*)
```

where *fd* is the open file descriptor of the device, *request* is what you want to do followed by a pointer to a buffer of data where appropriate. The data is either sent to the device or supplied by the device according to the request.

There have been attempts to organize the request code and document it, but finding out how to do something with a new device is usually not easy.

The `ioctl` function is particularly useful when working with the pseudo file system, see Chapter 9.

Summary

- If you think of a file as just a sequence or stream of bytes that can be read or written, then you have an idea that fits a great many sources and sinks of data.

- This idea is so powerful that under Linux/Unix you can view almost all data as an example of a file.

- C has a standard way of working with files – streams – and it provides a range of functions for working with file pointers such as fopen and fclose.

- C files are buffered and this can cause unexpected behavior. Use fflush to make sure that buffers are written out.

- Although not part of the C standard, file descriptors are part of Linux- and POSIX-compliant operating systems. They provide a lower-level, but OS-dependent, way of working with files.

- File descriptor functions are similar to C file functions, but they don't start with f and are simply open, close, read, write, and so on.

- As C files are actually opened as file descriptors under POSIX operating systems, you can find the descriptor corresponding to a stream using fileno.

- Files can be shared between processes.

- The state of Linux/Unix file locking is not good, but you can lock a range of bytes within a file as long as you are aware of the problems.

- A pipe is like a shared file but stored in memory. There are named and anonymous pipes.

- There are a range of file and directory manipulation commands that allow you to do things like rename files.

Chapter 9

The Pseudo File System

The idea that everything is a file doesn't seem strange until you meet the pseudo file system – also sometimes called the synthetic file system. This is a file system designed to wrap hardware, drivers, system state and just about anything that isn't a really a file, as a file.

The pseudo file system has folders and files and you can generally work with these as if they were perfectly normal. You can read/write and even use seek to move to a position in such a file. Of course, exactly what you can and cannot do varies according to the object being wrapped as a file or folder.

One of the big problems of the pseudo file system is that it is poorly documented and its behavior can vary a lot depending on the hardware it is implemented on. In this chapter we will look at the Linux pseudo file system. Unix and other operating systems have similar facilities, but there is no standard for the pseudo file system.

The Linux Pseudo Directories

There are a two well-known pseudo directories:

procfs

Usually mounted as /proc, contains a large number of directories concerned with the state of the system and has a subdirectory for every process running containing information about that process.

sysfs

Usually mounted as /sys, contains folders that expose the hardware and driver information.

There are also some lesser known ones including:

debugfs

Usually mounted as /sys/debug, is used by debugging utilities.

pipefs
Isn't mountable and is used to create pipes.

tmpfs
Usually mounted as /tmp/shm used to share memory areas.

It is also worth mentioning /dev which contains folders that correspond to device drivers of various sorts. This predates the sysfs file system and contains many pseudo directories that probably would be in sysfs if reinvented today.

What can you do with these file systems?

If the file is a wrapper for some status data then generally you can read it to find out the current values. For example, /proc/meminfo gives memory use statistics. You can open it and read it or just use the cat command:

```
cat /proc/meminfo
MemTotal:          949444 kB
MemFree:           250276 kB
MemAvailable:      588716 kB
Buffers:            94528 kB
Cached:            355420 kB
SwapCached:             0 kB
Active:            454272 kB
Inactive:         193148 kB
```

Most of the data is used by system utilities that report on the state of the system to the user.

Another useful directory is /proc/iomem which lists the addresses and uses of the physical memory. That is:

```
cat /proc/iomem
```

will display a memory map for the device that you are working with.

However, it doesn't always contain all of the information you might hope for.

For an example of a pseudo directory that you can read and write to, consider /sys/power/ which controls the power state of the machine. If you write any of the strings "disk", "freeze" or "standby" to the file /sys/power/state then the machine will go into hibernation, suspend-to-idle and standby states. If it doesn't support sleep states, the directory is missing.

160

Notice that you can use C standard file handling or POSIX file handling to access pseudo files, but sometimes only POSIX will do. In particular, the POSIX file functions don't buffer the data and this is sometimes what you need when writing to hardware.

How do you find out what is available in the pseudo file systems? The answer is that you look it up in the man pages for the relevant file system. However, how well any given feature is implemented varies. Sometimes you will find features omitted, half-implemented or augmented. You simply have to look at the file system and try things out.

Finding a PID by Name

As an example of the sort of things that the pseudo file system is used for, consider the question of how to find the PID of a program by name. That is, assuming that myProgram is running, what is its PID?

At first thought it seems likely that there would be a syscall for this action, after all there is getpid which returns the PID of the calling program, and getppid, which returns the PID of the parent process. You can, however, search the documentation in vain as there is no predefined way to get a PID of a named process.

The solution is to use the /proc pseudo directory.

This contains a directory for each running process with a name given by the PID. Within this directory are files and other directories that give information about the process. If you consult the man page for /proc you will find a file called comm which gives the command name for the process i.e. what the user types on the command line to get the program running. You can also use the cmdline file to discover exactly what the user typed including arguments.

So the method is to open the /proc directory and read each directory entry in turn - see the end of Chapter 8 for information on working with directories. This way we can step through the information on each process running in an effort to find the one with the required name.

Each directory entry contains the PID of the process and this can then be used to construct a path to /proc/*pid*/comm where *pid* is the name of the directory entry corresponding to the process with that pid. You can then open this file and read it to discover the name of the process with that *pid*. If this is the name that you are looking for you have found the PID.

The program is:

```c
#include <stdio.h>
#include <stdlib.h>
#include <string.h>
#include <dirent.h>
#include <sys/types.h>

int main(int argc, char** argv) {
    struct dirent *direntry;
    char path[200];
    char name[200];
    FILE *fp;
    DIR *dir = opendir("/proc/");

    while ((direntry = readdir(dir)) != NULL) {
        strcpy(path, "/proc/");
        strcat(path, direntry->d_name);
        strcat(path, "/comm");
        fp = fopen(path, "r");
        if (fp != NULL) {
            fscanf(fp, "%s", name);
            printf("%s-%s\n\r", direntry->d_name, name);
            fflush(NULL);
            fclose(fp);
        }
    }
    closedir(dir);
    return (EXIT_SUCCESS);
}
```

Notice that we have not checked for buffer overruns for simplicity. It is also necessary to check that the constructed path does correspond to an openable file as as it could be a directory or "." say - hence the test if(fp!=NULL).

The program simply prints the PID and the names of each process. You can easily use this example to construct a function that matches the name of each item against a target name and returns the PID.

Working with GPIO

One particularly important pseudo file system is /sys/class/gpio/. This is where any drivers to a device's GPIO (General Purpose I/O) lines are exposed to the user space.

To see what is in the folder, simply list it:

ls /sys/class/gpio

For example on a Raspberry Pi you will see something like:

```
pi@raspberrypi:    ls /sys/class/gpio
export  gpio4  gpiochip0  unexport
pi@raspberrypi:    ▮
```

The list includes the GPIO lines that are already in use by some process or other. Notice that the GPIO numbers are internal - how they relate to the hardware is something you have to discover from the machine's specification.

The steps in using a line are always the same:

1. Reserve or "export" the GPIO line, by writing its number to the export directory, so that no other process can use it. This also creates a gpio*n* directory which contains other directories that you can use to control the line.

2. You can then use this new directory to set its direction and read or write it.

3. When you have finished using it you have to unreserve or "unexport" it. This destroys the directory associated with the line.

You can do these steps from any language that supports file operations, including the shell. All of these steps are accomplished by reading and writing to what look like files.

For example in C:

```c
#include <stdio.h>
#include <string.h>
int main(int argc, char** argv) {
        int gpioNo = 4;
        FILE* fd = fopen("/sys/class/gpio/export", "w");
        fprintf(fd, "%d", gpioNo);
        fclose(fd);
        return 0;
}
```

Once you have the pin reserved, you will see a `gpio4` folder corresponding to it in `/sys/class/gpio`. Now that you have it reserved, you can set its direction and read/write it. To do this you have to read from or write to the appropriate sub folder of the gpio folder just created.

If you list all of the folders in `gpio4` you will see:

```
pi@raspberrypi:    ls /sys/class/gpio/gpio4
active_low  device  direction  edge        subsystem  uevent  value
pi@raspberrypi:    █
```

Each of these folders controls some aspect of the GPIO line's functioning. The most important are `direction`, in which the line can be set to `in` or `out`, and `value`, in which can be set to `0` or `1` for an output line and read as `0` or `1` for input line. There is also `active_low` which determines which way the logic operates. It determines if the line going low corresponds to a `1` or a `0`.

The following C program is taken from:

Raspberry Pi IoT in C (ISBN: 978-1871962468)

and is typical of the `sysfs` approach to using GPIO lines. It sets GPIO 4 to output and then toggles it high and low as fast as possible:

```c
#include <stdio.h>
#include <string.h>

int main(int argc, char** argv) {
    int gpioNo = 4;
    char buf[100];
    FILE* fd = fopen("/sys/class/gpio/export", "w");
    fprintf(fd, "%d", gpioNo);
    fclose(fd);
    sprintf(buf, "/sys/class/gpio/gpio%d/direction", gpioNo);
    fd = fopen(buf, "w");
    fprintf(fd, "out");
    fclose(fd);
    sprintf(buf, "/sys/class/gpio/gpio%d/value", gpioNo);
    fd = fopen(buf, "w");
    for (;;) {
        fd = fopen(buf, "w");
        fprintf(fd, "1");
        fclose(fd);
        fd = fopen(buf, "w");
        fprintf(fd, "0");
        fclose(fd);
    }
    return 0;
}
```

The program first exports `gpio4` and then writes `"out"` to its `direction` folder to set the line to output. After this the value file is open for writing and `"1"` and `"0"` are written to the file repeatedly.

You might be puzzled by the loop that opens the file, writes a value and then closes it. Why not just keep the file open? The reason is that the file buffer isn't flushed unless the file is closed. This is the usual way of dealing with the problem, but it is not very fast and it is part of the reason that `sysfs` has a bad reputation.

Typically the sysfs approach is slow. On a Raspberry Pi Zero, for example, it can take 500us to change the state of a GPIO line, which is very slow. We can, however, do much better by not closing the file every time we write to it. Instead we can use `fflush` to flush the file buffer:

If you change the for loop to:

```
for (;;) {
        fprintf(fd, "1");
                fflush(fd);
                fprintf(fd, "0");
        fflush(fd);
}
```

Now the it takes only 10us to change the state of a GPIO line, which is much better, but it is still 10 times slower than working with the line directly without pretending that it is a file.

The point is that opening and closing files is expensive in terms of overhead, but reading and writing isn't. If you are using sysfs it is worth keeping files open, which is not what most of the example sysfs programs do. They tend to provide a function that writes to the GPIO line by first opening the file, writing to it and then closing it. The program above is an improvement on this and an even better solution would be to use POSIX I/O functions, which are not buffered.

You might wonder why something as strange, and as slow, as the sysfs approach to GPIO lines is used? It is often suggested that the answer is portability as it is the same on all versions of Linux. Of course, differences in hardware generally mean that the line numbers are different and there are usually other considerations that make it necessary to customize the code. Another reason is that system designers believe that it is the only way to keep the system secure. The alternatives, like giving user space programs access to the memory areas needed to control the GPIO lines, are a security risk. This is certainly the case for the Linux-based Android Things system where sysfs is used because memory mapping is wrongly regarded as too insecure. As a result Android Things is very slow and this has undoubtedly contributed to its low rate of adoption.

Accessing Memory

If you are familiar with programming very simple processors then you will regard direct access to memory as almost a right. If you want to access memory location 0xFFFF then all you have to do is load up a pointer with the address and start making use of it. This is simple, but for most modern processors it isn't likely to work. The reason is that a modern processor is likely to make use of memory mapping to place physical memory at any logical address it cares to place it. If you try to access memory location 0xFFFF the chances are that it isn't part of your allocated address space and the result is an error.

So how can you access memory by physical address? The answer is that there is a pseudo file /dev/mem which represents the entire system memory by physical addresses. You can see what is installed at any memory address by reading /proc/iomem:

cat /proc/iomem.

The pseudo file /dev/mem is a character device file that is an image of the main memory. When you read or write byte *n* this is the same as reading and writing the memory location at physical byte address *n*. You can move the pointer to almost any memory location using lseek and read and write blocks of bytes using fread and fwrite, the exceptions being areas of memory inaccessible for security reasons. It is simple, but it takes some time to get used to the idea. For example to open the file to read and write it you might use:

```
int memfd = open("/dev/mem", O_RDWR | O_SYNC);
```

The O_RDWR opens the file for read and write and the O_SYNC flag makes the call blocking. After this you can lseek to the memory location you want to work with. For example, to go to the start of the GPIO registers in a Raspberry Pi 2 or later you would use:

```
uint32_t p = lseek(memfd, (off_t) 0x3f200000, SEEK_SET);
```

and for the Pi 1:

```
uint32_t p = lseek(memfd, (off_t) 0x20200000, SEEK_SET);
```

Notice that these are the base address plus 0x20 000. Next you could read the 32 bits starting at that location, i.e. the FSEL0 register:

```
int buffer[1];
int n = read(memfd, buffer, 4);
```

It is worth mentioning that not all processors make use of memory-mapped I/O. In particular the Intel x86 family makes use of some memory-mapped I/O and a separate port-based system. The I/O ports behave like a completely separate address and memory bus and no memory mapping is applied. If you want to work with this entirely separate set of ports then you can make use of the /dev/port pseudo file, which works in exactly the same way as /dev/mem. You can see what is installed at what address by reading the /proc/ioports pseudo file:

```
cat /proc/ioports
```

Memory Mapping Files

The Linux approach to I/O places the emphasis on files, but there are times when reading and writing a file to an external device like a disk drive is too slow. To solve this problem Linux has a memory mapping function which will read any portion of a file into user memory so that you can work with it directly using pointers. In principle, this is a very fast way to access any file, including the mem pseudo file.

This may seem be a very convoluted route to get at memory. First implement memory access as a file you can read and then map that file into memory so that you can read it as if it was memory - which it is. However, if you follow the story, it is logical. What is more it solves a slightly different problem very elegantly. It allows the fixed physical addresses of the peripherals to access the user space virtual addresses. In other words, when you memory map the mem file into user memory, it can be located anywhere and the address of the start of the register area will be within your program's allocated address space. This means that all of the addresses will change. Of course, as long as we work with offsets from the start of memory this is no problem - we update the starting value and use the same offsets.

Let's see how this works in practice, noting that the key function is mmap:

```
void *mmap(void *addr,size_t length,int prot,int flags,int fd,
                                      off_t offset);
```

This function memory maps the file corresponding to the file descriptor fd into memory and returns its start address. The offset and length parameters control the portion of the file mapped, i.e. the mapped portions starts at the byte given by offset and continues for length bytes.

There is a small complication in that, for reasons of efficiency, the file is always mapped in units of the page size of the machine. So if you ask for a 1-Kbyte file to be loaded into memory then on ARM processors, such as the Raspberry Pi, which have a 4-Kbyte page size, 4 Kbytes of memory will be allocated. The file will occupy the first 1 Kbytes and the rest will be zeroed.

You can also specify the address to which you would like the file loaded in your program's address space, but the system doesn't have to honor this request, it just uses it as a hint. Some programmers reserve an area of memory using `malloc` and then ask the system to load the file into it. However, as this might not happen it seems simpler to let the system allocate the memory and pass `NULL` as the starting address. The parameters `prot` and `flags` specify various ways the file can be memory mapped and there are a lot of options - see the man page for details.

Notice that this is a completely general mechanism and you can use it to map any file into memory. For example, if you have a graphics file `image.gif`, you could load it into memory to make working with it faster. Many databases use this technique to speed up their processing.

Now all we have to do is map `/dev/mem` into memory. First we need to open the `/dev/mem` device as usual:

```
uint32_t memfd = open("/dev/mem", O_RDWR | O_SYNC);
```

As long as this works we can map the file into memory.

Memory mapping `/dev/mem` means that you can work with fixed physical addresses anywhere in your user space. As well as being useful, it is also generally fast because of the way the hardware is used. It is a much better way to work with I/O devices than sysfs simply because it is faster, but it only works under Linux.

For example, in the case of the Raspberry Pi we want to map the file starting at either `0x20200000` for the Pi 1 or starting at `0x3F200000` for the Pi 2 or later. If we only want to work with the GPIO registers then we only need offsets of `0000` to `00B0` i.e. 176, bytes but as we get a complete 4-Kbyte page we might as well map 4 KBytes worth of address space:

```
uint32_t * map = (uint32_t *)mmap(NULL,4*1024,
      (PROT_READ | PROT_WRITE),MAP_SHARED,memfd,0x3f200000);
```

If you try this, remember to change the offset to be correct for the device you are using.

Notice that we haven't set an address for the file to be loaded into - the system will take care of it and return the address in `map`. We have also asked for read/write permission and allowed other processes to share the map. This makes `map` a very important variable because now it gives the location of the start of the GPIO register area in user space.

Now we can read and write a 3KByte block of addresses starting at the first GPIO register, i.e. FSEL0.

For example to read FSEL0 we would use:

```
printf("fsel0 %X \n\r",*map);
```

To access the other registers we need to add their offset, but there is one subtle detail. The pointer to the start of the memory has been cast to a uint32_t because we want to read and write 32-bit registers. However, by the rules of pointer arithmetic, when you add one to a pointer you actually add the size of the data type the pointer is pointing to.

In this case when you add one to map you increment the location it is pointing at by four, i.e. the size of a 32-bit unsigned integer. The rule is that with this cast we are using word addresses which are byte addresses divided by 4. Thus, when we add the offsets, we need to add the offset divided by 4. For example, to read the memory location at offset 0xFF you have to read from *(map+0x3F) because 0xFF/4=0x3F. You can read smaller units than 32-bit words from memory by casting the pointer to other types.

Shared Memory

You can use memory mapped files to allow processes to share memory - threads (see Chapter 12) share memory by default. The idea is much like pipes. You create a special file which is then associated with an area of memory using mmap as if it was a real file. Other processes can then open the same file and mmap it and use it to communicate.

To do this you need the shm_open function:

```
int fd = shm_open("filename",flags ,mode);
```

which creates a special file called *filename*, just like the usual open function. Once you have the file descriptor you have to use:

```
ftruncate(fd, size);
```

to set the file to a fixed size. Next you can use mmap to map the file into memory and start using it.

When you have finished with the memory mapping you can unmap it:

```
munmap(memptr, size);
```

You also need to close the file descriptor. If you leave the file in the filing system then it can be used again without being created. Alternatively you can unlink the file, after closing it, using:

```
shm_unlink("filename");
```

Here is a simple writer example:

```c
#define _POSIX_C_SOURCE 200112L
#include <stdio.h>
#include <stdlib.h>
#include <sys/mman.h>
#include <string.h>
#include <sys/stat.h>
#include <fcntl.h>
#include <unistd.h>
#include <sys/types.h>
#include <inttypes.h>

int main(int argc, char** argv) {
    int value = 0x55555555;
    int fd = shm_open("BackingFile", O_RDWR | O_CREAT, 0644);
    ftruncate(fd, 1000);

    uint8_t *memptr = mmap(NULL, 1000, PROT_READ |
                                PROT_WRITE, MAP_SHARED, fd, 0);

    for (int i = 0; i < 10; ++i) {
        value = ~value;
        memcpy(memptr,&value,4);
        sleep(1);
    }

    munmap(memptr, 1000);
    close(fd);
    shm_unlink("BackingFile");
    return (EXIT_SUCCESS);
}
```

You need to add the rt library to the linker to make this work.

This alternatively writes 0x55555555 and 0xAAAAAAAA to the shared memory. Notice the use of memcpy to copy the four bytes in the int to the start of shared memory.

A reading program is just as simple:

```c
#define _POSIX_C_SOURCE 200112L
#include <stdio.h>
#include <stdlib.h>
#include <sys/mman.h>
#include <string.h>
#include <sys/stat.h>
#include <fcntl.h>
#include <unistd.h>
#include <sys/types.h>
#include <inttypes.h>

int main(int argc, char** argv) {
    int value = 0x55555555;
    int fd = shm_open("BackingFile", O_RDWR, 0644);
    uint8_t *memptr = mmap(NULL, 1000, PROT_READ |
                                PROT_WRITE, MAP_SHARED, fd, 0);

    for (int i = 0; i < 10; ++i) {
        memcpy(&value,memptr,4);
        printf("%x\n", value);
        fflush(NULL);
        sleep(1);
    }

    munmap(memptr, 1000);
    close(fd);
    shm_unlink("BackingFile");
    return (EXIT_SUCCESS);
}
```

Notice that in this case the shm_open doesn't create the file, it simply opens it and it also doesn't have to set it to a size using ftruncate. You need to remember to add the rt library to the linker to make this work.

If you run the writer and then the reader you should see the pattern of values printed correctly. Notice that neither program has any error checks and neither makes use of locking to avoid the writer or reader being interrupted in the middle of an update. Given we are only writing 4 bytes this is unlikely but not impossible.

It is probably better to use pointers to the shared memory rather than using functions such as memcpy as this is more like how you work with memory created by malloc. For example:

```
uint32_t *memptr = mmap(NULL, 1000, PROT_READ | PROT_WRITE,
                                         MAP_SHARED, fd, 0);

int *value =memptr;
```

and in the read loop:

```
printf("%x\n", *value);
```

but notice if you use locking then you need to lock access to the shared memory. The lock time is reduced if you use local variables and only transfer them to the shared memory after their value has been computed.

Semaphore Locking

To add locking you need to make use of a semaphore which works between processes or threads. A semaphore is a more than just a lock, it is a way of signaling a state. A semaphore is created and set to a value. When a process waits on a semaphore it checks the value of the semaphore and as long as the value is greater than zero it decrements the value and continues - i.e. it has a lock. If the value is zero the process blocks and waits for the value to be greater than zero - i.e. it has to wait for the lock. Unlocking the semaphore immediately increments the value by one.

Semaphores come in named and unnamed versions. You need a named semaphore to lock between processes, but an unnamed semaphore will suffice for locking threads. To create a semaphore you first need to create a variable of type sem_t, then you use the sem_open function for a named semaphore or sem_init for an unnamed semaphore. A named semaphore is removed using sem_close and an unnamed semaphore is removed using sem_destroy.

After creation named and unnamed semaphores are used in the same way with sem_wait being an attempt to decrement and lock and sem_post being an unlock and increment. Notice that although we have been using the terms "lock" and "unlock", exactly what a semaphore is used for is up to you.

To create a named semaphore you use:

```
sem_t* semptr = sem_open(Name,flags,mode,value);
```

where `Name` is a null terminated string starting with / and not containing any additional slashes. It is the name of the semaphore used by all of the processes wanting to access it. The `flags` and `mode` parameters are as for opening a file. If you are creating the semaphore with `O_CREATE` then you have to supply `value` which is used to set the semaphore's initial value. If the semaphore already exists `mode` and `value` are ignored.

To wait on a semaphore or obtain a lock you use:

```
sem_wait(semptr);
```

to release a "lock" you would use:

```
sem_post(semptr);
```

When a process has finished with a semaphore it can close it using:

```
sem_close(semptr);
```

and if necessary it can be removed using:

```
sem_unlink(name);
```

where `name` is the name used to open it.

Notice that if you create a named semaphore with initial value 1 then only one process can acquire a lock and any process that tries to acquire a lock has to wait until the first process releases it.

Generally the initial value gives the number of processes that can lock the semaphore without having to wait.

Using a semaphore in this way the writer program is:

```c
#define _POSIX_C_SOURCE 200112L
#include <stdio.h>
#include <stdlib.h>
#include <sys/mman.h>
#include <string.h>
#include <sys/stat.h>
#include <fcntl.h>
#include <unistd.h>
#include <sys/types.h>
#include <inttypes.h>
#include <semaphore.h>

int main(int argc, char** argv) {
    int value = 0x55555555;

    int fd = shm_open("BackingFile", O_RDWR | O_CREAT, 0644);
    ftruncate(fd, 1000);

    uint8_t *memptr = mmap(NULL, 1000, PROT_READ |
                                PROT_WRITE, MAP_SHARED, fd, 0);

    sem_unlink("/mySemaphore");
    sem_t* semptr = sem_open("/mySemaphore", O_CREAT, 0644, 1);

    for (int i = 0; i < 20; ++i) {
        value = ~value;
        sem_wait(semptr);
        memcpy(memptr, &value, 4);
        sem_post(semptr);
        printf("%x\n", value);
        fflush(NULL);
        sleep(1);
    }

    munmap(memptr, 1000);
    close(fd);
    shm_unlink("BackingFile");
    return (EXIT_SUCCESS);

}
```

Notice that we unlink the semaphore just before we attempt to create it to make sure that we set its initial value. The writing program then tries to acquire a lock before writing to the memory location. If it acquires the lock, we can be sure that the reader isn't in the middle of reading data. It relinquishes the lock as soon as it can.

The reader program is very similar:

```c
#define _POSIX_C_SOURCE 200112L
#include <stdio.h>
#include <stdlib.h>
#include <sys/mman.h>
#include <string.h>
#include <sys/stat.h>
#include <fcntl.h>
#include <unistd.h>
#include <sys/types.h>
#include <inttypes.h>
#include <semaphore.h>

int main(int argc, char** argv) {
    int value = 0x55555555;

    int fd = shm_open("BackingFile", O_RDWR, 0644);

    uint8_t *memptr = mmap(NULL, 1000, PROT_READ |
                                PROT_WRITE, MAP_SHARED, fd, 0);

    sem_t* semptr = sem_open("/mySemaphore", O_CREAT, 0644, 1);

    for (int i = 0; i < 10; ++i) {
        sem_wait(semptr);
        memcpy(&value, memptr, 4);
        sem_post(semptr);
        printf("%x\n", value);
        fflush(NULL);
        sleep(1);
    }

    munmap(memptr, 1000);
    close(fd);
    shm_unlink("BackingFile");
    return (EXIT_SUCCESS);
}
```

In this case we do not unlink the semaphore before opening it because we don't want to change its value if the writer has already created it - it is assumed that the write is started first as if it isn't the attempt to read the shared memory fails. That is, the semaphore mechanism doesn't stop the reader from attempting to read before the writer has started. Again the reader locks the semaphore before reading and unlocks it as quickly as possible. For either program to work we have to add the pthread library via the linker.

Semaphores can be used to implement more complex types of synchronization and a full coverage of the topic would take a book in its own right. This chapter has given you a brief introduction to the many parts of the pseudo file system. In general there are two problems with making use of it. The first is discovering if there is a part of the system that covers the device or facility you want to access. The second is discovering if the machine you are working with implements it and how well.

Summary

- The general principle of "everything is a file" leads to the pseudo file system which wraps many hardware sources and sinks of data as files and folders.

- From an IoT point of view the most important of the pseudo directories is sysfs which provides access to the GPIO.

- Working with GPIO lines using sysfs is a matter of exporting the line you want to use and then using the folders and files created to manipulate it.

- Sysfs has a reputation for being slow, but this is mainly due to the closing and reopening of files on each access. If you make use of fflush or file descriptors then it is much faster, although still slower than direct access to the GPIO.

- To access memory directly with the cooperation of the memory management hardware you have to use the mem pseudo file. Reading and writing this file gives you direct access to memory.

- Any file can be loaded into a process's memory and accessed directly using pointers. This is faster than repeated disk accesses.

- If the mem pseudo file is loaded into a process's memory then you can have direct access to a machine's memory using pointers rather than file operations. This is the standard way of accessing memory-mapped I/O on most machines.

- A memory mapped file can be shared between processes.

- To lock a memory mapped file use a semaphore.

Chapter 10

Graphics

C is not a language known in the context of developing user interfaces, but even small systems occasionally need to communicate with their users. Often all that is needed is the display of a few digits to provide feedback on the current state. A common and low-cost way of doing this is to interface directly to a 7-segment LCD display driven directly by the GPIO lines. Any input is also often provided by physical switches and buttons and handled directly by programming GPIO lines.

In this sense the user interface is just an extension of the low-level GPIO programming in the rest of the system. However, with many small devices being equipped with a full HDMI or VGA graphics output, using a full screen display is a real alternative to the GPIO-driven user interface. This means we have to move to using full Linux graphics from C to create either simple displays at one end of the spectrum or full GUI interfaces, complete with touchscreen, trackball, mouse or keyboard input.

Choosing a GUI System

Graphics in Linux is the most difficult of topics. The reason is not that graphics programming is intrinsically hard, it can be, but because there are so many choices. Linux has no one right way to do graphics and as your needs get more sophisticated so do the choices. Linux has a hierarchy of approaches starting with the lowest level API - the framebuffer - which lets you write directly to the screen. Next you have X Windows and similar windowing subsystems which give you the ability to create and manage windows. Windowing systems don't give you the ability to create a GUI out of the box - they lack widgets and the infrastructure needed to use them. Beyond windowing systems you need a GUI system such as GTK or Qt, which generally works via a windowing system. When choosing a GUI system the problem is working out which has the right licensing terms and which is lightweight enough not to slow your program down. Then there is the question of which of these frameworks has the sort of longevity needed to base your program on. GUI frameworks are a popular hobby and come and go with the interests of their developers.

In this chapter we look at the lowest level of graphics, the framebuffer, which is rarely used in application programs because it is so low-level. However, for small systems it might provide the level of interaction with the hardware that you need. After this we look at using X-Windows to work cooperatively in a windowing environment and finally using GTK+ to create a full windowed GUI system. Obviously these topics are large and each deserves a book in its own right. The objective of this chapter is to provide enough information to get you started and more importantly to get you thinking in the right way to understand how to proceed with more complex programs.

The Framebuffer

The framebuffer is a pseudo file stored in /dev. If the system you are working with has a framebuffer there will be a file called fb0 or fb1 etc. This is a file-like interface to the graphics buffer - yes its a pseudo file and it can be memory mapped so that you can use it as a conventional memory based graphics buffer. However, if you want to you can treat it as a file and work with read, write and seek. You can also use commands such as cp to copy the entire file and hence take a screen dump. In Linux/Unix everything is a file.

To open the framebuffer you use:

```
int fd = open("/dev/fb0", O_RDWR);
```

assuming the framebuffer is fb0 and you want to both read and write it.
At this point you can't map it into memory because you don't know how big it is. The framebuffer has two structs that you can use to get and set information about the graphics mode and state. The fb_fix_screeninfo struct gives you the current state of the video hardware:

```
struct fb_fix_screeninfo {
  char id[16];                 /* identification string        */
  unsigned long smem_start; /* Address of frame buffer mem    */
  __u32 smem_len;              /* Length of frame buffer mem   */
  __u32 type;                  /* see FB_TYPE_*                */
  __u32 type_aux;              /* Interleave                   */
  __u32 visual;                /* see FB_VISUAL_               */
  __u16 xpanstep;              /* zero if no hardware panning  */
  __u16 ypanstep;              /* zero if no hardware panning  */
  __u16 ywrapstep;             /* zero if no hardware ywrap    */
  __u32 line_length;           /* length of a line in bytes    */
  unsigned long mmio_start; /* Start of Memory Mapped I/O     */
  __u32 mmio_len;              /* Length of Memory Mapped I/O  */
  __u32 accel;                 /*  specific chip/card we have  */
  __u16 capabilities;          /* see FB_CAP_                  */
  __u16 reserved[2];           /* Reserved                     */
};
```

Which of these fields is important depends on the graphics hardware in use.
The variable information is usually of much more direct use:

```
struct fb_var_screeninfo {
  __u32 xres;                    /* number of pixels in row      */
  __u32 yres;                    /* number of pixels in col      */
  __u32 xres_virtual;            /* virtual resolution           */
  __u32 yres_virtual;
  __u32 xoffset;                 /* offset from virtual to visible*/
  __u32 yoffset;                 /* resolution                   */
  __u32 bits_per_pixel;          /* bits per pixel               */
  __u32 grayscale;               /* 0 = color, 1 = grayscale,    */
                                 /* >1 = FOURCC                  */
  struct fb_bitfield red;        /* bitfield fb mem if true color,*/
  struct fb_bitfield green;      /* else only length significant */
  struct fb_bitfield blue;
  struct fb_bitfield transp;     /* transparency                 */
  __u32 nonstd;                  /* != 0 Non standard pixel format*/
  __u32 activate;                /* see FB_ACTIVATE_             */
  __u32 height;                  /* height of picture in mm      */
  __u32 width;                   /* width of picture in mm       */
  __u32 accel_flags;             /* (OBSOLETE) see fb_info.flags */
/* Timing: All values in pixclocks, except pixclock              */
  __u32 pixclock;                /* pixel clock in pico seconds  */
  __u32 left_margin;             /* time from sync to picture    */
  __u32 right_margin;            /* time from picture to sync    */
  __u32 upper_margin;            /* time from sync to picture    */
  __u32 lower_margin;
  __u32 hsync_len;               /* length of horizontal sync    */
  __u32 vsync_len;               /* length of vertical sync      */
  __u32 sync;                    /* see FB_SYNC_ *               */
  __u32 vmode;                   /* see FB_VMODE_ *              */
  __u32 rotate;                  /* angle we rotate cnter clkwise */
  __u32 colorspace;              /* colorspace for FOURCC modes  */
  __u32 reserved[4];             /* Reserved                     */
};
```

Most of the important information is in the first part of this struct. The
geometry of the image is determined by six fields:

```
xres;
yres;
xres_virtual;
yres_virtual;
xoffset;
yoffset;
```

The xres and yres values give you the number of pixels in a row and a
column in the framebuffer. The xres_virtual and yres_virtual values give

you the number of pixels displayed on the screen. In general the two are the same but if the screenbuffer is bigger than the screen can display then it is a portal into the screenbuffer and its location is given by the value of xoffset and yoffset. In most cases the actual and virtual are the same and the offsets are zero.

We also need to know the value of bits_per_pixel, which can be divided by 8 to give the number of bytes per pixel.

This almost gives us enough information to work out the size of the framebuffer and locate any given pixel. However there is one small but standard complication in such calculations. A row of pixels should take xres* bits_per_pixel/8 bytes to store but often padding bytes have to be added to make each row align on an address boundary. The number of bytes including padding is given in fb_fix_screeninfo.line_length. This is often called the stride because its the number of bytes you need to skip over to reach a pixel at the same x coordinate but at y+1.

Putting all this together gives the size of the framebuffer as:

yres* line_length

To map the file into memory all we need is:

```
int fd = open("/dev/fb0", O_RDWR);
struct fb_fix_screeninfo finfo;
struct fb_var_screeninfo vinfo;
ioctl(fd, FBIOGET_VSCREENINFO, &vinfo);
ioctl(fd, FBIOGET_FSCREENINFO, &finfo);
size_t size = vinfo.yres * finfo.line_length;
uint8_t *fbp = mmap(0, size, PROT_READ | PROT_WRITE,
                                    MAP_SHARED, fd,0);
```

The ioctl calls are the standard way to get the information into the structs. Using this we compute the total size of the buffer in bytes. The memory mapping is straightforward but notice that we have opted to work in byte addresses by using a pointer to uint8_t.

The next step is to work out where a pixel at coordinate x,y is stored in the buffer. First we need to decide if we are working in screen coordinates i.e. virtual coordinates or physical coordinates. If the screenbuffer is larger than the screen then this makes a difference. In most cases it makes sense to draw in the screen buffer and ignore the fact that only a portion is visible on the screen. Thus x and y are give the location of the pixel in an image of size xres and yres. The location of this pixel in the buffer is given by:

```
uint32_t location = x*vinfo.bits_per_pixel/8 + y*finfo.line_length;
```

This is the address of the first byte of the pixel.

Finally we need to create a color value to store in the pixel. The problem here is that the format used depends on the number of bits used for each pixel and how the RGBA values are packed. This is coded by the fields in fb_var_screeninfo:

```
struct fb_bitfield red;
struct fb_bitfield green;
struct fb_bitfield blue;
struct fb_bitfield transp;
```

and the fb_bitfield stuct is:

```
struct fb_bitfield {
  __u32 offset;       /* beginning of bitfield                */
  __u32 length;       /* length of bitfield                   */
  __u32 msb_right;    /* != 0 :Most significant bit is right   */
};
```

This is officially a legacy way of doing the job but it has been in use for so long that it is widely supported.

This allows you to pack the RGBA values correctly no matter what the format is. Pixels are always stored in an integer number of bytes and padding bits are added according. Suppose the red fb_bitfield was offset=16, length=8, msb_right=0 this would mean that the red color value was stored in the pixel starting at bit 16 and was 8 bits e.g 0x00RR0000. Suppose we have the color value stored in variables r, g, b and a, then we could assemble a 32 bit pixel value using:

```
uint32_t r=0x00,g=0x00,b=0xFF,a=0xFF;
uint32_t pixel =(r<<vinfo.red.offset) | (g<<vinfo.green.offset)
               | (b<<vinfo.blue.offset)| (a<<vinfo.transp .offset);
```

That is, shift by the offset and OR the results together. Notice that this simple way of packing a pixel color value doesn't take care of all of the possibilities - it doesn't deal with the possibility that the color values could be less than 8-bits or that the most significant bit could be on the right. However, this is typical of a 32 bit RGBA pixel format. In any real application you would have to do a lot more bit manipulation to ensure that your program worked with a range of display modes.

We can now store the pixel value in the framebuffer:

```
*((uint32_t*) (fbp + location)) = pixel;
```

Notice that we have to cast the pointer to ensure that the pixel is stored as a 4-byte value.

The modern way of doing the same job is to specify a FOURCC code. This is a set of four-character codes that specify the pixel format without specifying it in the way that the old API does. You simply have to know what a particular FOURCC code means and implement it. For example, the FOURCC code RGBA or 0x41424752 specifies the same format as used in the example above. The framebuffer signals that it supports FOURCC by setting a bit in the capability field - most don't.

It is time to put all of this information together and draw something on the screen.

Drawing a Line

As an example we can create a function that draws a pixel of a given color value on the screen and then use it to draw a line:

```
#include <stdio.h>
#include <stdlib.h>
#include <linux/fb.h>
#include <fcntl.h>
#include <sys/ioctl.h>
#include <sys/mman.h>
#include <inttypes.h>
struct fb_fix_screeninfo finfo;
struct fb_var_screeninfo vinfo;
size_t size;
uint8_t *fbp;

void setPixel(uint32_t x, uint32_t y, uint32_t r, uint32_t g,
                               uint32_t b, uint32_t a) {
 uint32_t pixel = (r << vinfo.red.offset)|(g << vinfo.green.offset)|
                  (b << vinfo.blue.offset)|
                   (a << vinfo.transp .offset);
 uint32_t location = x*vinfo.bits_per_pixel/8 + y*finfo.line_length;
 *((uint32_t*) (fbp + location)) = pixel;
}

int main(int argc, char** argv) {
 int fd = open("/dev/fb0", O_RDWR);
 ioctl(fd, FBIOGET_VSCREENINFO, &vinfo);
 ioctl(fd, FBIOGET_FSCREENINFO, &finfo);
 size = vinfo.yres * finfo.line_length;
 fbp = mmap(0, size, PROT_READ | PROT_WRITE, MAP_SHARED, fd, 0);
 uint32_t x = 0;
 uint32_t y = 400;
 for (x = 0; x < 800; x++) {
   setPixel(x, y, 0xFF, 0xFF, 0x00, 0xFF);
 }
 return (EXIT_SUCCESS);
}
```

The program assumes that the graphics are in 32-bit per pixel color mode. If this isn't the case then to set the mode, just after the two existing `ioctl` calls, add:

```
vinfo.grayscale = 0;
vinfo.bits_per_pixel = 32;
ioctl(fd, FBIOPUT_VSCREENINFO, &vinfo);
ioctl(fd, FBIOGET_VSCREENINFO, &vinfo);
```

Notice that the line drawn on the screen goes over any windows that might be in its way and it isn't persistent in the sense that if anything writes over it, such as a window, it is wiped out.

Bounce

As a very simple demonstration of using the framebuffer, let's bounce a ball around the screen - the whole screen, not just in a window. The basic idea is very simple - save the contents of a small block of the screen, draw a "ball" in this block and finally restore the original contents of screen.

We need some graphics utility functions to get started. The `getRawPixel` and `setRawPixel` functions simply work with a 32-bit RGBA value:

```
uint32_t getRawPixel(uint32_t x, uint32_t y) {
  uint32_t location = x * (vinfo.bits_per_pixel / 8) +
                                 y * finfo.line_length;
  return *((uint32_t*) (fbp + location));
}
uint32_t setRawPixel(uint32_t x, uint32_t y, uint32_t pixel) {
  uint32_t location = x * (vinfo.bits_per_pixel / 8) +
                                 y * finfo.line_length;
  *((uint32_t*) (fbp + location)) = pixel;
}
```

Using these it is easy to write a setPixel to a color function:

```
void setPixel(uint32_t x, uint32_t y, struct color c) {
  uint32_t pixel = (c.r << vinfo.red.offset)|
                      (c.g << vinfo.green.offset) |
                        (c.b << vinfo.blue.offset) |
                          (c.a << vinfo.transp .offset);
  setRawPixel(x, y, pixel);
}
```

We don't need a `getPixel` function in this program. We do need a `setBlock` function to draw the ball:

```
void setBlock(uint32_t x, uint32_t y, uint32_t L, struct color c) {
  for (int i = 0; i < L; i++) {
    for (int j = 0; j < L; j++) {
        setPixel(x + i, y + j, c);
    }
  }
}
```

It draws a square block of width L in color c with top left-hand corner at x,y. We also need a function to get a block of pixels and a function to restore them:

```
void saveBlock(uint32_t x, uint32_t y, uint32_t L,
                                    uint32_t block[]) {
  for (int i = 0; i < L; i++) {
    for (int j = 0; j < L; j++) {
      block[i+j*L] = getRawPixel(x + i, y + j);
    }
  }
}
void restoreBlock(uint32_t x, uint32_t y, uint32_t L,
                                    uint32_t block[]) {
  for (int i = 0; i < L; i++) {
    for (int j = 0; j < L; j++) {
      setRawPixel(x + i, y + j, block[i+j*L]);
    }
  }
}
```

The pixel data is stored in a one-dimensional array simulating a two-dimensional array to avoid the problems of passing a variable size two-dimensional array.

Now we can start on the main program. First we need the includes and some data structures:

```
#define _POSIX_C_SOURCE  199309L
#include <stdio.h>
#include <stdlib.h>
#include <linux/fb.h>
#include <fcntl.h>
#include <sys/ioctl.h>
#include <sys/mman.h>
#include <inttypes.h>
#include <time.h>
#define BLOCKSIZE 10

struct fb_fix_screeninfo finfo;
struct fb_var_screeninfo vinfo;
uint8_t *fbp;
uint32_t block[BLOCKSIZE*BLOCKSIZE];
struct color {
    uint32_t r;
    uint32_t g;
    uint32_t b;
    uint32_t a;
};
```

186

The fbp variable is a global pointer to the start of the framebuffer. First we need to set up the framebuffer:

```
int main(int argc, char** argv) {
    int fd = open("/dev/fb0", O_RDWR);
    ioctl(fd, FBIOGET_VSCREENINFO, &vinfo);
    ioctl(fd, FBIOGET_FSCREENINFO, &finfo);
    vinfo.grayscale = 0;
    vinfo.bits_per_pixel = 32;
    ioctl(fd, FBIOPUT_VSCREENINFO, &vinfo);
    ioctl(fd, FBIOGET_VSCREENINFO, &vinfo);
    fbp = mmap(0, vinfo.yres * finfo.line_length, PROT_READ |
                                  PROT_WRITE, MAP_SHARED, fd, 0);
```

With the framebuffer set up we can write a bounce program ignoring the details of how the graphics are being created:

```
struct color c = {0xFF, 0x00, 0x00, 0xFF};
int x = 600;
int y = 400;
int vx = -1;
int vy = -1;
struct timespec pause;
pause.tv_sec = 0;
pause.tv_nsec = 20 * 1000*1000;
saveBlock(x, y, BLOCKSIZE,block);
for (;;) {
    restoreBlock(x, y, BLOCKSIZE, block);
    x = x + vx;
    y = y + vy;
    if (x <= 0) {
        x = 0; vx = -vx;
    }
    if (y <= 0) {
        y = 0; vy = -vy;
    }
    if ((x + BLOCKSIZE) >= vinfo.xres) {
        x = vinfo.xres - BLOCKSIZE - 1;
        vx = -vx;
    }
    if ((y + BLOCKSIZE) >= vinfo.yres) {
        y = vinfo.yres - BLOCKSIZE - 1;
        vy = -vy;
    }
    saveBlock(x, y, BLOCKSIZE, block);
    setBlock(x, y, BLOCKSIZE, c);
    nanosleep(&pause, NULL);
    }
    return (EXIT_SUCCESS);
}
```

The if statements check to see if the ball is about to go off the screen and if it is then it is bounced by reversing the appropriate velocity and settings its position to be on the edge of the screen. The speed of the bounce can be determined by the time delay used in nanosleep. The ball will bounce around the screen, overwriting, but not destroying, anything else on the screen. There are various system "glitches" that can spoil the effect. In particular, the activation of any screensaver will result in the ball leaving a trail behind.

If you are familiar with other graphics environments, you might be wondering how to synchronize your graphics update to the screen refresh. You can try looking up the ioctl FBIO_WAITFORVSYNC call, which waits for a vertical sync to occur. The problem is that many graphics cards do not implement it.

Framebuffer Text PSF 1

This example is included because increasingly IoT devices have access to VGA/HDMI graphics and increasingly often there is a need to display data or status messages using the framebuffer. Think of it as an alternative to adding a 7-segment or similar display. The only new feature to add to the basic framebuffer functions described in the previous sections is the use of a font file. There are many different types of font and font file formats, but for this simple application a bitmap font is the simplest to use. Linux makes use of PSF files for bitmapped console fonts. These are generally stored in /usr/share/consolefonts but this location varies. The selection of fonts you will find also varies. Add to this the fact that there are two versions of PSF format and you can see that things might not be so straightforward.

The first problem is we have to read a gzipped file. The simplest way to do this is to use the zlib library which is preinstalled on many Linux distributions. You need to add:

```
#include <zlib.h>
```

and you need to add the library file z to the linker. Once you have done this you can use the gzopen function exactly like the open function but in this case it will uncompress a gzipped file as you read from it using gzread. There is also a gzclose command and everything works exactly the same as the file descriptor functions, apart from the fact that the file is decompressed on the fly.

The PSF version 1 format is very simple and consists of a header followed by the font data. The header corresponds to the struct:

```
struct psf_header {
    uint8_t magic[2];
    uint8_t filemode;
    uint8_t fontheight;
};
```

For a version 1 format file the magic bytes are `0x36` and `0x04` and you should check that this is so before reading the rest of the file. The `filemode` byte tells you how many characters there are in the file and if there is any Unicode information:

```
0 : 256 characters, no unicode_data
1 : 512 characters, no unicode_data
2 : 256 characters, with unicode_data
3 : 512 characters, with unicode_data
```

In this example we can ignore any Unicode data. The font data follows the header and consists of `fontheight` bytes for each character in the font. These are the pixel rows of the character. So to get the font data into an array we would do something like:

```
gzFile font = gzopen(
                "/usr/share/consolefonts/Lat15-VGA8.psf.gz", "r");
gzread(font, &header, sizeof (header));
uint8_t chars[header.fontheight * 256];
gzread(font, chars, header.fontheight * 256);
```

The font file being used returns `filemode` = 2 and so it has 256 characters and unicode data that follows the font which we are ignoring. If you use a different font file, check the `filemode` and adjust the number of characters accordingly.

We can use the font data to find the 8x`fontheight` pixel data for any character ch using:

```
row = chars[ch * header.fontheight + j];
```

where j gives the row number from the top of the character.

To draw the character on the screen, we simply test each bit in each row in turn and draw a block if it is a `1`:

```
for (int j = 0; j < header.fontheight; j++) {
        row = chars[ch * header.fontheight + j];
        for (int i = 0; i < 8; i++) {
            if (row & 0x80) {
                setBlock(x1, y, BLOCKSIZE, c);
            }
            row = row << 1;
            x1 = x1 + BLOCKSIZE;
        }
        y = y + BLOCKSIZE;
        x1 = x;
    }
```

where `setBlock` is the function given in the previous section.

From this basic "draw a character" technique, we can easily create a function to do the same job and a function to draw all of the characters in a string. The complete program is:

```c
#define _POSIX_C_SOURCE  199309L
#include <stdio.h>
#include <stdlib.h>
#include <linux/fb.h>
#include <fcntl.h>
#include <sys/ioctl.h>
#include <sys/mman.h>
#include <inttypes.h>
#include <zlib.h>
#define BLOCKSIZE 10

struct fb_fix_screeninfo finfo;
struct fb_var_screeninfo vinfo;

uint8_t *fbp;
uint32_t block[BLOCKSIZE*BLOCKSIZE];

struct color {
    uint32_t r;
    uint32_t g;
    uint32_t b;
    uint32_t a;
};

uint32_t setRawPixel(uint32_t x, uint32_t y, uint32_t pixel) {
    uint32_t location = x * (vinfo.bits_per_pixel / 8) + y *
finfo.line_length;
    *((uint32_t*) (fbp + location)) = pixel;
}

void setPixel(uint32_t x, uint32_t y, struct color c) {
    uint32_t pixel = (c.r << vinfo.red.offset) | (c.g <<
vinfo.green.offset) | (c.b << vinfo.blue.offset) | (c.a <<
vinfo.transp .offset);
    setRawPixel(x, y, pixel);
}

void setBlock(uint32_t x, uint32_t y, uint32_t L, struct color c) {
    for (int i = 0; i < L; i++) {
        for (int j = 0; j < L; j++) {
            setPixel(x + i, y + j, c);
        }
    }
}
```

```
struct psf_header {
    uint8_t magic[2];
    uint8_t filemode;
    uint8_t fontheight;
};
struct psf_header header;

void displayChar(char ch, int x, int y, struct color c, uint8_t
chars[]) {
    uint8_t row;
    int x1 = x;
    for (int j = 0; j < header.fontheight; j++) {
        row = chars[ch * header.fontheight + j];
        for (int i = 0; i < 8; i++) {
            if (row & 0x80) {
                setBlock(x1, y, BLOCKSIZE, c);
            }
            row = row << 1;
            x1 = x1 + BLOCKSIZE;
        }
        y = y + BLOCKSIZE;
        x1 = x;
    }
}

void displayString(char s[], int x, int y, struct color c, uint8_t
chars[]) {
    int k = 0;
    while (s[k]) {
        displayChar(s[k], x, y, c, chars);
        x = x + BLOCKSIZE * 9;
        k++;
    }
}
```

```
int main(int argc, char** argv) {

    int fd = open("/dev/fb0", O_RDWR);
    ioctl(fd, FBIOGET_VSCREENINFO, &vinfo);
    ioctl(fd, FBIOGET_FSCREENINFO, &finfo);

    vinfo.grayscale = 0;
    vinfo.bits_per_pixel = 32;
    ioctl(fd, FBIOPUT_VSCREENINFO, &vinfo);
    ioctl(fd, FBIOGET_VSCREENINFO, &vinfo);

    fbp = mmap(0, vinfo.yres * finfo.line_length, PROT_READ |
                            PROT_WRITE, MAP_SHARED, fd, 0);

    gzFile font = gzopen(
            "/usr/share/consolefonts/Lat15-VGA8.psf.gz", "r");

    gzread(font, &header, sizeof (header));

    uint8_t chars[header.fontheight * 256];
    gzread(font, chars, header.fontheight * 256);

    struct color c = {0xFF, 0x00, 0x00, 0xFF};
    int x = 50;
    int y = 400;
    displayString("Hello World!", x, y, c, chars);

    return (EXIT_SUCCESS);
}
```

If you try this out you will find the message overwrites everything currently on the screen. If you want to restore the screen you need to save its original state before writing over it. You can also change the size of the font by changing BLOCKSIZE. As the font is defined in 8-bit rows, making it much bigger makes it look very blocky.

To do better you either need a vector font, such as Truetype, or you need a custom bitmap font at the correct resolution. You can improve the vertical resolution using alternative PSF 1 files, but the horizontal resolution is always 8 bits.

An easy alternative is to use a PSF 2 font which is the subject of the next section.

Framebuffer Text PSF 2

To increase the horizontal resolution you have move to PSF 2, which is slightly more difficult due to the need to read more than one byte per character row. For example, you can convert the example program to a PSF 2 font by changing the displayChar function to:

```
void displayChar(char ch, int x, int y, struct color c, uint8_t
chars[]) {
    uint8_t row;
    int x1 = x;
    int stride = header.charsize / header.height;
    int bits;
    for (int j = 0; j < header.height; j++) {
        bits = 0;
        for (int i = 0; i < stride; i++) {
            row = chars[ch * header.charsize + i + j * stride];
            for (int b = 0; b < 8; b++) {
                if (bits == header.width)continue;
                if (row & 0x80) {
                    setBlock(x1 + bits*BLOCKSIZE, y, BLOCKSIZE, c);
                }
                row = row << 1;
                bits++;
            }
        }
        y = y + BLOCKSIZE;
        x1 = x;
    }
}
```

The displayString function needs to be changed to:

```
void displayString(char s[], int x, int y, struct color c, uint8_t
chars[]) {
    int k = 0;
    while (s[k]) {
        displayChar(s[k], x, y, c, chars);
        x = x + BLOCKSIZE * header.width;
        k++;
    }
}
```

You also need to change the definition of the header to:

```
struct psf2_header {
    unsigned char magic[4];
    unsigned int version;
    unsigned int headersize; /* offset of bitmaps in file */
    unsigned int flags;
    unsigned int length; /* number of characters */
    unsigned int charsize; /* number of bytes for each character */
    unsigned int height, width; /* max dimensions in bits */
};
struct psf2_header header;
```

Of course, you need a PSF 2 font to try it out with:

```
gzFile font = gzopen(
        "/usr/share/consolefonts/Lat15-Terminus32x16.psf.gz", "r");
```

You can see a complete listing of this version of the program at the book's page on www.iopress.info.

Windowing Systems - X11

The framebuffer is a very primitive access to the graphics hardware. At the next level up in the hierarchy we have the window managers and X11 is the longest serving. It was created back in 1984 at MIT and has been stuck at version 11 since 1987, hence X11. The X Window System was a revolutionary way of implementing graphics and it is what is responsible for the ease of remote desktop implementation on Linux/Unix machines. X11 provides all of the facilities you need to create and manage windows including input. You can draw within a window, but X11 doesn't provide any widgets such as buttons and hence it doesn't determine a complete GUI.

X11 uses a client-server architecture and this was revolutionary at a time when network communications were generally slow. The idea is that the client sends graphics commands to an X11 server, which might be installed on the same machine or on another machine accessed via a network connection.

Notice that this is not the usual sense of "server" because the X11 server is generally installed on the machine in front of the user and the client is the one that is perhaps located elsewhere. The client sends X11 drawing commands to the server and the server occasionally sends back notifications of user actions, such as mouse clicks and keystrokes.

When the server and client are resident on the same machine, communication is via a named pipe. When they are running on different machines, communication is via sockets, see the next chapter.

The standard way of writing programs that make use of X11 is to make use of the Xlib library, but there is an alternative in the form of the XCB library. In this chapter the focus will be on Xlib because so many other programs are based on it. While the X11 system is usually installed by default, the development system involving Xlib generally isn't. You can install it on Debian based systems using something like:

```
sudo apt install libx11-dev
```

As long as it is installed, you will have access to Xlib.h and other header files and to the X11 library, which has to be added to the linker.

The big problem with getting to grips with X11 is that its client-server architecture means you have to do things in a slightly different way from writing or reading directly into a framebuffer. For example, to minimize any transmission protocol overheads, any commands or requests that you issue are usually stored in a buffer, the request buffer. To send the requests to the server you have to use Xflush, which is non-blocking, or Xsync, which is blocking and waits for the server to complete all of the requests. In many cases you don't need to explicitly flush the buffer because it happens whenever the client handles an event from the server.

You also need to know that X11 maintains a hierarchy of windows and every window is a child of some other window. All children of the root window are "top-level" windows and these are managed by the window manager, which can have some unexpected effects. For example, although you specify a position when creating a window, it is usually ignored because the window manager knows best where to place your new window. In the same way, you might not get a window of the size you requested.

Device, Screen and Window

With all these warnings in place, it is time to get started on a simple example. The first step in any X11 client is to open an X display using:

```
display=XOpenDisplay(displayname)
```

Servers can support multiple devices and you can pick which one you want to work with, or you can simply pass NULL, or the X11 macro None, and accept the default. A display can support multiple screens, but generally only one keyboard and mouse.

So to open the default display you would use:

```
Display *dpy = XOpenDisplay(None);
```

The function returns None if it cannot open a display and you need to test for this.

Once you have the display there are a large number of functions that you can use to discover its characteristics. For example, you can get the default screen number using:

```
int screen=DefaultScreen(dpy);
```

A screen is only guaranteed to support two colors - black and white - and you can get the color codes to be used for these from the display:

```
int blackColor = BlackPixel(dpy, screen);
int whiteColor = WhitePixel(dpy, screen);
```

Now we are ready to create a window. This is a two-step process. We first create the data structure that defines the window and then we map it into the display so that it is rendered. The simplest way to create a window is to use:

```
Window w=XCreateSimpleWindow(dpy, parent, x, y, width, height,
                             border_width, border, background)
```

The window is a child of parent, positioned at x,y, of size width by height and with a border of the specified width and color. The border is additional to the window manager's border and hence rarely used. There is a more complete function to create a window but XCreateSimpleWindow inherits all unspecified attributes from the parent window. To create a top-level window we can use:

```
DefaultRootWindow(dpy);
```

to get the root window. So for example:

```
Window w = XCreateSimpleWindow(dpy, DefaultRootWindow(dpy),
                x, y, 500, 400, 0, blackColor, blackColor);
```

creates a 500 by 400 pixel top-level window at x,y with no border and black background. Of course, the window manager will probably override your position values and probably the size values as well.

The window is created in an unmapped, i.e. hidden, state. To make it visible on the screen you have to map it to the display:

```
XMapWindow(dpy, w);
```

You can hide the window again using the XUnmapWindow function, which doesn't destroy the window. If you want to destroy a window and all its children then you need to use XDestroyWindow function.

We can't start to use the window until it is fully mapped. The problem is that this can be a relatively slow process. The correct way to wait for the mapping to be complete is to wait on a notification from the server, but for the moment we can ignore notifications or events by simply putting in a delay long enough to ensure that the window is mapped. This is not the normal way of doing the job, but it is simple and for the moment it gets us started.

Graphics Functions

Once the window is mapped, we can ask for a graphics context. This is a fairly standard idea in graphics systems. A graphics context is a set of properties, like foreground color and so on, that allows you to draw on a window. In other graphics systems it would be called a brush or a pen.

You can create multiple graphics contexts per window and use each one to draw in a different style, or you can modify a single graphics context each time you need a new style. You can also use a graphics context with any drawable that is the same sort of graphic as the context was created for. The only real problem is that an X11 graphics context contains a great many attributes you can change. In many cases all you need is a default graphics context that you then use to modify a few simple things like foreground color.

To get a default graphics context you can use:

```
GC gc = XCreateGC(dpy, w, 0, 0);
```

you have to specify the display and the window. The final two parameters can be used to modify the graphics context. In this case all we need to do is set the foreground color, i.e. the color used to draw:

```
XSetForeground(dpy, gc, whiteColor);
```

notice that in this case you only need the display and the graphics context.

With a foreground color set, we can now draw things using any of the many graphics functions. For example, to draw a point use:

```
XDrawPoint(dpy, w, gc, x, y);
```

Other useful drawing functions are:

```
XDrawLine(dpy, w, gc, x1,y1, x2,y2);
XDrawRectangle(dpy, w, gc, x, y, width, height);
XDrawArc(dpy, w, gc, cx,cy, width,height, angle1, angle2);
XDrawString(dpy, w, gc, x, y, string, nchars);
```

There are also Fill versions of the rectangle and arc drawing functions and most drawing functions have a version which will draw multiple items specified in array.

There are many other graphics functions available, consult the man pages and other documentation.

An Example

Putting all of this together we can write a simple demonstration program:

```c
#include <stdio.h>
#include <stdlib.h>
#include <unistd.h>
#include <X11/Xlib.h>
#include <X11/Xutil.h>

int main(int argc, char** argv) {
    Display *dpy = XOpenDisplay(None);
    int screen = DefaultScreen(dpy);

    int blackColor = BlackPixel(dpy, screen);
    int whiteColor = WhitePixel(dpy, screen);

    Window w = XCreateSimpleWindow(dpy, DefaultRootWindow(dpy),
            200, 600, 500, 500, 0, blackColor, blackColor);

    XMapWindow(dpy, w);
    XFlush(dpy);
    sleep(1);
    GC gc = XCreateGC(dpy, w, 0, 0);
    XSetForeground(dpy, gc, whiteColor);
    XDrawLine(dpy, w, gc, 10, 10, 200, 20);
    XDrawRectangle(dpy, w, gc,30, 200, 100, 200);
    XFillRectangle(dpy, w, gc,200, 200, 100, 200);
    XDrawString(dpy, w, gc, 35, 300, "Hello X World", 13);
    XFlush(dpy);
    sleep(10);
    return (EXIT_SUCCESS);
}
```

Notice that we need the XFlush after the window is mapped to make the system display the window. The one-second wait after the XFlush is to make sure that the window has been mapped. As already discussed, this is not the usual way to do this job, but it avoids having to use events. The final sleep(10) is required so you can see the results as when a process ends any windows it owns are closed.

If you are using NetBeans as a remote compiler then it is important that you run the compiled program from the command line - it cannot be run with NetBeans.

Color

The X11 system is particularly sophisticated when it comes to specifying and managing color. As already mentioned, X11 only guarantees two colors - black and white, although for any given output device there might be other high contrast colors that serve in place of black and white. Other colors are display-dependent and defined in a color map, a table of all the colors the device can display.

You can get a default color map using:

```
Colormap cmap = DefaultColormap(dpy,screen);
```

Your program can work in terms of 16-bit RGB values - this gives you the ability to define any color to a high precision. When you want a color specified as RGB, use a function to look up a color that is as close as possible in the color map. This returns the bit pattern you have to store in a pixel to display the color. To make this work we have to use the XColor struct:

```
typedef struct {
 unsigned long     pixel;
 unsigned short    red, green, blue;
 char              flags;
 char              pad;
} XColor;
```

Store the RGB values you want in the red, green and blue fields. The flags specify which of the red, green or blue fields are to be used. You call the XAllocColor function with the color map and the XColor struct with the values of red, green and blue you have specified and it fills in the pixel field with the color value you should use.

For example, in the previous example if we wanted to draw everything in red you would use something like:

```
Colormap cmap = DefaultColormap(dpy,screen);
XColor color;
color.red=0xFFFF;
color.green=0;
color.blue=0;
XAllocColor(dpy, cmap, &color);
XSetForeground(dpy, gc, color.pixel);
```

As well as RGB, you can use other systems of color specification. You can even use named colors, which are the same as the color names used by CSS.

The function:

```
XAllocNamedColor(dpy, cmap, name,&color,&exact)
```

will fill in the pixel field in `color` to be the closest match that the hardware supports and the exact RGB values in `exact`. For example, to set the color to red you could use:

```
XColor color,exact;
XAllocNamedColor(dpy, cmap,"red",&color,&exact);
XSetForeground(dpy, gc, color.pixel);
```

The subject of color in X11 is a big one. Not only is it sophisticated, it is often much more than you need. The few functions described here are enough to get you a fairly long way.

Events

The final feature of X11 we have to deal with is events. The X11 server sends events to the client to keep it informed of what is happening and to signal user interaction with the window. Whenever you encounter a GUI framework you will nearly always encounter events in one form or another. The reason is that user actions are inherently asynchronous with the operation of your program. In other words, you cannot predetermine when a user will click a button or which button will be clicked. Your program has to respond to what the user does and this generally means what function is called and when it is called depends on what the user does.

X11 has a very basic form of event handling compared to other frameworks. In fact, it is so simple that if you have encountered other asynchronous frameworks you may well misunderstand it.

The server keeps a queue of events which your program can examine and read. It does this by calling the XNextEvent function. This takes the first event from the queue and returns it. If the queue is empty then the function blocks until there is an event available. If you want to examine the event queue without blocking, you can use XPeekEvent. In addition you can specify which events you want to handle in a number of different ways. The XSelectInput function can be used after a window has been created with an event_mask to specify which events are handled.

For example, in a previous example a sleep(10) was used to give the system enough time to map a window. This is not the usual way of doing the job as the system will issue a MapNotify event after the window has been displayed. So the usual way of making sure a window is mapped is to first specify that you want to accept all StructureNotify events using:

```
XSelectInput(dpy, w, StructureNotifyMask);
XMapWindow(dpy, w);
XFlush(dpy);

for(;;) {
   XEvent e;
   XNextEvent(dpy, &e);
   if (e.type == MapNotify)  break;
}

GC gc = XCreateGC(dpy, w, 0, 0);
```

Notice that the for loop polls the event queue until it receives the MapNotify event. The event struct has fields that give information about the event in addition to the type field.

This is an untypical use of events in that you specifically want to know that a specific event has occurred. Asynchronous programs nearly always take a very standard form. First there is some initialization which sets up the graphics and then the program starts an event loop which reads an event and calls an appropriate function to handle it:

```
while(1){
    XNextEvent(dpy, &e);
    switch(e.type){
      case ButtonPress:
                handle mouse button pressing
                break

      case MotionNotify:
                handle mouse move
                break
        .   .   .

      default:
                unknown event - ignore
                break
    }
}
```

The loop runs forever, or at least until the user selects an option which triggers an event that the program treats as a terminate command. The event handling loop usually has a large number of case clauses to deal with everything that can happen while the program is running.

For example, to draw on a window you can write an event loop that draws a point each time the mouse button is clicked:

```
XSelectInput(dpy, w, ButtonPressMask);
while (1) {
    XEvent e;
    XNextEvent(dpy, &e);
    switch (e.type) {
        case Expose:
            /* handle this event type... */
            break;
        case ButtonPress:
            XDrawPoint(dpy, w, gc, e.xbutton.x, e.xbutton.y);
            break;
        default: /* unknown event type - ignore it. */
            break;
    }
}
```

Notice the ButtonPress event is generated for any mouse button press. You can find out which button using the event struct.

You can look up the range of events and how to handle them in the documentation but there is one event that deserves special mention - Expose. When a window is moved to cover up your window the system does nothing to preserve its contents. When it is uncovered the section that was covered will appear blank. The Expose event is sent to the window to signal that it is now uncovered and, if it needs to, now is the time to redraw its erased content.

The Expose event occurs at other times, but it is always a signal to draw or redraw content. The XEvent struct contains fields x,y, width and height, which specify the minimum rectangle that needs to be redrawn. Clearly, in many cases, your only option is to store a copy of the graphic and restore it in response to an Expose event. The idea is simple, but the implementation may be more involved than you initially imagine.

GTK - a GUI Framework

The X11 window system is one step up in complexity from the framebuffer, but it doesn't provide any widgets by way of buttons, textboxes and so on. You could implement graphics for all of these components, but it is much easier to simply adopt one of the available frameworks - the hard question is which one. For C, the GIMP Toolkit (GTK) has a lot in its favor. It is fully open source under the GNU Lesser General Public License (LGPL), which allows it to be used in proprietary applications without any license fees or royalty. It is also implemented in C and hence easy to use from C. The final thing in its favor is that it has been in existence for a long time and it is used by many well-known projects including the GNOME desktop environment and products. There is also an interactive drag-and-drop designer called GLADE that produces XML that can be read into GTK to produce the layout.

The biggest problem with using GTK is getting a development environment prepared for it. It has so many dependencies by way of header files and libraries. First you need to make sure the development system is installed. On Debian systems this is as simple as:

```
sudo apt-get install libgtk-3-dev
```

You could add all of the header files and libraries one by one but in this case the pkg-config utility makes the job much easier. This collects metadata about installed libraries. For example, the command:

```
pkg-config --cflags gtk+-3.0
```

gives you all the compiler flags you need to compile against the gtk library and:

```
pkg-config --libs gtk+-3.0
```

lists all of the library files needed as compiler options.

The good news is that GCC knows all about pkg-config and you can include it in the compiler options and it will be expanded for you. So to compile against GTK you could use:

```
gcc `pkg-config --cflags gtk+-3.0` -o example-0 example-0.c
                                   `pkg-config --libs gtk+-3.0`
```

Notice that the back ticks are required. GCC automatically expands the compiler flags and libraries.

If you are using NetBeans things are even easier - all you have to do is use the project's Properties and select Linker, Libraries and then click the button "Add Pkg-Config Libraries..." You can then select gtk+- 3.0 from the list that you are presented with. From this point on the project will have no problem finding the header files and libraries.

A First Window

Now we are all set up, we can create a window to try it out. Notice that, while it is like using X11, GTK builds in more of the asynchronous behavior typical of a GUI. For example, you have to pass it pointers to functions that will be called to do particular jobs in response to events as they occur.

In addition, to start a GTK application you have to make a call to gtk_application_new which creates all of the data structures needed for a basic GUI. After this you start the event queue running using g_application_run.

This is a blocking call and GTK beginners often worry where their programs fit into the picture? The answer is that as the event queue processes events it calls functions that you have provided as handlers. When you work with an asynchronous system your program is always just a collection of event handlers.

What this all means is that the simplest GTK program is:

```
#include <stdio.h>
#include <stdlib.h>
#include <gtk/gtk.h>

int main(int argc, char** argv) {

  GtkApplication *app = gtk_application_new(
          "info.i-programmer.example", G_APPLICATION_FLAGS_NONE);
  int status = g_application_run(G_APPLICATION(app), argc, argv);
  g_object_unref(app);
  return status;
}
```

You can try this out, but the application comes to an end immediately as there is nothing to display and hence no events to process. There are a number of functions that let you add windows to the application but you can only do this after the application has been activated by the call to g_application_run and, of course, this is a blocking call, so you can't. The solution is that you have add a window to the app after it has been activated by adding an event handler for the activate event.

This is done using:

g_signal_connect(app, *signal*, *function*)

to connect the *signal*, i.e. the event, in the app to the *function*.

For example, the `activate` event can be handled by defining a handler function:

```
static void activate(GtkApplication* app, gpointer user_data) {
    GtkWidget *window = gtk_application_window_new(app);
    gtk_window_set_title(GTK_WINDOW(window), "Window");
    gtk_window_set_default_size(GTK_WINDOW(window), 200, 200);
    gtk_widget_show_all(window);
}
```

This creates a window, customizes it then shows it.

To set this as the event handler, we need to extend `main` with:

```
 g_signal_connect(app, "activate", G_CALLBACK(activate), NULL);
```

Now if you run the program you will see a window appear with the title "Window". The program will end when you close the window.

From here much of using GTK follows the same pattern - create an object, connect events to event handlers and arrange for it to be displayed. For example, let's add a button:

```
GtkWidget *button = gtk_button_new_with_label ("Click Me");
g_signal_connect (button, "clicked", G_CALLBACK (printHello), NULL);
gtk_container_add (GTK_CONTAINER (window), button);
```

and the click event handler is:

```
static void printHello(GtkWidget *widget,gpointer data){
    gtk_button_set_label ((GtkButton*)widget,"Hello World");
}
```

If you add this to the previous program and run it you will see a button with the label "Click Me". When you click it the label changes to "Hello World". The only problem is that the button fills the entire window. How can we set the size and position of the button?

This is where GTK once again surprises many beginners who are expecting to be able to set size and position in an absolute way. The problem that most GUI frameworks face is that windows can be moved and resized by users and this means that absolute layouts are a problem. Instead of absolute positioning and sizing they generally take over the task of layout for you. In GTK you have a range of containers into which you can put widgets. Each container provides a way of working out the best layout of the widgets it contains.

For example, there is GtkButtonBox, which is specifically provided for creating small groups of buttons, mostly of the same size. To create a reasonable looking button in a windows layout we need to add a GtkButtonBox containing the button:

```
GtkWidget *button = gtk_button_new_with_label("Click Me");
g_signal_connect(button, "clicked", G_CALLBACK(printHello), NULL);
GtkWidget *button_box =
                    gtk_button_box_new(GTK_ORIENTATION_HORIZONTAL);
gtk_container_add(GTK_CONTAINER(button_box), button);
gtk_container_add(GTK_CONTAINER(window), button_box);
gtk_widget_show_all(window);
```

The complete program is:

```
#include <stdio.h>
#include <stdlib.h>
#include <gtk/gtk.h>

static void printHello(GtkWidget *widget, gpointer data) {
  gtk_button_set_label((GtkButton*) widget, "Hello World");

}

static void activate(GtkApplication* app, gpointer user_data) {
  GtkWidget *window = gtk_application_window_new(app);
  gtk_window_set_title(GTK_WINDOW(window), "Window");
  gtk_window_set_default_size(GTK_WINDOW(window), 200, 200);

  GtkWidget *button = gtk_button_new_with_label("Click Me");
  g_signal_connect(button, "clicked", G_CALLBACK(printHello), NULL);
  GtkWidget *button_box = gtk_button_box_new(
                                GTK_ORIENTATION_HORIZONTAL);
  gtk_container_add(GTK_CONTAINER(button_box), button);
  gtk_container_add(GTK_CONTAINER(window), button_box);
  gtk_widget_show_all(window);
}

int main(int argc, char** argv) {
  GtkApplication *app = gtk_application_new(
          "info.i-programmer.example", G_APPLICATION_FLAGS_NONE);
  g_signal_connect(app, "activate", G_CALLBACK(activate), NULL);
  int status = g_application_run(G_APPLICATION(app), argc, argv);
  g_object_unref(app);
  return status;
}
```

Glade

You can carry on working on building a GUI in this procedural way, i.e. calling functions to add objects to the layout and adding event handlers, but there is a great deal to learn. GTK is a big framework with lots of objects and lots of attributes to modify. It isn't difficult, but becoming an expert can take a long time and this may not be justified if you just want to add a simple GUI interface to a project.

A good alternative way of adding a GUI interface without having to master GTK is to use Glade. This is an interactive GUI designer that can be used to place widgets on a window and customize them by entering their attributes in a table. The resulting layout can be saved to a file as an XML description of the GTK objects needed to create the interface. You can then write code that loads the file, creates the objects and adds event handlers. This is much simpler than writing the code to create and customize all the objects in the first place. Another very big advantage is that you can tweak the user interface by simply editing the Glade file and running your program. In many cases no changes to the code will be required.

To see how this works let's implement the Hello World button example in the previous section. First you will need Glade. This is available for Windows, but you will need to install GTK for Windows and other utilities. This isn't difficult, but the Linux version is much easier to install. On a Debian system all you need is:

```
sudo apt-get install glade
```

When you run Glade you first have to start a new project, then place a top-level window, in this case a `GtkApplicationWindow`, on the design surface.

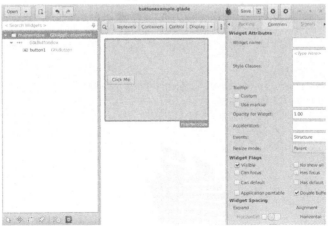

207

You can give the window, or any of the widgets you place on it, an ID - `mainwindow` in the example. This ID can be used by your code to access the widget at runtime - see later.

To complete the example you need to put a `buttonbox` and a button on the window. Give the button an ID of `button1`. Then select the button and select the Signals tab. Here you can enter the name of the functions you want to handle the events listed. In this example we will use the original method of connecting handlers with signals.

Once you have customized the layout, you can save it under the name `buttonexample` - it automatically gets a `.glade` extension. You can examine the contents of the file and you should find it understandable and even editable:

```xml
<?xml version="1.0" encoding="UTF-8"?>
<!-- Generated with glade 3.20.0 -->
<interface>
  <requires lib="gtk+" version="3.20"/>
  <object class="GtkApplicationWindow" id="mainwindow">
    <property name="can_focus">False</property>
    <property name="default_width">440</property>
    <property name="default_height">250</property>
    <child>
      <object class="GtkButtonBox">
        <property name="visible">True</property>
        <property name="can_focus">False</property>
        <property name="layout_style">start</property>
        <child>
          <object class="GtkButton" id="button1">
            <property name="label" translatable="yes">
                                    Click Me</property>
            <property name="visible">True</property>
            <property name="can_focus">True</property>
            <property name="receives_default">True</property>
          </object>
          <packing>
            <property name="expand">True</property>
            <property name="fill">True</property>
            <property name="position">2</property>
          </packing>
        </child>
      </object>
    </child>
  </object>
</interface>
```

Now we can turn our attention to the code. There are a number of different ways of working with a Glade file, but the steps are usually the same - first create a GtkBuilder and use it to instantiate all of the graphics objects described in its .glade file:

```
GtkBuilder *builder = gtk_builder_new();
gtk_builder_add_from_file(builder, "buttonexample.glade", NULL);
```

Notice for this to work the .glade file has to be in the same directory as the executable. After this the builder object can be used to access the graphics objects and then you can do the final configuration.

The complete program is:

```
#include <stdio.h>
#include <stdlib.h>
#include <gtk/gtk.h>

static void printHello(GtkWidget *widget, gpointer data) {
  gtk_button_set_label((GtkButton*) widget, "Hello World");
}

static void activate(GtkApplication* app, gpointer user_data) {
  GtkBuilder *builder = gtk_builder_new();
  gtk_builder_add_from_file(builder, "buttonexample.glade", NULL);
  GtkWindow *window =
      (GtkWindow*) gtk_builder_get_object(builder, "mainwindow");
  GtkButton* button =
      (GtkButton*) gtk_builder_get_object(builder, "button1");
  g_signal_connect(button, "clicked", G_CALLBACK(printHello), NULL);
  gtk_window_set_application(window, app);
  gtk_window_present(window);
}

int main(int argc, char** argv) {
  GtkApplication *app = gtk_application_new(
          "info.i-programmer.example", G_APPLICATION_FLAGS_NONE);
  g_signal_connect(app, "activate", G_CALLBACK(activate), NULL);
  int status = g_application_run(G_APPLICATION(app), argc, argv);
  g_object_unref(app);
  return status;
}
```

Notice that main is exactly the same as before, but the activate event handler is slightly different to allow for the way that the window is displayed. If you run the program you should find that it works in exactly the same way as before, but now you can change the GUI simply by editing the Glade file, saving it and rerunning.

You can also use Glade to connect events with event handlers. All you have to do is enter the name of the event handling functions in the Signals tab for all the appropriate events. You then have to make sure that the functions exist in your program and call:

```
gtk_builder_connect_signals(builder, NULL);
```

to connect the functions to the events.

The only complication is that the `builder` needs a symbol table to work out the connection between function names and function addresses - remember there are no symbols in a compiled program. There are two ways to provide symbols, but the only one that is cross-platform is to use `gtk_builder_add_callback_symbol` to explicitly add symbols to the `builder`. For example in our case we could use:

```
gtk_builder_add_callback_symbol (builder,
                    "printHello",G_CALLBACK(printHello));
```

You can see that, because of the need to add all the function handler names, it isn't much of a simplification over the manual method of making the connection.

Given the complexity of GTK, it is worth getting to know Glade. It makes constructing GUI interfaces for programs much easier.

Graphics Beyond GTK

There are a great many graphics libraries, but many have a very C++ orientation. Apart from GTK, the most obvious graphics system is OpenGL, or Mesa which is easy to use from C. You probably don't need OpenGL unless you are planning to create some exceptional graphics or work in 3D. For general 2D graphics and for GUI construction, GTK is enough. Other useful libraries of note are LibGD, which provides easy to use functions for creating bitmaps, Cairo for a PostScript-like 2D drawing library and OpenCV if machine vision is what you need.

Summary

- Selecting a graphics system for Linux is difficult because there is so much choice and many different levels of operation.

- The framebuffer gives you direct access to the graphics buffer.

- You can use it to write directly to the screen and it doesn't take account of windows or any other part of the GUI.

- It is possible to use font files to write text to the framebuffer.

- The standard window system is X11 and it has a client-server architecture with the program that does the drawing as the client, and the program that does the rendering on a device as the server.

- X11 can be used via the Xlib library.

- X11 can also handle user input and for this you have to implement an event handling loop.

- The GTK Framework is a complete GUI system with windows, buttons and events.

- The structure of almost any GUI framework makes your program asynchronous and this can be confusing at first.

- You can use GTK via function calls, but it is much easier to use the Glade drag-and-drop editor.

Chapter 11

Connecting With Sockets

Sockets are a general-purpose way of communicating over networks and similar infrastructure. Essentially they are a generalization of files to things other than storage devices. They aren't part of the C standard, but are available on all POSIX-compliant operating systems. As well as sockets, POSIX systems also support other file-like ways to communicate – in particular, pipes, see Chapter 8, can be thought of as streams of bytes that are produced by one process and consumed by another. In this sense a pipe is an inter-process communication tool. Sockets can also be used in this way, but they can also be used to send streams of bytes from one machine to another using a range of different communications media. For example, X11 makes a connection between a client and server using a pipe when they are on the same machine and sockets when they are on different machines.

In this chapter we focus on using sockets to send data over the internet but it is worth keeping in mind that they are more versatile that this might suggest. All of the code described will work under any POSIX system including Raspbian and Linux running on x86. It doesn't work as described under Windows or MinGW. To make it work under Windows you either have to use CygWin or the native WinSock library, which is slightly different from the POSIX socket library as explained later.

To send some web data, an HTML page or JSON data, most programmers think of a web server and that the next step is to install and configure Apache. This is usually far too big a solution to a small problem to be implemented on a small machine. However, it is very easy to implement a simple web server or a web client using sockets. All sockets do is transport data from one point to another, so you can use them to communicate using almost any standard protocol, like HTTP, or a custom protocol of your own devising. Put simply, a socket is a stream of bytes that you can send over a communication channel.

Socket Basics

The basic steps in using a socket are fairly simple:

1. Create socket
2. Connect the socket to an address
3. Transfer data.

Sockets connect to other sockets by their addresses. The simplest case is where there are just two sockets, or two endpoints, communicating. Once the connection is made, the two sockets at each end of the connection operate in more or less the same way. In general one of the sockets, the client, will have initiated the connection and the other, the server, will have accepted it.

There is a conceptual difference between a client and a server socket. A server socket is set up and then it waits for clients to connect to it. A client socket actively seeks a connection with a server. Once connected, data can flow in both directions and the difference between the two ends of the connection becomes less. That is, the difference between client and server is only about who initiates the connection.

The key idea is that a socket is implemented to make it look as much like a standard POSIX file as possible. This conforms with a general principle of Linux/Unix that any I/O facility should follow the conventions of a file.

Socket Functions

There are several basic socket functions that are needed for specific purposes:

Create a socket

```
sockfd= socket(int socket_family, int socket_type, int protocol);
```

This returns a socket descriptor, an int which you use in other socket functions. The socket_family is where you specify the type of communications link to be use and this is where sockets are most general. There are lots of communications methods that sockets can use, including AF_UNIX or AF_LOCAL, which don't use a network, but allow inter-communication between processes on the same machine. In most cases, you are going to be using AF_INET for IPv4 or AF_INET6 for IPv6 networking.

The socket_type specifies the general protocol to be used. In most cases you will use SOCK_STREAM which specifies a reliable two-way connection - for IP communications this means TCP/IP is used. For some applications you might want to use SOCK_DGRAM, which specifies that the data should be sent without

214

confirming that it has been received. This is a broadcast mechanism that corresponds to UDP for IP communications.

The `protocol` parameter selects a sub-protocol of the socket type. In most cases you can simply set it to 0. As we are going to be working with sockets that basically work with the web, we will use `AF_INET` and `SOCK_STREAM`.

Connect a socket to an address

To connect a socket as a client of another use the `connect` function:

```
int connect(int sockfd,const struct sockaddr *addr,
                                    socklen_t addrlen);
```

The `sockfd` parameter is just the socket file descriptor returned from the socket function. The `addr` parameter points at a `sockaddr` struct which contains the address of the socket you want to connect to. Of course `addrlen` just specifies the size of the struct. The socket address type depend on the underlying communications medium that the socket uses, but in most cases it is just an IP address.

Bind a socket to an address

To assign a server socket to the address it will respond to, use `bind`:

```
int bind(int sockfd, const struct sockaddr *addr,socklen_t addrlen);
```

Beginners often ask what the difference is between `connect` and `bind`. The answer is that `connect` makes a connection to the socket with the specified address whereas `bind` makes the socket respond to that address. Put another way, use `connect` with a client socket and `bind` with a server socket.

Reading and Writing

As an open socket is just a file, you can use the standard `read` and `write` functions that you would use to work with a file. There are two additional functions, `send` and `recv`, which work in the same way as `write` and `read` but have an additional final parameter that can be used to control exactly how the transaction is performed. If you set the file parameter to 0 then `send` and `recv` are identical to `write` and `read`. Under some C standards you may also need:

```
#include <unistd.h>
```

To emphasize the unity between the file system and sockets, the examples in this chapter use `read` and `write`, but they could just as easily use `recv` and `send` with 0 as the final parameter. It is worth noting that Windows sockets do not support `read` and `write` but they do work with `recv` and `send` and if you are developing a cross-platform program then it might be easier to use these alternatives.

Listen and Accept

There is one small matter that we have to deal with that takes us beyond simple file use semantics. If you have opened a socket and bound it to an IP address then it is acting as a server socket and is ready to wait for a connection. How do you know when there is a connection, and how do you know when to read or write data? Notice this problem doesn't arise with a client socket because it initiates the complete connection and sends and receives data when it is ready.

The function:

```
int listen(int sockfd, int backlog);
```

sets the socket as an active server. From this point on it listens for the IP address it is bound to and accepts incoming connections. The backlog parameter sets how many pending connections will be queued for processing. The actual processing of a connection is specified by:

```
int accept(int sockfd, struct sockaddr *addr, socklen_t *addrlen);
```

The accept command provides the address of the client trying to make the connection in the sockaddr structure. It also returns a new socket file descriptor to use to talk to the client. The original socket carries on operating as before. Notice that this is slightly more complicated than you might expect in that it is not the socket that you created that is used to communicate with the client. The socket you created just listens out for clients and creates a queue of pending requests. The accept function processes these requests and creates new sockets used to communicate with the client.

This still doesn't solve the problem of how the server detects that there are clients pending. This is a complicated question with many different solutions. You can set up the listening socket to be either blocking or non-blocking. If it is blocking then a call to accept will not return until there is a client ready to be processed. If it is non-blocking then a call to accept returns at once with an error code equal to EAGAIN or EWOULDBLOCK. So you can either use a blocking call or you can poll for clients to be ready.

A more complex approach would be to use another thread to call the poll() function which performs a wait with no CPU overhead while the file descriptor isn't ready, see Chapter 14 for an example.

A Web Client

We now have enough information to implement our first socket program, a web client. It has to be admitted that a web client isn't as common a requirement as a web server, but it is simpler and illustrates most of the points of using sockets to implement an HTTP transaction.

The first thing we have to do is create a socket and the TCP needed for an HTTP transaction:

```
int sockfd = socket(AF_INET, SOCK_STREAM, 0);
```
To allow this to work you have to add:

```
#include <sys/socket.h>
```
Next we need to get the address of the server we want to connect to. For the web this would usually be done using a DNS lookup on a domain name. To make things simple, we will skip the lookup and use a known IP address. Example.com is a domain name provided for use by examples and you can find its address by pinging it. At the time of writing it was hosted at:

```
93.184.216.34
```
This could change so check before concluding that "nothing works".

There are three fields in the address structure. The first is:

```
struct sockaddr_in addr;
```
Then comes sin_family, which is set to:

```
addr.sin_family = AF_INET;
```
to indicate an internet IPv4 address.

The next field is the port number of the IP address, but you can't simply use:

```
 addr.sin_port = 80;
```
because the bit order used on the Internet isn't the same as used on most processors. Instead you have to use a utility function that will ensure the correct bit order:

```
addr.sin_port = htons(80);
```

The function name stands for "host to network short" and there are other similarly named functions.

The actual address is defined in the in_addr field. This is a struct with only one field, s_addr, a 32-bit representation of an IP address. The format is fairly simple. Regard the 32-bit value as four bytes with each byte coding one value of the "dotted" IP address. That is, if the IP address is w.x.y.z then w, x, y and z are the bytes of s_addr. For example, the IP address of example.com is 93.184.216.34 and converting each value into its byte equivalent in hex gives 5d.b8.d8.22, which would be the hex value we have to store in s_addr

217

if it wasn't for the fact that the bytes are stored in reverse order. So, the hex equivalent of the IP address is `0x22d8b85d` and this is used to initialize the address struct:

```
addr.sin_addr.s_addr = 0x22d8b85d;
```

To make all this work you need to add:

```
#include <sys/types.h>
```

and:

```
#include <netinet/in.h>
```

With the address worked out and safely stored we can now make the connection:

```
connect(sockfd, &addr, sizeof (addr));
```

This will return 0 if it successfully connects and we do need to test for this condition. You will also get a type warning because the pointer to the `addr` structure isn't as defined in the function. In fact there are many variations which you could pass and it is the standard idiom to cast them to the function's pointer type:

```
connect(sockfd, (struct sockaddr *) &addr, sizeof (addr));
```

Finally we need to check for an error:

```
if(connect(sockfd,(struct sockaddr*)&addr,sizeof(addr))<0)return -1;
```

As long as there is no error then we can start to send and receive data. But what data? The answer is that it all depends on the protocol you are using. There is nothing about a socket that tells you what to send. It is a completely general I/O mechanism. You can send anything, but if you don't send what the server is expecting you won't get very far.

The web uses the HTTP protocol and this is essentially a set of text formatted headers that tell the server what to do and a set of headers that the server sends back to tell you what it has done. The most basic transaction the client can have with the server is to send a `GET` request for the server to send a particular file. Thus the simplest header is:

```
char header[] = "GET /index.html HTTP/1.1\r\n\r\n";
```

which is a request for the server to send `index.html`. However, in most cases we do need one more header, `HOST`, which gives the domain name of the server. Why do we need to do this? Simply because HTTP says you should, and many websites are hosted by a single server at the same IP address. Which website the server retrieves the file from is governed by the domain name you specify in the `HOST` header.

This means that the simplest set of headers we can send the sever is:

```
char header[] = "GET /index.htm HTTP/1.1\r\n
                        HOST:example.org\r\n\r\n";
```

which corresponds to the headers:

```
GET /index.html HTTP/1.1
HOST:example.com
```

An HTTP request always ends with a blank line. If you don't send the blank line then you will get no response from most servers. In addition the HOST header has to have the domain name with no additional syntax - no slashes and no http: or similar.

With the headers defined we can send our first HTTP request using write as if the socket was just another file to write data to:

```
int n = write(sockfd, header, strlen(header));
```

Of course to use the strlen function we need to add:

```
#include <string.h>
```

The server receives the HTTP request and should respond by sending the data corresponding to the file specified, i.e. index.html. We can read the response just as if the socket was a file:

```
char buffer[2048];
n = read(sockfd, buffer, 2048);
printf("%s", buffer);
```

You can make this more complicated by checking the number of bytes read and reading more if the buffer is full. In fact you get more than the HTML as you get the entire HTTP response including the response headers:

```
HTTP/1.1 200 OK
Cache-Control: max-age=604800
Content-Type: text/html
Date: Sun, 14 Aug 2016 15:30:44 GMT
Etag: "359670651+gzip+ident"
Expires: Sun, 21 Aug 2016 15:30:44 GMT
Last-Modified: Fri, 09 Aug 2013 23:54:35 GMT
Server: ECS (ewr/15F9)
Vary: Accept-EncodinX-Cache: HIT
x-ec-custom-error: 1
Content-Length: 1270

<!doctype html>
<html>
<head>
```

and so on...

Notice the blank line marking the end of the header and signaling that the data payload follows.

The complete program is:

```c
#include <stdio.h>
#include <stdlib.h>

#include <sys/socket.h>
#include <string.h>
#include <sys/types.h>
#include <netinet/in.h>

int main(int argc, char** argv) {
 int sockfd = socket(AF_INET, SOCK_STREAM, 0);
 struct sockaddr_in addr;addr.sin_family = AF_INET;
 addr.sin_port = htons(80);
 addr.sin_addr.s_addr = 0x22d8b85d;
 if (connect(sockfd, (struct sockaddr *)
                &addr,sizeof (addr)) < 0)return -1;
 char header[] = "GET /index.html HTTP/1.1\r\n
                        Host:example.org\r\n\r\n";
 int n = write(sockfd, header, strlen(header));
 char buffer[2048];
 n = read(sockfd, buffer, 2048);
 printf("%s", buffer);
 return (EXIT_SUCCESS);
}
```

Of course, we can do much better than this simple example. For one thing each socket operation needs to be checked for errors. Here we only check for the mostly likely error that the sever refuses the connection.

A WinSock Web Client

In case you need to support Windows, it is worth knowing how relatively easy it is to convert a POSIX sockets program to use WinSock. As the previous example stands it does not run under Windows using either MinGW or Visual Studio and the Windows native libraries. To convert it to work is fairly easy. First you have to replace:

```c
#include <sys/socket.h>
```

by:

```c
#include <winsock2.h>
```

You also have to make sure that the GCC compiler links the program to the appropriate library and MinGW provides a library for WinSock. Simply add wsock32.a which you should find in mingw/lib to the libraries.

The only other changes your program needs to make is to use recv and send in place of read and write and you need to start with a call to WSAStartup to initialize the sockets system with an integer value that specifies the WinSock version you want to use and a struct to accept data about the system:

```
WSADATA wsaData;
WSAStartup(0x202, &wsaData) ;
```

0x202 specifies that you need at least WinSock 2.2.

Putting all this together the program becomes:

```
#include <stdio.h>
#include <stdlib.h>
#include <string.h>
#include <winsock2.h>

int main(int argc, char** argv) {
 WSADATA wsaData;
 WSAStartup(0x202, &wsaData) ;
 int sockfd = socket(AF_INET, SOCK_STREAM, 0);
 struct sockaddr_in addr;
 addr.sin_family = AF_INET;
 addr.sin_port = htons(80);
 addr.sin_addr.s_addr = 0x22d8b85d;
 if (connect(sockfd, (struct sockaddr *) &addr,
                       sizeof (addr)) < 0)return -1;
 char header[] = "GET /index.html
                   HTTP/1.1\r\nHost:example.org\r\n\r\n";
 int n = send(sockfd, header, strlen(header),0);
 char buffer[2048];
 n = recv(sockfd, buffer, 2048,0);
 printf("%s", buffer);
 return (EXIT_SUCCESS);
}
```

Now that you have a basic WinSock client working you can read the documentation and find out how to handle errors and close the socket after use, both of which are slightly different to POSIX sockets.

Connecting Using a URL

There is also a utility function that will perform a DNS lookup for you or convert an IP address specified so you don't need to specify an IP address struct. Surprisingly this is almost an easier way to do things and it has become the standard way to set up a socket. The getaddrinfo function not only looks up the URL using DNS, it also constructs all of the structs you need to open a socket and connect. It will also return as many address specifications as you request, IPv4 and IPv6 for example.

The function specification is:

```
int getaddrinfo(const char *node,
                const char *service,
                const struct addrinfo *hints,
                struct addrinfo **res);
```

and you need to add:

```
#include <netdb.h>
```

If you compile with C99 or C11 selected then you will find that none of the following works. You need to add:

```
#define _GNU_SOURCE
```

to the start of the file.

You pass getaddrinfo the IP address or the DNS name, i.e. either "93.184.216.34" or "www.example.com", as node. The service can be specified as a port address "80" or as a service name "http". The hints struct is used to specify what sort of socket and address you are going to use. The result is a linked list of structs pointed at by addrinfo. The only slightly complication in using getaddrinfo is that you might have more than one result - one for IPv4 and one for IPv6, say - and then you have to work out which one to actually use.

The result struct contains structs that you need to both open the socket and to connect. For example, setting up the hints as:

```
struct addrinfo hints;
memset(&hints, 0, sizeof hints);
hints.ai_family = AF_INET ;
hints.ai_socktype = SOCK_STREAM;
```

asks for structs to be made for a TCP IPv4 socket.

We can now get the address details we need:

```
struct addrinfo *servinfo;
int status = getaddrinfo("www.example.com", "80",&hints,
                         &servinfo);
```

Notice that you could use the IP address as a string. As long as this works the result should be a linked list with a single entry. In this case `servinfo` points to the first and only `addrinfo` struct. If there are any additional structs they are pointed at by:

```
servinfo->next
```

which is `NULL` if there is no `next` struct.

Using the single result is easy. To create the socket we use:

```
int sockfd = socket(servinfo->ai_family,
                    servinfo->ai_socktype,
                    servinfo->ai_protocol);
```

and to connect to the server we use:

```
connect(sockfd,
        servinfo->ai_addr,
        servinfo->ai_addrlen);
```

This is so much simpler that whenever you need a socket connected to a given URL or IP address and port you tend to fall into the idiom of writing:

```
struct addrinfo hints;
memset(&hints, 0, sizeof hints);
hints.ai_family = AF_INET ;
hints.ai_socktype = SOCK_STREAM;
struct addrinfo *servinfo;
int status = getaddrinfo("www.example.com", "80",&hints, &servinfo);
int sockfd = socket(servinfo->ai_family,
                    servinfo->ai_socktype,
                    servinfo->ai_protocol);
connect(sockfd,
        servinfo->ai_addr,
        servinfo->ai_addrlen);
```

The only minor complication is that you need to remember to free the linked list once you are finished with it using:

```
freeaddrinfo(servinfo);
```

As before this all works on any POSIX system including Linux on x86, Raspbian and so on. It doesn't work without some modifications under Windows, even with the help of MinGW.

To make it work you need to add:

```
#define _WIN32_WINNT 0x501
#include <ws2tcpip.h>
```

to the start of the file and add the library file ws2_32.a, which you should find in mingw/lib, to the libraries.

The complete POSIX listing is:

```
#define _GNU_SOURCE
#include <stdio.h>
#include <stdlib.h>
#include <unistd.h>
#include <sys/socket.h>
#include <string.h>
#include <sys/types.h>
#include <netinet/in.h>
#include <netdb.h>

int main(int argc, char** argv) {
 struct addrinfo hints;
 memset(&hints, 0, sizeof hints);
 hints.ai_family = AF_INET;
 hints.ai_socktype = SOCK_STREAM;

 struct addrinfo *servinfo;
 int status = getaddrinfo("www.example.com", "80",&hints,
                              &servinfo);
 int sockfd = socket(servinfo->ai_family,
                     servinfo->ai_socktype,
                     servinfo->ai_protocol);

connect(sockfd,
        servinfo->ai_addr,
        servinfo->ai_addrlen);

 char header[] = "GET /index.html
                     HTTP/1.1\r\nHost:example.org\r\n\r\n";
 int n = write(sockfd, header, strlen(header));
 char buffer[2048];
 n = read(sockfd, buffer, 2048);
 printf("%s", buffer);
 return (EXIT_SUCCESS);
}
```

A Server

A server is more or less the same as a client from an implementation point of view. The only real difference is that it has to wait until a client connects before dealing with a transaction.

The first step is to create the socket and this follows the same pattern as for the client. We could simply set up the address structures and create a socket, but now we know how to use getaddrinfo it is easier to use this to do the job automatically and flexibly:

```
struct addrinfo hints, *server;
memset(&hints, 0, sizeof hints);
hints.ai_family = AF_INET;
hints.ai_socktype = SOCK_STREAM;
hints.ai_flags = AI_PASSIVE;
getaddrinfo(NULL, "1024", &hints, &server);
```

The AI_PASSIVE flag assigns the current system's IP address. You can easily get address structures for alternative addresses such as IPv6 using this, but for simplicity we just ask for an IPv4 address. Notice the specification of port 1024, which isn't the usual HTTP port. The reason for using it is that ports below 1024 are restricted and programs need to be run as root to use them. If you want to use 80 for an HTTP server socket you have to compile the program and run it using sudo, or however you give a program root access in the operating system you are using. After the call to getaddrinfo, the structs we need to create sockets are ready to be used:

```
int sockfd = socket(server->ai_family,
                    server->ai_socktype,
                    server->ai_protocol);
bind(sockfd, server->ai_addr,
             server->ai_addrlen);
listen(sockfd, 10);
```

You can see how easy getaddrinfo makes everything. The call to bind assigns the socket the IP address of the machine on port 1024 and listen starts things going with a queue of ten pending clients.

We can now use accept to wait for a client to connect:

```
struct sockaddr_storage client_addr;
socklen_t addr_size = sizeof client_addr;
int client_fd = accept(sockfd,
                       (struct sockaddr *) &client_addr,
                        &addr_size);
```

At this point our program is blocked waiting for a client to connect to the socket. If you want to keep processing things then you need to use a socket in non-blocking mode, see later.

For the moment we can assume that when accept returns there is a new socket descriptor in client and details of the client in `client_addr`. Again for simplicity, we are not going to check to see who the client is, just serve them a web page. The client will first send the server an HTTP GET packet, assuming they do want to GET a web page. We can read this in using:

```
char buffer[2048];
int n = read(client_fd, buffer, 2048);
printf("%s", buffer);
```

The data in the GET headers tell the server which file is required and you can do some string handling to process it to get the name. In this case we are going to send the same HTML file no matter what the client asked for. To do this we need some HTTP headers defining what we are sending back and some HTML to define the page we are sending. The simplest set of headers that work is:

```
char headers[] = "HTTP/1.0 200 OK\r\n
        Server: C\r\n
        Content-type: text/html\r\n\r\n";
```

which corresponds to sending:

```
HTTP/1.0 200 OK
Server: C
Content-type: text/html
```

with a blank line to mark the end of the headers.

Notice that we have swapped to HTTP 1.0 because this is simpler and works with a smaller set of headers. If you want to support HTTP 1.1 then you need to specify the Content-Length header and the Connection header.

Some sample HTML:

```
char html[] = "<html><head><title>Hello HTTP World</title>
    </head><body><p>Hello HTTP World</p></body></html>\r\n";
```

The HTML could be anything you need to construct a page.

Now we can assemble the data and send it to the client:

```
char data[2048] = {0};
snprintf(data, sizeof data, "%s %s", headers, html);
n = write(client_fd, data, strlen(data));
close(client_fd);
```

If you put all of this together and run the program you will find that the server waits until a client, any web browser, connects. To connect use:

```
http://IPAddress:1024/
```

The web page will then be displayed in the browser.

Of course, this only works once. To make the whole thing continue to work we have to put the entire client handling code into a loop:

```
for (;;) {
    int client_fd = accept(sockfd,
        (struct sockaddr *) &client_addr, &addr_size);
    int n = read(client_fd, buffer, 2048);
    printf("%s", buffer);
    fflush(stdout);
    n = write(client_fd, data,  strlen(data));
    close(client_fd);
}
```

The only problem with this loop is that accept is a blocking call which means you can't include any additional processing in the loop. Sometimes this doesn't matter. For example, if this was a processing loop for a sensor then the sensors could be read after a client connected and the web data served.

If this isn't the case we need to make the call to accept non-blocking. The simplest way of doing this is to OR SOCK_NONBLOCK in the call to socket:

```
int sockfd = socket(server→ai_family,
                    server->ai_socktype| SOCK_NONBLOCK,
                    server->ai_protocol);
```

Note that this only works under Linux. If you want Unix compatibility then use ioctl via the fcntl function:

```
fcntl(sockfd, F_SETFL, O_NONBLOCK);
```

Following this the call to accept will return immediately and the value of client_fd is negative if there is no client waiting:

```
for (;;) {
    int client_fd = accept(sockfd,
        (struct sockaddr *) &client_addr, &addr_size);
    if (client_fd > 0) {
        int n = read(client_fd, buffer, 2048);
        printf("%s", buffer);
        fflush(stdout);
        n = write(client_fd, data, strlen(data));
        close(client_fd);
    }
}
```

Notice that this polling loop is a bad idea if the machine is a general purpose system as it uses 100% of one core's time. However, if the system is dedicated to doing a single job, this is the most logical and effective solution. In this case the polling loop also implements other repetitive and essential tasks.

In a more general context, the problem of how to handle incoming client connects has two solutions that divide opinion on which is better. Servers like Apache create a new thread for each client that has to be served. This is efficient, but handling lots of threads and cleaning up after threads terminate can be a problem. Node.js, on the other hand, uses a single thread to deal with all client requests and manages things using events. Event handling is basically an elaboration on the polling loop shown above and it is claimed that event-based servers can be faster than thread-based ones. Use whichever method suits your application.

The complete listing for the server with non-blocking calls is:

```
#define _GNU_SOURCE
#include <stdio.h>
#include <stdlib.h>
#include <unistd.h>
#include <sys/socket.h>
#include <string.h>
#include <sys/types.h>
#include <netinet/in.h>
#include <netdb.h>

int main(int argc, char** argv) {

    struct addrinfo hints, *server;
    memset(&hints, 0, sizeof hints);
    hints.ai_family = AF_INET;
    hints.ai_socktype = SOCK_STREAM;
    hints.ai_flags = AI_PASSIVE;
    getaddrinfo(NULL, "1024", &hints, &server);

    int sockfd = socket(server→ai_family,
                        server->ai_socktype| SOCK_NONBLOCK,
                        server->ai_protocol);
    bind(sockfd, server->ai_addr, server->ai_addrlen);

    listen(sockfd, 10);
    struct sockaddr_storage client_addr;
    socklen_t addr_size = sizeof client_addr;
    char buffer[2048];
    char headers[] = "HTTP/1.0 200 OK\r\nServer:C\r\n
                      Content-type: text/html\r\n\r\n";
```

```
char html[] = "<html><head><title>Hello HTTP World</title>
        </head><body><p>Hello HTTP World</p></body></html>\r\n";
char data[2048] = {0};
snprintf(data, sizeof data, "%s %s", headers, html);

for (;;) {
    int client_fd = accept(sockfd,
            (struct sockaddr *) &client_addr, &addr_size);
    if (client_fd > 0) {
        int n = read(client_fd, buffer, 2048);
        printf("%s", buffer);
        fflush(stdout);
        n = write(client_fd, data, strlen(data));
        close(client_fd);
    }
}
return (EXIT_SUCCESS);
}
```

Notice the use of snprintf – the safe version of sprintf which is like printf but sends the output to a string.

A WinSock Server

To make all of this work with WinSock you have to make the usual changes.

Replace:

`#include <sys/socket.h>`

by:

`#include <winsock2.h>`

You also need to add:

```
#define _WIN32_WINNT 0x501
#include <ws2tcpip.h>
```

to the start of the file and add the library files wsock32.a and ws2_32.a which you should find in mingw/lib to the libraries.

As before, the only other changes your program needs to make is to use recv and send in place of read and write and you need to start with a call to WSAStartup to initialize the sockets system:

```
WSADATA wsaData;
WSAStartup(0x202, &wsaData) ;
```

where 0x202 specifies that you need at least WinSock 2.2.

In addition you need to use:

`ioctlsocket(sockfd, FIONBIO , 0);`

to set the socket to non-blocking.

```c
#define _WIN32_WINNT 0x501
#include <ws2tcpip.h>
#include <stdio.h>
#include <stdlib.h>
#include <string.h>
#include <fcntl.h>
#include <winsock2.h>
int main(int argc, char** argv) {
    WSADATA wsaData;
    WSAStartup(0x202, &wsaData);
    struct addrinfo hints, *server;
    memset(&hints, 0, sizeof hints);
    hints.ai_family = AF_INET;
    hints.ai_socktype = SOCK_STREAM;
    hints.ai_flags = AI_PASSIVE;
    getaddrinfo(NULL, "1024", &hints, &server);
    int sockfd = socket(server->ai_family,
            server->ai_socktype,
            server->ai_protocol);
    ioctlsocket(sockfd, FIONBIO, 0);
    int result = bind(sockfd, server->ai_addr, server->ai_addrlen);
    listen(sockfd, 10);
    struct sockaddr_storage client_addr;
    socklen_t addr_size = sizeof client_addr;
    int client_fd = accept(sockfd, (struct sockaddr *) &client_addr,
                                                &addr_size);
    char buffer[2048];
    char headers[] = "HTTP/1.0 200 OK\r\nServer: C\r\n
                            Content-type: text/html\r\n\r\n";
    char html[] = "<html><head><title>Hello HTTP World</title>
        </head><body><p>Hello HTTP World</p></body></html>\r\n";
    char data[2048] = {0};
    snprintf(data, sizeof data, "%s %s", headers, html);
    for (;;) {
        int client_fd = accept(sockfd,
                (struct sockaddr *) &client_addr, &addr_size);
        if (client_fd > 0) {
            int n = recv(client_fd, buffer, 2048, 0);
            printf("%s", buffer);
            fflush(stdout);
            n = send(client_fd, data, strlen(data), 0);
            close(client_fd);
        }
    }
    return (EXIT_SUCCESS);
}
```

Summary

- Sockets are a general way of making a connection between two programs, perhaps running on different machines.

- Sockets are a POSIX standard, but not a C standard. Windows supports a modified form of sockets via WinSock.

- To use sockets you have to create a socket, connect it to an address and then transfer data.

- Sockets come in two general types – client sockets, which actively connect to another socket and transfer data, and server sockets, which wait for a connection and then service it.

- You create a socket using the socket function and you have to specify the type of connection and the detailed protocol in use.

- To connect a socket you use the connect function, which accepts a struct which specifies the address of the socket to connect to.

- A server socket has to be bound to an address, using the bind function, which it listens on for a client trying to connect.

- A server socket also has a listen function, which activates it ready for a client to try to connect. The server then uses the accept function to create a connection.

- Once a socket is connected to another socket data can be transferred as if it was a file. It is very easy to create a web client or a web server.

- The simplest way to create a server is to use a blocking call to the accept function and leave the thread idle waiting for a client to connect.

- A more useful way to handle the connection is in non-blocking mode which allows the thread to do something else while waiting.

Chapter 12

Threads

C has no standard way of multi-tasking and no standard way of handling interrupts, hard or soft. Until recently you could mostly ignore this deficit on small machines because they hardly had the power to run one thread of execution, let alone multiple threads. Also any use of interrupts would have been highly hardware-specific. Increasingly even small machines run Linux using multiple cores and the environment is multi-threaded even if your C program isn't.

In this chapter we look at how POSIX systems handle the problem of threading, i.e. more than one task running potentially at the same time.

The C11 standard introduced its own standard threading, which is similar to POSIX, but lacking some facilities. For the moment, the POSIX approach is the more practical and better supported.

The subject of multi-tasking and parallel programming is a large one and this chapter doesn't aim to be complete. It is an introduction to the ideas and techniques you need to understand why creating multi-threaded programs is difficult and the general approaches for getting it right. In most cases the best advice is to try to avoid multi-tasking altogether, but if you can't or you think it is desirable then keep it as simple as possible. Reasoning about even simple parallel systems that interact is hard – if they are complex it becomes very nearly impossible.

Why Multi-task?

It seems almost obvious that getting a program to do more than one thing at a time is a good idea. It obviously speeds things up. In practice this isn't quite so obvious. Multi-tasking on a machine that has only one CPU is often slower than an equivalent program that doesn't attempt it. The reason is that there is an overhead in switching between tasks. If the machine has multiple cores then you can achieve a faster performance, but even here usually not as much as you would expect. The reason is that interacting tasks generally need to cooperate and share resources and the time this requires can reduce the speed increase and in some cases eliminate it altogether. The bottom line is that no matter how attractive multi-tasking appears from a common sense point of view, it often doesn't deliver what you expect and it increases the complexity of your program. In fact many programmers are of the opinion that multi-tasking, including interrupts, should never be used in any embedded system even if they are available.

To Thread or Fork

The first thing to say is that the modern idea of a thread is not fundamental to POSIX operating systems. Unix introduced the fork function which makes a complete copy of a running program. The two copies are identical and the new process continues to run from the same location in the program. The child process doesn't inherit any outstanding I/O nor memory locks from the parent process and it has a unique process ID.

This doesn't seem particularly useful until you know that fork returns -1 if there is an error, 0 in the child's program and a positive integer, the child's PID, in the original parent program. This means, you can write code which behaves differently in each copy.

For example:

```
#include <stdio.h>
#include <stdlib.h>
#include <sys/types.h>
#include <unistd.h>
int main(int argc, char** argv) {
    if (fork() == 0)
        printf("Hello from Child\n");
    else
        printf("Hello from Parent\n");
    return (EXIT_SUCCESS);
}
```

The reason for this strange way of doing things is lost in the past, probably due to the limited memory available back then. Most programmers when first exposed to the idea of the fork are concerned about the idea that there are two copies of a program running and the distinction between them is just which part of the if statement is executed. In practice, the pattern was generally fork followed by the child doing an exec call to load another program.

Why not just use exec to load a program without a fork? The answer is that you can do this, but the new program simply overwrites the current program and a new process isn't created.

When you use a fork, the new process is fairly well separated from the original. There are ways that the two can communicate, pipes and shared memory for example, but they don't share resources. A thread on the other hand is a process that lives in the same environment as other threads of execution. When a process is started it has a single thread of execution but there are system calls that allow you to create new threads. Most operating systems do threading in their own way, but the standard POSIX threading specification is fairly well supported and it is generally referred to as Pthreads.

You can use fork and even lower-level system calls such as `clone` and so on to implement multi-tasking, but Pthreads is fairly modern and a good choice if you are working with Linux or any POSIX-compliant operating system. It doesn't work under Windows, which has its own threading system, but there are libraries that provide some compatibility.

The advantage of using threads over processes created using fork is that threads involve a smaller overhead when the operating system switches its attention to a new thread. Threads are often described as lightweight processes. It is also usually easier to allow communication between threads via their shared memory space. This is also the big disadvantage of threads – if a thread corrupts the memory in some way then all of the threads could be affected.

A group of threads or processes may be implemented on a single processor. In this case the operating system shares the processor's time by scheduling threads and processes to run for a short time. In this case all but one thread in one process is executing at any one time and all of the others are suspended. This situation is much easier to reason about as there is only one thing happening at any given moment. Today's processors, however, often support multiple cores, each one capable of running a thread. If the processor has n cores there can be n threads running at the same time and this makes the interaction between the threads much more difficult to analyze.

Pthreads

Pthreads is standard on all POSIX systems, including Linux. To use it we need to include the pthreads library:

```
#include <pthread.h>
```

and also specify the name of the library that you want the linker to add to your program. To do this right click on the project and select properties. Select Build,Linker in the dialog box that appears, click the three dots in the Libraries section, click Add Library and specify pthread.

The key function for thread creation is:

```
int pthread_create(&pthread_t,options,&function,&param);
```

The first parameter is used to return the id of the thread. The second parameter can be set to NULL unless you want to modify the way the thread is created. The third parameter is a pointer to the function to be executed by the new thread and the final parameter is a pointer to a parameter to pass to the function. The function returns 0 if it worked and a negative value otherwise.

Let's create a minimal thread creation program.

First we need a function to pass to the thread:

```
void *hello(void *p){
    printf("Hello Thread World");
}
```

Notice that the function accepts a void pointer and returns a void pointer. This means that the input parameter and the return result can be anything you care to use. However, you also need to keep in mind that returning a pointer to a dynamic object that the function created will fail as the object will be destroyed when the function terminates.

The main program can be as simple as:

```
int main(int argc, char** argv) {
    pthread_t pthread;
    int param=0;
    int id=pthread_create(&pthread,NULL,hello,&param);
    return (EXIT_SUCCESS);
}
```

However, if you run this program you won't see the message printed. The reason is that when the main program terminates all of its threads are also terminated and so the new thread never gets a chance to print anything. You might think that making the main program pause long enough would be enough, but because printf is writing to a buffer you still see nothing. To see the message you have to keep the main program running long enough for the thread to do its work and you need to `fflush` the buffer.

The complete program is:

```
#include <stdio.h>
#include <stdlib.h>
#include <pthread.h>

void * hello(void *p){
    printf("Hello Thread World");
}
int main(int argc, char** argv) {
    pthread_t pthread;
    int param=0;
    int id=pthread_create(&pthread,NULL,hello,&param);
    for(;;){fflush(NULL);};
    return (EXIT_SUCCESS);
}
```

Although we have just allowed the thread function to terminate there is an explicit exit function:

```
pthread_exit(void *retval);
```

and this also sets the pointer to the return value. Compare this to `exit`, which terminates the entire process, i.e. all of the threads. As explained later, the return value is accessible to threads that have joined the thread.

It is important to realize that all of the threads are on an equal footing. There is no master thread and the thread that was used to start the program is just another thread. Anything you can do in the main thread you can do in a thread you have created, including creating other threads, and vice versa. That is, although we tend to think about the main or default thread as special, it isn't.

For example, when you call `pthread_exit` in the main program then the main thread will end but the process will continue to run until all of the threads have exited and the process has ended.

This means that our simple example could have been written:

```
int main(int argc, char** argv) {
    pthread_t pthread;
    int param=0;
    int id=pthread_create(&pthread,NULL,hello,&param);
    pthread_exit(NULL);
}
```

The Thread Attributes Object

Much of the time a default thread will do, and you can pass NULL as the second argument to create. However, you do need to be able to customize the threads you create. To do this you have to pass a thread attributes object which is essentially a struct that you have to set using special functions.

You can create a thread attributes object using:

```
int pthread_attr_init(*attr);
```

and you can destroy it using:

```
int pthread_attr_destroy(*attr);
```

where attr is a pthread_attr_t.

So for example:

```
pthread_attr_t attrObj:
pthread_attr_init(&attrObj);
```

creates a thread attribute object set to the defaults. In this case:

```
int id=pthread_create(&pthread,&attrObj,hello,&param);
```

has the same effect as:

```
int id=pthread_create(&pthread,NULL,hello,&param);
```

To set values different from the defaults you have to call set functions and, to discover what the attribute is, there are corresponding get functions.

For example, to get the current size of the stack that will be used for threads created using this thread attribute object:

```
int pthread_attr_getstacksize(*attr, *stacksize);
```

The stack size will be stored in stacksize and to set it use:

```
int pthread_attr_setstacksize(*attr,stacksize);
```

Once you have finished using the thread attribute object you should destroy it.

This use of an abstract "object" to store attributes or state is something you will encounter again in other parts of Pthreads.

Joinable And Detached Threads

It is important to understand what threads share and what constitutes their own "property". When a thread is created it gets its own use of the CPU registers, its own stack, signal mask and priority. It shares open files, user id and group, signals and signal handlers and all non-local variables. Notice that each thread you start gets its own stack and this means that each thread will consume a larger amount of memory than you might imagine – 10Mbytes or more per thread.

One way of thinking about this is that the function that is being executed has its own local variables which are allocated on its own stack, but it has access to all of the variables that it would have access to if it was running on the same thread as the main program. That is, it has access to any variables allocated on the heap and variables with global scope.

The next question is what happens to all of the thread's resources when it terminates? By default threads are created as "joinable" and in this case the thread's resources are kept after the thread terminates. You can also create "detached" threads which automatically clear up their resources when they terminate.

Joinable threads can be the source of memory leaks if the process goes on running and keeps starting threads which terminate. Each terminated joinable thread keeps its stack allocation, for example. Of course, all resources are reclaimed when the process ends. To free the resources of a joinable thread you have to join it. A thread can call the join function to wait for another thread to complete. The join function also returns the thread's return value which is kept after the thread has terminated. You can think of joinable threads as keeping their state intact until some other thread wants to make use of their data, after which their resources are deallocated.

In:

```
int pthread_join(thread,**returnval);
```

the first parameter is a pthread_t, which identifies the thread to be joined and the second parameter is a pointer to a pointer to the returned value.

Notice that if *thread* has already terminated then join returns at once with the returnval pointer. If the join returns without an error you can be sure that the thread has terminated and that you have its returnval.

If multiple threads try to join to the same thread at the same time the result is undefined – simply because one of the joins will be executed first and the thread's resources, including its return value, will be removed.

Notice that a thread can join multiple threads and wait for them to complete one after another:

```
int pthread_join(thread1,**returnval);
int pthread_join(thread2,**returnval);
int pthread_join(thread3,**returnval);
```

This first waits for thread1 to terminate, then waits for thread2, and finally for thread3. Notice that this still works if thread2 or thread3 terminate before thread1.

For an example of using pthread_join see the next section.

This leaves open the question of how you implement more complicated waiting for threads, such as waiting for the first thread in a group to finish, no matter which one it is – see later.

A detached thread removes its resources as soon as it exits and hence it cannot be the subject of a join. You can change a default joinable thread into a detached thread using:

```
int pthread_detach(thread);
```

where thread is a pthread_t that identifies the thread.

If you want to create detached threads rather than convert a joinable thread you need to use the thread attributes object and the setdetachstate function:

```
pthread_attr_t attrObj;
pthread_attr_init(&attrObj);
pthread_attr_setdetachstate(&attrObj, PTHREAD_CREATE_DETACHED);
pthread_t pthread;
int param = 0;
int id = pthread_create(&pthread, &attrObj, hello, &param);
```

The thread so created using attrObj is detached and you will get an error if you try to join it. You can also use PTHREAD_CREATE_JOINABLE to create a joinable thread, but this is the default.

The distinction between joinable and detached threads is initially puzzling, but the reasons for using each type is very clear:

- ◆ If you want to get a value back from a thread then make it joinable.

- ◆ If you create a joinable thread then join it, otherwise you risk creating a zombie thread that holds on to its resources.

- ◆ The only way a joinable thread releases its resources is if it is joined or if the process terminates.

- ◆ Create a detached thread whenever you don't want to use the thread's returned value.

Threads and Scope - Thread Local

A subject that is often ignored in introductions to threads is which variables are accessible from any particular thread. Which variables can a thread access is very simple because it has the same answer in a single threaded program. A thread can access the local variables of any function it executes. A thread executing a different function cannot access the local variables in any other function. That is, local variables are still local when functions are executed by multiple threads. Notice that each thread has its own stack and hence any local variables it creates are accessible only by it.

Global variables, however, are another matter. A global variable can be accessed from any function in the program unless a local variable of the same name is declared. In most cases a global variable is a way of sharing information between functions. For example, a global state variable can be used to make sure that all functions have access to and can modify the current state indicator. Global variables are shared between all of the functions in a program. If any of those functions are executed by another thread then we immediately have the problem of race conditions - two threads might try to modify the shared data at the same time with the result that the final value might be wrong or inconsistent. The solution, of course, is to use locks to restrict access and this is the topic of the next section.

Global variables are resources shared between all threads. Often in a program functions form groups that are intended to be executed on the same thread. For example, a group of functions might implement a state machine with one function per state. Which one is called might be controlled by a state variable which needs to be shared by all of the functions in the group - i.e. it needs to be global. However, the state variable does not need to be shared by other threads executing the same group of functions. In other words, you may have multiple state machines running at the same time using the same group of functions each with its own thread. The only problem is that the global state variable is shared by all of the threads and so all of the state machines have the same state!

What is needed is a way to create a variable that is global to all of the functions but not shared between threads - this is a thread local storage variable. Thread local storage provides global variables that are accessible from all of the functions in a program but not shared between threads - each thread has its own copy of the global variable.

You can create a thread local in Pthreads using:

```
__thread
```

as a qualifier on any static or global variable. This is a widely supported POSIX standard but there are other ways of doing the job and in particular C11 introduced its own way that works if you are using C11 threading.

As an example, let's try two simple counting threads sharing a global counter variable:

```
#include <stdio.h>
#include <stdlib.h>
#include <pthread.h>

int counter;

void * count(void *p) {
    for (int i = 0; i < 5000; i++) {
        counter++;
    }
    return &counter;
}

int main(int argc, char** argv) {
    pthread_t pthread1;
    int id1 = pthread_create(&pthread1, NULL, &count, NULL);

    pthread_t pthread2;
    int id2 = pthread_create(&pthread2, NULL, &count, NULL);

    void *returnval1;
    void *returnval2;
    pthread_join(pthread1, &returnval1);
    pthread_join(pthread2, &returnval2);

    printf("%d\n", *(int*) returnval1);
    printf("%d\n", *(int*) returnval2);
    return (EXIT_SUCCESS);
}
```

You can see that the counter variable is global and both threads increment it 5000 times. It might appear that the result of printing the two return values would be 5000 each time. However, as both threads access the variable in an uncontrolled way sometimes things go wrong as both threads access the count variable at the same time - take the same value it contains, increment it and store the same incremented value back. What should have been an increment by two becomes an increment by one. If you run the program you

242

will get results in the 6000 region indicating the simultaneous updates aren't that rare.

Now if you change the declaration of count to:

```
__thread int counter;
```

and rerun the program you will see that returnval1 prints 5000 and returnva2 prints 5000 also. Each thread has its own copy of the global count variable and there is no sharing and hence no interaction. Of course the variable is still global and any other function executed on the same thread will have access to its value.

A thread local variable is safe to use within a thread but how do we correct the counter program with a shared global so that we always get the right answer - the most obvious answer is use a lock but there is another.

Atomic Operations and Locks

As we have just discovered, a problem with multi-threaded programs is the possibility that two or more threads will try to change a shared resource in non-coordinated way. For example, if two threads are writing strings to the same file there is a good chance the strings will be written to the file all mixed together as they take turns at writing to the file in a disorganized way.

Clearly what matters is whether an operation can be interrupted by another thread or not. Operations that cannot be interrupted are called "atomic". For example storing a single int to memory is atomic and the action will be completed in one step and another thread cannot change the state of the memory location in the middle of it being changed. The big problem is that different architectures result in different operations being atomic.

Consider again the operation of adding one to a memory location as in the counter example in the previous section. On some machines it might take a transfer to a register, add one and then transfer back to memory. As this is three operations it isn't an atomic operation as another thread could modify the memory location by adding one while the first thread was in the middle of doing the same thing. That is, thread1 could add 1 while thread2 was adding 1 and the outcome would be that the memory location was incremented by 1. If adding 1 was an atomic operation the result would be 2.

So far we have seen that non-atomic operations can result in the wrong answer i.e. the count isn't what you expect it to be, but it can also give rise to inconsistent results. For example, this is a risk whenever you update a complex data structure such as a struct. If the struct is shared then one thread might be updating all of the fields and this clearly isn't a naturally atomic operation as it involves any number of writes to the struct. If another thread starts to read data from the struct then it is very possible that it will read a partially updated record and process it as if it was valid.

For example, if we used two threads to update the record:

```
struct person {
    char name[25];
    int age;
} me;
```

then it is very easy to detect an invalid record. The thread function is designed to repeatedly "erase" the record's data:

```
void * resetRec(void *p) {
    for (;;) {
        strcpy(me.name, "xxxxx");
        me.age = 0;
    }
}
```

The main program simply starts the thread:

```
pthread_t pthread;
int id = pthread_create(&pthread,NULL, resetRec, NULL);
```

and then starts a similar loop to the thread, but in this case setting the struct to some reasonable data:

```
    for (int i = 0;; i++) {
        strcpy(me.name, "Harry");
        me.age = 18;
        if (strcmp(me.name, "Harry") == 0 && me.age != 18) {
            printf("error %s %d %d", me.name, me.age, i);
            exit(0);
        }
    }
```

The if in the loop checks that the data in the struct is logical. If everything is working it can only be xxxxx and 0 or Harry and 18. If the if statement detects a Harry and anything other than 18 it prints the error message and stops.

If you put all of this together and try it out you will find that it fails after at most a few thousand loops. Surprisingly, you will also discover that the struct is set to xxxxx and 0. What this means is that the thread changed the struct halfway through the if statement's condition – after it has tested for Harry and before it tests for age. This is a failure mode you might not have expected. What is the solution to this problem?

The most well known answer is locking but placing a lock around a set of operations can also be thought of as converting that operation into an atomic operation.

Mutex

We have already encountered one locking mechanism in an earlier chapter, the semaphore. The mutex, however, is one of the simplest and most used forms of locking. A mutex can be locked by a single thread. If another thread tries to obtain the lock on the mutex it is suspended and waits until the thread that has the lock releases it. Notice the mutex variable has to be accessible to all of the threads that are going to use it and it has to have the same lifetime. Only the thread that locked the mutex can unlock it and the thread that has the lock cannot try to lock it again – both are undefined behavior. Finally, it has to be kept in mind at all times that mutex locking is cooperative and voluntary. If a thread wants to do something it can ignore any locking that you have provided. A mutex also only works within a single process, i.e. it is a way of synchronizing threads within a process. If you need to synchronize processes then you need to use pthread's semaphore.

You can create a `mutex` in two ways. You can declare it and initialize it to a default:

```
pthread_mutex_t mymutex = PTHREAD_MUTEX_INITIALIZER;
```

Generally it is better to declare the `mutex` outside of any functions, i.e. as a static variable. This ensures that it is initialized and ready to be used.

The second way is to use an initialization function:

```
pthread_mutex_t mymutex;
pthread_mutex_init ( &mymutex, &attr);
```

The advantage of this is that you can use an attribute object to specify how you want the `mutex` to be initialized. You can only initialize a mutex once. Once you have finished using a mutex, you can remove it with `pthread_mutex_destroy`.

A mutex is initially created unlocked. To lock it you can use:

```
pthread_mutex_lock (&mymutex);
```

If the mutex is already locked the thread is suspended and it waits for the lock to become free. In other words, the lock function only returns when it has the lock on the mutex.

The thread that locked the mutex can unlock it using:

```
pthread_mutex_unlock (&mymutex);
```

The unlock function always returns at once and the thread that unlocked the mutex continues. The operating system, at some undefined time, will select one of the threads that are waiting on the lock to wake up. That thread then acquires the lock and its call to `mutex_lock` returns. The other threads, if there are any, continue to wait. Notice that there is no way to know which waiting thread is started, or exactly when, and this shouldn't make any difference to your program.

Going back to our counting example, adding a mutex to the increment is easy:

```
int counter;
pthread_mutex_t mymutex=PTHREAD_MUTEX_INITIALIZER;

void * count(void *p) {
    for (int i = 0; i < 5000; i++) {
        pthread_mutex_lock (&mymutex);
        counter++;
        pthread_mutex_unlock (&mymutex);
    }
    return &counter;
}
```

Now when you run the program the answer is always 10,000 as the two threads cannot interfere with each other's update. Problem solved, but it might not be an acceptable solution. In this case the time between unlocking and locking is very small and once a thread gains the lock any other thread only has a very small window of opportunity in which to acquire the lock. In this sense, the program is closer to one where the first thread to gain the lock keeps it until all 5000 updates have been completed. Locking is safe but it may not be fair in the sense that other threads may not get a chance to progress after the first thread gains the lock.

It is up to the operating system to make sure that the threads waiting on the lock get a turn, but there are no guarantees that this will happen. If one thread holds the lock for most of the time, the other threads suffer "starvation" as they cannot acquire the lock often enough to make progress. In most programs the lock is acquired for a short time and then released, making starvation unlikely. If you have to deal with a greedy thread problem then you need something more sophisticated than a mutex – possibly a condition variable, see later.

A quick fix is to use the yield function from sched.h which is also a POSIX standard. This causes the thread to release the processor and allow another thread to start. If you include:

```
sched_yield();
```

after each of the calls to unlock then you will discover that each of the threads has a more equal share of the processor's time, but the overall efficiency goes down due to the overhead involved in yielding after each increment.

In the real world it can be very difficult to work out what is happening but the principle is easy - make sure that a lock is held for the minimum time by each thread, and that on average it is unlocked for more time than it is locked.

Using a mutex is very easy – getting it right can be more difficult. For example, in the previous case of updating a struct the problem is that the struct has to updated atomically. The solution is to make both updates subject to acquiring a lock.

That is:

```
pthread_mutex_t my_mutex=PTHREAD_MUTEX_INITIALIZER;
void * resetRec(void *p) {
    for ( j=1;;j++) {
       pthread_mutex_lock(&my_mutex);
        strcpy(me.name, "xxxxx");
        me.age = 0;
        pthread_mutex_unlock(&my_mutex);
    }
}
```

The main program does the same thing and locks the update to the struct:

```
int main(int argc, char** argv) {
    pthread_t pthread;
    int id = pthread_create(&pthread,NULL, resetRec, NULL);
    for (int i = 0;; i++) {
        pthread_mutex_lock(&my_mutex);
        strcpy(me.name, "Harry");
        me.age = 18;
        pthread_mutex_unlock(&my_mutex);

        if (strcmp(me.name, "Harry") == 0 && me.age != 18) {
            printf("error %s %d %d", me.name, me.age,i);
            exit(0);
        }
    }
    return (EXIT_SUCCESS);
}
```

If you try this out you will discover that it still doesn't work. After a few thousand iterations the program will halt and print xxxxx, 0, 3456. We have stopped the problem of the two updates creating an invalid record, but we haven't stopped the problem of the struct being changed by the thread during the if statement's testing of its two fields, name and age. It can be very difficult to ensure that access to shared variables is fully protected. There is a tendency to think that we only have to lock when two threads are trying to perform the same or similar operation on a shared resource. In practice you need to lock whenever a thread accesses a shared resource.

To make it all work `unlock` in the main program has to be moved to after the `if`. This means that the amount of time that the `mutex` is unlocked by the main program is very small. Notice that the amount of time that the thread releases the lock is also very small and starvation of the second thread is now very likely.

There are some more advanced mutex features. For example, there is the:

```
pthread_mutex_trylock(&mymutex);
```

function which always returns at once, but with an error if the lock hasn't been acquired. This can be used to allow a thread to get on with some work while it waits for the lock to come free. The default mutex is a fast mutex, which doesn't check to see which thread locked it when attempting a lock. This means if the same thread tries to lock it a second time it is suspended and it is never able to unlock the mutex. Another type of mutex is a recursive mutex, which counts the number of times a thread has locked it and requires the same number of unlocks to free the mutex. There is also a separate `rwlock` that can be locked for reading only or for writing only.

Condition Variables

Condition variables seem to be hard to understand and tricky to use when you first meet them. However, they allow you to do things that are difficult to do any other way. A join allows one thread to wait for another to complete, but a condition variable allows any number of threads to wait for another thread to signal a condition. If you are familiar with a language and environment that supports events, then you can think of a condition variable as something like an event. When the condition is signaled then threads waiting on it are woken up. If you know the theory of concurrent programming then it might be helpful to know that a mutex plus a condition variable implements a monitor.

You can declare a condition variable using:

```
pthread_cond_t  myConVar = PTHREAD_COND_INITIALIZER;
```

You can also use the `pthread_cond_init` function and a condition attribute object to customize the condition variable.

Condition variables are always used in conjunction with a mutex to control access to them. To wait on a condition variable you use:

```
pthread_cond_wait(&myConVar , &mymutex);
```

You need to lock the mutex before calling the function. This means that the thread might wait if another thread is trying to use the condition variable.

Most of the time the mutex isn't locked because the wait function puts the thread into a wait state and automatically unlocks the mutex.

All of the threads waiting on the condition variable are suspended until another thread uses the signal function:

```
pthread_cond_signal(&myConVar);
```

In this case the mutex has to be locked before calling the function and unlocked after it. The signal function causes at least one of the threads that are waiting to be restarted. This vagueness of "at least one" is often a problem as it changes the behavior according to the system the program is running on.

If you want to be sure to unblock all of the waiting threads then use:

```
pthread_cond_broadcast(&myConVar);
```

In either case multiple threads are started up one at a time and the thread that is started has the mutex in a locked state.

There is one final problem. The specification says that spurious wakeups from wait states can occur. This means you cannot assume that when a thread is restarted from a wait, some other thread has necessarily signaled or broadcast. As a result you generally have to set up a global variable that indicates that a signal or broadcast has occurred and test it to make sure that this is a real wake up call. If it isn't then you can wait on the condition variable again.

You can call signal or broadcast even if there are no threads waiting on the condition. The call only affects the threads currently waiting at the time the call is made – there is no memory that the condition has been signaled.

This is a very simple mechanism, but it can be used in many different ways. Let's take a look at some of the most common.

First Thread to Finish

You can easily wait for all threads to finish using join as was shown earlier in this chapter. However, the related problem of waiting for the first thread of a group to finish is a harder problem, but one easily solved using a condition variable.

The general idea is that each thread in the group is started and then the thread that wants to wait for the first thread to finish waits on the condition variable that they all share. Each thread calls cond_signal as soon as it has finished and this wakes up the waiting thread. As the other threads finish they too signal, but by this time there are no waiting threads.

First we need functions for two threads:

```c
void * threadA(void *p) {
    sleep(rand()%5);
    pthread_mutex_lock(&my_mutex);
    threadid=1;
    pthread_cond_signal(&myConVar);
    pthread_mutex_unlock(&my_mutex);
}
```

This function simply waits for a random number of seconds between 0 and 4, then it locks the mutex and changes a shared global variable which is used to indicate which thread has finished. Notice that access to the global variable is also locked by the mutex. Next it signals on the condition variable, which starts the thread that is waiting and finally it unlocks the mutex. Notice the use of sleep, which is a POSIX function that causes a thread to be suspended for the specified number of seconds.

The threadB function is the same, but it sets threadid to 2.

In the main program we need to declare the mutex, condition variable, and the global variable:

```c
pthread_mutex_t my_mutex = PTHREAD_MUTEX_INITIALIZER;
pthread_cond_t myConVar = PTHREAD_COND_INITIALIZER;

int threadid=0;
```

The main program starts the two threads going and then waits:

```c
int main(int argc, char** argv) {
    srand(time(0));

    pthread_t pthreadA;
    pthread_create(&pthreadA, NULL, threadA, NULL);
    pthread_t pthreadB;
    pthread_create(&pthreadB, NULL, threadB, NULL);

    pthread_mutex_lock(&my_mutex);
    while (threadid == 0) pthread_cond_wait(&myConVar, &my_mutex);
    printf("%d", threadid);
    pthread_mutex_unlock(&my_mutex);
    return (EXIT_SUCCESS);
}
```

Notice that the call to pthread_cond_wait is in the form of a while loop. The reason is that the wait can end without any thread signaling. To make sure that it isn't a spurious wake-up, we have to check that threadid has been set to something other than 0. If it is still 0 then the wait is restarted. Finally we print the value of threadid and unlock the mutex. Notice you can't unlock the mutex until the value of threadid has been printed as one of the other threads might update it.

The complete program is:

```
#include <stdio.h>
#include <stdlib.h>
#include <pthread.h>
#include <unistd.h>

pthread_mutex_t my_mutex = PTHREAD_MUTEX_INITIALIZER;
pthread_cond_t myConVar = PTHREAD_COND_INITIALIZER;

int threadid = 0;

void * threadA(void *p) {
    sleep(rand() % 5);
    pthread_mutex_lock(&my_mutex);
    threadid = 1;
    pthread_cond_signal(&myConVar);
    pthread_mutex_unlock(&my_mutex);
}

void * threadB(void *p) {
    sleep(rand() % 5);
    pthread_mutex_lock(&my_mutex);
    threadid = 2;
    pthread_cond_signal(&myConVar);
    pthread_mutex_unlock(&my_mutex);
}

int main(int argc, char** argv) {
    srand(time(0));
    pthread_t pthreadA;
    pthread_create(&pthreadA, NULL, threadA, NULL);
    pthread_t pthreadB;
    pthread_create(&pthreadB, NULL, threadB, NULL);

    pthread_mutex_lock(&my_mutex);
    while (threadid == 0) pthread_cond_wait(&myConVar, &my_mutex);

    printf("%d", threadid);
    pthread_mutex_unlock(&my_mutex);
    return (EXIT_SUCCESS);
}
```

Now that you have seen how this works you should be able to modify the program so that the main program only resumes when all of the threads have completed. All you have to do is change the update of the global variable and the signal to:

```
threadid++;
if(threadid==2) pthread_cond_signal(&myConVar);
```

With this change each thread increments the global variable, but only wakes the main thread up when it reaches 2 and both threads have terminated.

You might want to use this in place of joins if you want to create detached threads.

Scheduling

In nearly all cases there will be more threads than processors to run them. The operating system has to ensure that every thread makes progress by assigning each one time on a processor. The operating system interrupts running threads, stores their state and starts another thread by restoring its stored state. Exactly how this is done depends on the operating system and its scheduling policy. POSIX defines a standard for specifying the scheduling policy a particular process runs under, but says nothing about scheduling threads. Linux, however, considers threads to be a type of process and so supports a POSIX-like set of functions to control the way threads are run. What follows applies specifically to Linux.

Every Linux thread is assigned a scheduling policy and a static priority. The normal scheduling algorithm that Linux uses, SCHED_OTHER, applies to all threads with static priority zero.

If you are not using real-time scheduling then all the threads run at priority zero. In place of a static priority, each thread is assigned a dynamic priority, which increases each time it is passed over for execution by the scheduler. The scheduler gives the thread with the highest dynamic priority an opportunity to run for one quantum of time or for one time slice. A thread can be suspended before its time slice is up because it has to wait for I/O or because it is blocked in some other way. Any time a thread makes a system call it is also a candidate to be suspended in favor of another thread.

You have only a little control over the computation of the dynamic priority. All you can do is set its initial value using the **nice** command or **setpriority**.

The normal scheduling algorithm doesn't provide much control over what runs. It is "fair" in the sense that all threads get a turn at running, but it isn't possible to set a thread to have a high priority so that it runs in preference to all others. To do this we need to look at the real time scheduling options.

The most important is SCHED_FIFO and sometimes the closely related SCHED_RR. These apply to real time threads with static priorities 1(low) to 99(high).

The first thing to note is that a thread with priority greater than zero will always run in preference to a thread with priority zero and so all real-time threads will run before a thread using the normal scheduling algorithm.

What happens in FIFO is that the system maintains queues of threads that are ready to run at each priority. It then looks for the list with the highest priority with threads ready to run and it starts the thread at the head of the list. When a thread is started it is added to the back of its priority queue. Once a FIFO thread gets to run it can be preempted by a thread with a higher static priority that is ready to run.

If a FIFO thread is suspended because of a higher priority thread it goes back at the head of the queue. This makes it the next thread to resume. This is the sense in which the schedule is FIFO (First In First Out) - if a thread is suspended by another thread of higher priority that becomes runnable then it is restarted as soon as the thread that replaced it is suspended or stops running.

Finally, if a thread explicitly yields (by calling yield) it goes to the end of its priority queue.

This sounds like chaos, but if you think about it for a moment and start simply you will see that it provides most of what you are looking for. By default all of the standard threads are priority zero and scheduled by the normal scheduler. Now consider what happens if you start a FIFO scheduled thread with priority 1. It starts and is added to the end of the priority 1 queue. Of course, it is the only priority 1 process and so it starts immediately on one of the cores available. If the process never makes a call that causes it to wait for I/O or become blocked in some other way, then it will execute without being interrupted by any other process. In principle this should ensure that your process never delivers anything but its fastest response time.

This is almost, but not quite, true. There are more complex situations you can invent with threads at different priorities according to how important they are but this gets complicated very quickly.

A modification to SCHED_FIFO is the Round Robin scheduler, SCHED_RR. for. In this case everything works as for SCHED_FIFO except that each running process is only allowed to run for a single time slice. When the time slice is up, the thread at the head of the priority queue is started and the current thread is added to the end of the queue. You can see that this allows each thread to run for around one time slice in turn.

In most cases for real-time programming with the Raspberry Pi, the SCHED_FIFO scheduler is what you need and in its simplest form. Its complete set of scheduling commands supported by #include <sched.h> are:

sched_setscheduler	Set the scheduling policy and parameters of a specified thread
sched_getscheduler	Return the scheduling policy of a specified thread
sched_setparam	Set the scheduling parameters of a specified thread
sched_getparam	Fetch the scheduling parameters of a specified thread
sched_get_priority_max	Return the maximum priority available in a specified scheduling policy
sched_get_priority_min	Return the minimum priority available in a specified scheduling policy
sched_rr_get_interval	Fetch the quantum used for threads that are scheduled under the round-robin scheduling policy
sched_yield	Cause the caller to relinquish the CPU, so that some other thread be executed
sched_setaffinity	Set the CPU affinity of a specified thread
sched_getaffinity	Get the CPU affinity of a specified thread
sched_setattr	Set the scheduling policy and parameters of a specified thread
sched_getattr	Fetch the scheduling policy and parameters of a thread

The scheduling types supported are:

SCHED_OTHER   the standard time-sharing policy
SCHED_BATCH   for "batch" style execution of processes
SCHED_IDLE   for running very low priority background jobs
SCHED_FIFO   a first-in, first-out policy
SCHED_RR   a round-robin policy

where only the final two are real time schedulers.

Also notice that all the scheduling functions return an error code which you should check to make sure things have worked. For example to set the current thread to FIFO scheduling with a `priority` struct you need to use:

```
sched_setscheduler(pid,sched,&priority);
```

where *pid* is the thread id and if it is 0 then the calling thread is used.

For example:

```
#include <sched.h>
...

const struct sched_param priority = {1};
sched_setscheduler(0, SCHED_FIFO, &priority);
```

If this is the only thread with a priority as high as 1 then it will not be interrupted by other threads and only the kernel will cause short interruptions in its running – typically a few tens of microseconds every now and again. Even if there are other threads with the same or higher priorities, as long as there are sufficient cores to run them, the thread will still not be interrupted.

Deadline Scheduling

For real time tasks FIFO scheduling is appropriate. However, if you are using a modern version of Linux there's a better choice. Earliest Deadline Scheduling (EDS) is new recently introduced (Kernel 3.14) Linux scheduling policy. Due to its recent introduction and because it isn't a POSIX scheduling method, it isn't widely used, but it does have many good properties for realtime tasks.

A `SCHED_DEADLINE` thread is associated with three parameters – *runtime*, *period* and *deadline*. The thread will receive *runtime* nanoseconds of execution every *period* nanoseconds and *deadline* specifies in nanoseconds how delayed into the period the allocation can be. If a thread takes longer than its runtime period the operating system suspends it and restarts it at its next activation period.

It is also useful to know that in this case `sched_yield` suspends the thread until its next time period starts. This means you can give time back to the system if you have overestimated how long a task should take.

Notice that times are specified in nano seconds (ns) but micro seconds (us) are more reasonable for describing how long a real world task is likely to take.

For example, if runtime is 10 us, period 100 us and deadline 20 us you can be sure that the thread will get 10 us every 100us and the maximum delay from the start of the 100 us period is 20 us. If the thread is, say, setting a hardware line high at the start of the 10us and low at the end, the pulses will be 10us wide and repeat every 100us, but with a jitter of 20 us from the start of the 100us period, i.e. a pulse could be up to 20us late. This only works if the system isn't overloaded and there are enough CPUs to satisfy all of the demands. As long as the system isn't overloaded then the scheduling algorithm is proven to meet the specifications of period and deadline.

You may be wondering how Linux can manage to operate with threads that have different scheduler policies?

The answer is that Linux has a modular scheduler which can be expanded by the addition of new classes. At the moment there are four scheduler classes - idle, cfs, rt and dl in order of priority. Any Deadline tasks are scheduled first, then FIFO, then Round Robin and finally Normal. What this means is that if there are any runnable Deadline threads these take precedence of any other type of thread. However, to keep the system running, Linux only allows Deadline tasks to add up to 95% of the available computing time. This leaves no less than 5% for the other schedulers.

To set deadline scheduling you have to use the Linux-specific calls and these are not available as easy-to-call functions in the GNU libraries. Fortunately it is very easy to use a direct Linux syscall:

```
int sched_setattr(pid, struct sched_attr *attr, flags);
```

where *pid* is the Linux process id and not the thread id returned by Pthreads. If this is 0 then the current thread is used. The second parameter is a pointer to a new struct which sets the properties of the scheduling policy. flags is an integer which is currently unused and should be set to 0.

To make use of this function we need a definition of the new struct. While there is a definition in one of the Linux-specific headers, it is simpler to include it in your program:

```
struct sched_attr {
    uint32_t size;
    uint32_t sched_policy;
    uint64_t sched_flags;
    int32_t sched_nice;
    uint32_t sched_priority;
    uint64_t sched_runtime;
    uint64_t sched_deadline;
    uint64_t sched_period;
};
```

with size as the size of the struct and policy specifying the policy using the same constants as used earlier plus the new SCHED_DEADLINE. The flags field is only used for one obscure thing and can mostly be set to zero and ignored. The next two fields control what happens under SCHED_OTHER/BATCH and SCHED_FIFO/RR respectively. The final three fields control SCHED_DEADLINE. To use these constants you need to add:

```
#include <linux/sched.h>
```

The function call has to be implemented as a Linux syscall so you also need to add:

```
#include <sys/syscall.h>
int sched_setattr(pid_t pid, const struct sched_attr *attr,
                                        unsigned int flags) {
    return syscall(__NR_sched_setattr, pid, attr, flags);
}
```

There is also a related getattr call:

```
int sched_getattr(pid_t pid,struct sched_attr *attr,
                     unsigned int size,unsigned int flags){
    return syscall(__NR_sched_getattr, pid, attr, size, flags);
}
```

The whole idea of EDS is that any task that has to be done on a regular basis can be given a guarantee that it will not miss its appointments. For example, suppose you need to check that a sensor is within range every few seconds. The actual reading takes little time, but in a priority based scheduler it could be that a high priority task blocks access to the CPU for so long that multiple readings are missed. You can be sure that the deadlines will be met because the scheduler computes the feasibility of the requested schedule and setattr will return with an EBUSY error when you add a thread that makes it impossible.

To see how this works let's implement a simple task that prints "sensor" every two seconds. The first problem is specifying the times to allocate. Currently these have to satisfy:

```
        sched_runtime <= sched_deadline <= sched_period
```

and all times have to be greater than 1024 ns and smaller than 2^{63} ns. Notice that this implies that the uncertainty in when the task runs is at least the execution times – which means a small execution time is best.

We have selected two seconds for `sched_period` and the runtime to print the message is likely to be less than 10 ms, so the deadline can be 11 ms. Thus the `struct` can be initialized as:

```
struct sched_attr attr = {
    .size = sizeof (attr),
    .sched_policy = SCHED_DEADLINE,
    .sched_runtime = 10 * 1000 * 1000,
    .sched_period = 2 * 1000 * 1000 * 1000,
    .sched_deadline = 11 * 1000 * 1000
};
```

The task will be repeated every two seconds and can be up to 11 ms late.

The thread function is simply:

```
sched_setattr(0, &attr, 0);
for (;;) {
    printf("sensor\n");
    fflush(0);
    sched_yield();
};
```

Notice that after we set the scheduling policy the thread simply loops printing the message. The key point is that in this case the `yield` causes the thread to be suspended until the start of its next time period.

Putting all of this together gives:

```
#define _GNU_SOURCE
#include <stdio.h>
#include <stdlib.h>
#include <sys/syscall.h>
#include <linux/sched.h>
#include <pthread.h>
#include <stdint.h>

struct sched_attr {
    uint32_t size;
    uint32_t sched_policy;
    uint64_t sched_flags;
    int32_t sched_nice;
    uint32_t sched_priority;
    uint64_t sched_runtime;
    uint64_t sched_deadline;
    uint64_t sched_period;
};
```

```c
int sched_setattr(pid_t pid, const struct sched_attr *attr,
                                         unsigned int flags) {
    return syscall(__NR_sched_setattr, pid, attr, flags);
}

void * threadA(void *p) {
    struct sched_attr attr = {
        .size = sizeof (attr),
        .sched_policy = SCHED_DEADLINE,
        .sched_runtime = 10 * 1000 * 1000,
        .sched_period = 2 * 1000 * 1000 * 1000,
        .sched_deadline = 11 * 1000 * 1000
    };
    sched_setattr(0, &attr, 0);
    for (;;) {
        printf("sensor\n");
        fflush(0);
        sched_yield();
    };
}

int main(int argc, char** argv) {
    pthread_t pthreadA;
    pthread_create(&pthreadA, NULL, threadA, NULL);
    pthread_exit(0);
    return (EXIT_SUCCESS);
}
```

In this case the main program simply stops its thread leaving the Deadline thread to run every two seconds. In a real instance the main program could continue to run using any of the other scheduling policies.

If you try and run the above program the chances are you will simply see "sensor" printed as fast as your machine can print it. The reason is that to use Deadline scheduling you have to run the program with root privileges. The setattr fails, and the thread is run under the default scheduling policy. , You should always test the return value of setattr for an error.

To make the program work it has to be run as root or similar. This is easy to arrange in a production environment, but during development it can be more difficult. If you are running the program using NetBeans and a remote build machine then simplest solution is to arrange for SSH to work with root as the user.

To do this log on to the machine using SSH and use:

```
sudo passwd root
```

to set a password for `root`. Next edit the `ssh.config` file:

```
sudo nano /etc/ssh/sshd_config
```

to allow `root` to log on via SSH. Find `PermitRootLogin` and uncomment the line and set it to `yes`:

```
PermitRootLogin yes
```

Save the file, reboot and set NetBeans up to use a remote Build Host using root and the password to log in.

Now if you run the program you should see the message printed every two seconds. The advantage of logging in as root is that you can also make use of the debug facilities without making any changes.

Deadline scheduling means you really don't need to use a full realtime version of Linux or an RT operating system. It is good enough for most situations where you have a set of short duration repetitive tasks.

Summary

- Multi-tasking is becoming increasingly common, even on small machines.

- The original way of creating new processes is to use a fork which creates a new copy of the currently running process. Today it is more common to use threads, which are more efficient and closer bound than a fork.

- Although C11 has a standard for threading, the original Pthreads library is still the most common way of implement threading.

- Pthreads supports joinable and detached threads. A joinable thread can return a result to a thread that waits on its completion, whereas a detached thread cannot do this.

- To avoid simultaneous access to resources you need to use locking. The mutex is one of the most basic locking devices.

- A more complex locking device is the condition variable, which can be used to synchronize threads that can wait on the condition variable.

- Threads and processes need to be scheduled by the operating system. Linux has a real time scheduling policy called FIFO, which is worth using, but the slightly less commonly used earliest deadline scheduling (EDS) is better.

Chapter 13

Cores, Atomics & Memory Models

Modern processors are much more complex than the simple, single core, design you typically find in a small embedded processor. This technology has slowly trickled down to lower-cost devices so that today even a low-cost SBC can not only run Linux, but do so with multiple cores. This makes threading even more challenging because, instead of just seeming to run concurrently by the operating system's scheduling algorithms, they really can be running at the same time on different cores. That is, a modern processor is capable of true parallel processing.

Not only are multiple cores a common feature of low-cost SBCs, each core can also have a sophisticated pipeline processor which can reorder instructions to get the best performance. This means that you can no longer rely on operations occurring in the order that you specified them, even within the same thread. To deal with this we need to introduce ways of specifying instruction order via memory barriers.

Finally, modern processors often provide alternatives to using locking to control access to resources. C11 introduced atomic operations, atomics, to take advantage of this.

Managing Cores

So far we have been ignoring the possibility that there is more than one processor. With the advent of multi-core CPUs, however, even low-end systems tend to have two or more cores and some support logical or hyperthreading cores which behave as if they were separate processors. This means that your multi-threaded programs are true parallel programs with more than one thing happening at any given time. This is a way to make your programs faster and more responsive, but it also brings some additional problems.

Processor architecture is far too varied to go into details here, but there are some very general patterns that are worth knowing about. Using this knowledge you should be able to understand, and make use of, the specific architecture of any particular machine.

263

Even relatively small machines have multiple processing cores. A core is a complete processor (P) but a core can also contain more than one processing unit (PU). A processing unit isn't a complete processor; it has its own set of registers and state, but it shares the execution unit with other PUs. At any one time there is generally only one PU running a program and if it is blocked for any reason another one can take over. A good description is that a PU is a hardware implementation of a thread, hence another term for the technique – hyperthreading.

The processor or "socket" that hosts the cores also has a set of hierarchical caches. Often there is a single cache shared between all the cores and each core also has its own caches. The details vary greatly but what is important to know is that cache access is fast but access to the shared cache is slower and access to the main memory is even slower.

It is also important to notice that as each core runs code out of its own isolated cache, you can think of them as isolated machines. Even when they appear to be operating on the same variable, they are in fact working with their own copy of the variable. This would mean that each core had its own view of the state of the machine if it wasn't for cache coherency mechanisms. When a core updates its level 1 (L1) cache then that change is propagated to all of the L1 caches by special cache coherency hardware. This means that even though updates to a variable by each cache occur in an isolated fashion, the change is propagated and all threads see the same updated value. What is not guaranteed by cache coherency is the order of update of different variables, which can be changed by the hardware for efficiency reasons.

Under Linux you can discover the architecture of the machine using the lstopo tool provided by the Portable Hardware Locality (HWLOC) project, which creates a graphical representation of the cores and processing units available. For example:

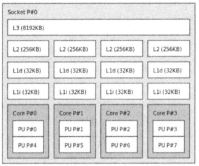

This machine has four cores or Processors and each core has two processing units – it is hyperthreaded. The machine can run a total of eight threads without having to involve the operating system. You can see that each core has two L1 caches – one for data and one for instructions. It also has a bigger second level, L2, cache all to itself and a very big shared L3 cache. Not all processors have multiple processing units. The Raspberry Pi 3 has a BCM2837B0 with four cores with one processing unit per core.

You can often simply ignore the structure of the processor and allow the operating system to manage allocation of threads to cores. Threads are generally created with a natural CPU affinity. This means that the operating system will assign a thread to a core and from then on attempt to run the thread on the same core. So in most cases you can let the operating system manage a machine's cores, but sometimes you know better.

The reasons why you would want to manually allocate threads to cores are usually very specific to the application. For example, you might have a computation-bound thread and an I/O-bound thread. Clearly, scheduling these on the same single core with two processing units would allow the computational thread to make use of the core when the I/O thread was waiting for the external world. Other reasons include placing a high priority thread into a core that no other thread was allowed to use so that it isn't interrupted, placing a thread into a core that has preferential access to particular hardware, and so on.

Another consideration is warm versus cold cache. When a thread starts running on a core then none of the data it needs will be in the cache and so it will run slowly. Slowly it transfers the data and instructions it uses, its working set, into the cache and the cache "warms up". If the thread is switched out of the core and another thread takes it over then restoring the original thread to the original core means that it is still possible that the cache has the data that it requires – the cache is still warm.

Affinity

The operating system tries to keep threads associated with particular cores, but sometime you need to enforce this. There is no standard POSIX way of determining which core a thread will use, but there is a Linux extension of the Pthreads library that does the job. The setaffinity function:

```
int pthread_setaffinity_np(pthread_t thread, size_t cpusetsize,
                                   const cpu_set_t *cpuset);
```

sets the specified thread to run on one of a set of possible CPUs as specified by the cpuset – the affinity mask.

The getaffinity function will return the affinity mask of the specified thread:

```
int pthread_getaffinity_np(pthread_t thread, size_t cpusetsize,
                           cpu_set_t *cpuset);
```

Notice the thread is specified as a Pthread id. You can also use a Linux process id if you use the alternative get and set functions defined in sched.h:

```
int sched_setaffinity(pid_t pid,size_t cpusetsize,
                               const cpu_set_t *mask);
int sched_getaffinity(pid_t pid,size_t cpusetsize,
                               cpu_set_t *mask);
```

In practice, the Pthreads function calls the functions defined in sched.h.

The only thing we need to know is how to set the affinity mask. This uses a single bit to control access to each of the physical and logical cores. You can't simply set or reset these bits. You have to use the set of macros designed for the job. There are a large number of these, but the ones that you use most often are:

```
CPU_ZERO(& cpuset);      set all bits to 0
CPU_SET(n,& cpuset);     sets the bit corresponding to core n
CPU_CLR(n,&cpuset);      resets the bit corresponding to core n
```

How do you find out which core corresponds to which bit in the mask?

As long as your system is set up correctly you should be able to get details by reading the /proc/cpuinfo file or you could use the lstopo tool.

For example, suppose you want to run two threads on separate cores. First we need two functions to run:

```
volatile int j;
volatile int i;

void * threadA(void *p) {
    for (i = 0;; i++) {
    };
}

void * threadB(void *p) {
    for (j = 0;; j++) {
    };
}
```

These simply run a for loop with a global counter to let us know how many times the loop has been executed. The global counters have to be marked as volatile to stop the compiler optimizing the empty loops away.

To set the thread affinity we need to use the macros:

```
cpu_set_t cpuset;
CPU_ZERO(&cpuset);
CPU_SET(1, &cpuset);
```

This sets the mask to core 1. Next we start the first thread and set its affinity:

```
pthread_t pthreadA;
pthread_create(&pthreadA, NULL, threadA, NULL);
pthread_setaffinity_np(pthreadA, sizeof (cpu_set_t), &cpuset);
```

The second thread is to run on core 2 so we need to change the mask and then start the thread:

```
CPU_ZERO(&cpuset);
CPU_SET(2, &cpuset);
pthread_t pthreadB;
pthread_create(&pthreadB, NULL, threadB, NULL);
pthread_setaffinity_np(pthreadB, sizeof (cpu_set_t), &cpuset);
```

Now we can let the main thread sleep for a few seconds and print the value of the counters to give an indication of how many loops each thread has performed.

The complete program is:

```
#define _GNU_SOURCE
#include <stdio.h>
#include <stdlib.h>

#include <pthread.h>
#include <sched.h>
#include <unistd.h>

volatile int j;
volatile int i;

void * threadA(void *p) {
    for (i = 0;; i++) {
    };
}

void * threadB(void *p) {
    for (j = 0;; j++) {
    };
}
```

```
int main(int argc, char** argv) {
    cpu_set_t cpuset;
    CPU_ZERO(&cpuset);
    CPU_SET(1, &cpuset);

    pthread_t pthreadA;
    pthread_create(&pthreadA, NULL, threadA, NULL);
    pthread_setaffinity_np(pthreadA, sizeof (cpu_set_t), &cpuset);

    CPU_ZERO(&cpuset);
    CPU_SET(2, &cpuset);
    pthread_t pthreadB;
    pthread_create(&pthreadB, NULL, threadB, NULL);
    pthread_setaffinity_np(pthreadB, sizeof (cpu_set_t), &cpuset);

    sleep(5);

    printf("%d,%d", i, j);
    return (EXIT_SUCCESS);
}
```

If you run the program you will find that each thread executes roughly the same number of loops. Now if you set the second thread to run on the same core by changing:

```
CPU_SET(2, &cpuset);
```

to:

```
CPU_SET(1, &cpuset);
```

and run it again, you will discover that each thread now loops for about half the previous total. This is what you would expect as each of the two threads now only gets to run on the core for half of the total time.

If you run the same program without setting affinities you will discover that for a lightly loaded machine they will automatically be allocated to different cores and as the load goes up they will eventually share a core.

In the case of a hyperthreaded processor, placing the two threads on two processing units in the same core has the same result as running them both on one core, as neither has any voluntary idle time and so they get to share the core equally. It is instructive to try this program out after assigning different scheduling policies and priorities to the threads.

There are Linux tools that will allow you to discover what core a process is running on and change its affinity. There is also the `cpuset` facility which can be used to dynamically change what cores are used. However, if your goal is to allocate a single core to a single important thread then the best and simplest way of doing this is to first prohibit Linux from using the core by adding:

```
isolcpus=core_number
```

to the boot loader. You can use a comma separated list of cores not to use.

For example, to disable core 3 you would edit `/etc/default/grub` and change the line:

```
GRUB_CMDLINE_LINUX_DEFAULT="quiet splash"
```

to:

```
GRUB_CMDLINE_LINUX_DEFAULT="quiet splash isolcpus=3"
```

You also have to use:

```
sudo update-grub
```

and reboot.

For the Raspberry Pi the Linux configuration is stored in `/boot/cmdline.txt`. Simply add `isolcpus=3` to the end of the list and reboot. When the machine starts up, core 3 will not be used by the system. You can, however, still use thread affinity to run a user thread on core 3. There are other ways, such as `cpu setc`, to disable a core dynamically, but these suffer from problems such as not moving any thread that is already running.

For fixed tasks the best way to do the job is `isolcpus`. You can find out what cores are isolated using:

```
cat /sys/devices/system/cpu/isolated
```

The system will still occasionally interrupt a thread running on an isolated core, but the interference is much less than encountered in normal scheduling.

You can discover which cores are being used for interrupt handlers using the command:

```
cat /proc/interrupts
```

This gives you a list of interrupt numbers and the cores that have handled them. Some interrupts have names rather than numbers and these are the ones that you can't tamper with. Isolated cores only handle interrupts that are essential – rescheduling interrupts for example.

It is sometimes possible to control which cores are used for particular interrupts – as long as they have an interrupt number and as long as they support IO-APIC, and many don't - there are none on the Raspberry Pi for example. To discover which cores a particular interrupt can be handled by use:

```
cat /proc/irq/n/smp_affinity
```

where *n* is the interrupt number. This returns a bit mask with the lowest order bit corresponding to core 0. You can set the bit mask to determine which processors will handle the interrupt using:

```
echo m > /proc/irq/n/smp_affinity
```

where *n* is the interrupt number and *m* is the new mask.

For example, to have all timer interrupts, irq 17, handled by Core 0 you would use:

```
echo "1" > /proc/irq/17/smp_affinity
```

Note that if the interrupt is not IO-APIC compatible you will get a read/write error. You also have to give the entire command as root e.g. use sudo -i.

Memory Barrier and Fences

Modern processors use many techniques to keep executing code. One of the most effective is reordering instructions.

For example, if you write:

```
a=1;
b=2;
```

then you would expect a to be assigned before b, but the hardware can change the order if it finds an advantage – perhaps one of the variables in question is already in the cache.

A reordering of this sort clearly makes no difference to your program – as long as it is single threaded or as long as a and b aren't shared with other threads. Consider, however, what would happen if another thread executed:

```
if(b==2) do something assuming a==1;
```

Now suppose the processor reordered the assignments:

```
b=2;
a=1;
```

Now the second thread might detect that b was 2 and start working on the assumption that a was 1 before a was actually set to 1.

When you first met this sort of possibility there is a tendency to think that things just got so complicated that you can't possible write a working program.

The truth of the matter is that you don't usually have to worry about reordering:

- If you are writing a single threaded program you can ignore it.
- If you are writing a multi-threaded program and sharing variables using Pthread locks you can ignore it. All Pthread locks enforce the ordering of operations before the lock to be what you would expect.

You only have to worry about reordering if:

- you are sharing variables between threads without using locks

or:

- if you are accessing hardware via memory locations, even with a single thread, without using locks

If you share variables between threads without using locks then you do not get the guarantee of ordering that they provide. If you access hardware via memory locations, even from a single thread, then reordering is possible and the hardware might not like having data written in the wrong order e.g. an initialization command should be given before going on to make use of the hardware.

To allow you to cope with reordering problems, hardware generally implements a memory barrier or fence – an instruction that you can use to impose an order when you need to. Notice that a memory barrier is not the same as a barrier in Pthreads which is just another form of locking. There are a number of different types of memory barrier and the subject is too complicated to go into much detail here.

Roughly speaking, an acquire barrier stops any load/store that is after the barrier being moved before the barrier, and a release barrier stops any load/store before the barrier being moved after the barrier.

A full memory barrier stops load/stores before or after being reordered around the barrier. Notice that load/stores can still be reordered, but they cannot move across the barrier.

The key idea is that when you issue a memory barrier instruction you can be sure that all of the stores or loads up to that point have been completed.

For example, to stop the reordering problem with the previous example we could write:

```
a=1;
memory barrier
b=2;
```

Now when the core gets to the memory barrier it has to wait for all of the previous assignments to be complete. This means that b=2 has to happen after a=1.

Of course if you use a lot of memory barriers then the core will be unable to optimize its time and your programs will run slower.

So how do you issue a memory barrier instruction?

There is no standard way of doing this and you might have to resort to assembler.

The GCC compiler does have a built in function that will issue a full memory barrier:

```
__sync_synchronize();
```

and this works on many systems including x86 and ARM. Other compilers have similar extensions.

You probably only need to use this to access memory-mapped hardware as shared variables are best locked and this implicitly applies a barrier.

For example, if you have a pointer to a hardware register then a typical way to access the hardware is:

```
__sync_synchronize();
*p=value;
__sync_synchronize();
value=*p;
```

and so on.

As explained in the next section you cannot rely on declaring p volatile to stop the hardware reordering the access. You need a physical memory barrier.

C11 has another way of implementing memory barriers.

Compiler Reordering and Optimization

To add to the complications of reordering, the hardware isn't the only source of reordering. The compiler can reorder instructions independently of the dynamic reordering performed by the hardware. That is, your program may have been reordered before it gets to the hardware with a similar set of potential problems.

The key fact is that even if you are not working with a multiprocessor system the compiler may still reorder your code.

The good news is that a memory barrier will act as a signal to the compiler not to modify the order – that is, a hardware barrier is also a software barrier.

However, in a single processor system you might still need to stop compiler reordering and hence you need a software barrier.

It is often assumed that if you declare a variable volatile then it will not be optimized by the compiler. This is partly true in the sense that the compiler will refrain from removing a volatile variable that it regards as redundant and it will keep in reads or writes that would otherwise have been optimized away. However, the compiler is still allowed to modify the order of access to a volatile object, and if that volatile object is say a hardware register this is not desirable. The minimum a compiler is expected to do is treat the next sequence point as a software barrier.

That is, a compiler may reorder the use of a volatile object only between sequence points. If you are not sure what a sequence point is then see: ***Fundamental C: Getting Closer To The Machine*** (ISBN: 978-1871962604)

As a full expression is a sequence point, declaring a variable volatile is often all we need to ensure that it isn't reordered. That is, a sequence of read/writes to a volatile variable cannot be reordered by the compiler.

However, a volatile variable does not stop the compiler reordering non-volatile variables around the volatile assignments. That is, volatile is not a software memory barrier – unless the compiler decides to treat it as such.

Also note that volatile is not a physical memory barrier – the processor can still reorder volatile access.

If you are using a memory-mapped hardware register you cannot rely on volatile to preserve the order of access in a multi-core system, you need a physical memory barrier.

It is also worth mentioning that compilers often introduce ways of specifying a software barrier. For example, GCC uses its inline assembler:

```
asm volatile("" ::: "memory");
```

to specify a software memory barrier. The compiler will not reorder load/stores across this instruction. Note that this adds nothing to the generated code, it simply tells the compiler not to reorder. See Chapter 15 for more about `asm`.

There is also a C11 standard function for a memory barrier – see the next section.

Should you worry about compiler reorderings?

Probably not as much as you might think at first. The reason is that if you are using a multi-core system then you have to use physical barriers, and these stop compiler reordering meaning you can forget about software barriers. In a single processor system, declaring a variable volatile often gives you all the protection you need.

However, it is important to realize that in a multiprocessor system volatile does not protect you from hardware based reordering – use a physical barrier.

C11 Atomics

So far we have been looking at the way that the hardware and compilers handle threading and multi-core architectures. The C11 standard was the first to introduce multiprocessing features to the C language. It can be argued that these weren't particularly successful, but they are standard and they are being improved over time. The ideas introduced in C11 were radical and influenced by current research. Instead of using explicit locks to control access to shared resources we use atomic operations – sometimes shortened to atomics.

The real question is, should you use the new C11 features?

If you can use C11 and if the compiler you are using supports atomics then, as long as it works in practice, it is an improvement over using locks and non-standard memory barriers. It is also worth knowing that GCC has its own atomics library that can be used without adopting C11.

The one proviso to using atomics is that you have to keep things as simple as possible. If you write complex messy code then the chances are that you will encounter one of the many "gotchas" inherent. If you can use atomics then your reward is a potentially faster and simpler multi-threaded system.

An atomic operation is one that cannot be interfered with by another thread. Once an atomic operation starts you can be sure that it will complete as if the thread was running on a single core processor. Modern processors have hardware features which allow the direct and efficient implementation of atomics. Older processors have to depend on the compiler to generate locks to force the operations to be atomic. Atomics are often referred to as "lock free" but in many ways it is better to think of them as implementing implicit locking – it is equivalent to obtaining a lock at the start of the operation and releasing it at the end.

What this means is that at best atomics are faster, and at worse you are using locks without having to go through the steps of creating, locking and releasing.

If implemented without the use of a lock, an atomic can be five to ten times faster than using a Pthreads mutex.

In principle C11 atomics were designed to work with C11 threads but you can also use it with Pthreads, which is what we are going to do in the rest of this chapter.

First we need to look at what operations not being atomic does to your program. Consider the following function:

```
int a = 0;
void * count(void *p) {
    for (int j = 0; j < 10000; j++) {
        a++;
    }
}
```

All it does is increment an int. If this function is run as two threads we would expect the shared variable to be incremented to 20000:

```
int main(int argc, char** argv) {
    pthread_t pthreadA;
    pthread_t pthreadB;
    pthread_create(&pthreadA, NULL, count, NULL);
    pthread_create(&pthreadB, NULL, count, NULL);
    pthread_join(pthreadA, NULL);
    pthread_join(pthreadB, NULL);
    printf("%d", a);
    return (EXIT_SUCCESS);
}
```

If you try this out you will discover that a is typically 12000 or less depending on the machine. If you do get 20000 then increase the number of loops because the machine is fast enough to run threadA without threadB getting started.

What is happening?

You might think that a++ was an atomic operation, but it translates to a load and a store more akin to a=a+1. If threadA loads a at the same time threadB loads a then only one increment occurs where two were intended.

Before atomics the solution would have been to put a lock around a++. With atomics all you have to do is declare a atomic i.e. change the declaration to:

```
_Atomic int a = 0;
```

and add:

```
#include<stdatomic.h>
```

then it all works, and 20000 is printed indicating that no increments were lost.

You can also use:

```
_Atomic(int) a=0;
```

Declaring a atomic means that a load and save to the variable has to be completed before any other thread can gain access to the variable. As already stated it is as if there was a lock around the increment, one that the other threads in the program have to obey.

You get all of this with such a small change – just make the int an atomic int. You can change any int type or struct into an atomic type in the same way. There are usually no atomic floats, double, complex or arrays – but this might change.

For any type that you define as atomic the system might well change its size to accommodate any lock state that needs to be stored. You have to treat atomic types as different from the original type. Integer atomic types have increment and decrement operators i.e. ++ and --, and compound assignment e.g. += as read-modify-write atomic operations.

For example, if a is atomic:

a++, a-- and a+=1 are all safe to use as they will complete without allowing another thread to modify a, i.e. they are atomic.

Notice that a being atomic doesn't help with expressions that a just happens to be involved in. That is, b=a+1 isn't atomic even if a and b are.

For example, if you change the increment in the for loop to:

```
b=a+1;
a=b;
```

then you will discover that this is not atomic and the final count is not 20000. Even:

```
a=a+1;
```

is not atomic.

However:

```
a+=b;
```

is atomic even if b isn't.

In other words, you have to be careful what operations you assume are atomic - it is the update to the atomic variable that is atomic and that update has to be part of a compound assignment or an increment/decrement.

If you are wondering about reordering problems it is worth saying that these "default" atomics are a full physical barrier and all load/store instructions cannot be moved across the barrier. There are ways of specifying more relaxed reordering – see later.

There are also a range of atomic functions that can be used to implement more varied atomics.

For example:

```
atomic_fetch_add(&atomic,value)
atomic_fetch_sub(&atomic,value)
atomic_fetch_or(&atomic,value)
atomic_fetch_xor(&atomic,value)
atomic_fetch_and(&atomic,value)
atomic_store(&atomic,value)
```

all perform the operation on the atomic in an atomic way.

For example to add one to a:

```
atomic_fetch_add(&a,1);
```

There is also:

```
var=atomic_load(&atomic);
```

which atomically stores the current value of atomic in var and:

```
var= atomic_fetch_exchange(&atomic,value)
```

which atomically stores the current value of atomic in var and stores value in atomic.

The atomic type can be volatile if necessary and the value is simply the non-atomic version of the type. The types can be integer types or pointers.

Two more complicated functions are:

```
atomic_compare_exchange_strong(&atomic, &expected, value);
atomic_compare_exchange_weak(&atomic, &expected, value);
```

which atomically compares atomic to expected and if they are the same in a bitwise sense, stores value in atomic. If they are not the same it stores expected in atomic – the functions return true for equality. The function is roughly equivalent to the following pseudo code:

```
if(atomic==expected) atomic=value;
else atomic=expected;
```

The weak form is included to allow for some architectures where the comparison will fail even though atomic is equal to expected. The weak version is faster but you have to include it in a loop if you expect it to behave like the strong form.

There is also a special Boolean type, atomic_flag, that is guaranteed to be implemented in a lock free way but what you can do with it is limited to:

```
var=atomic_flag_test_and_set(&atomicflag);
```

and:

```
atomic_flag_clear(&atomicflag);
```

The first function returns the current value of the atomicflag – true or false – and then sets it to true. The second simply clears the atomicflag to false. You also have to use a special macro to initialize a new atomic_flag:

```
atomic_flag flag = ATOMIC_FLAG_INIT;
```

If you don't initialize in this way you have undefined behavior.

As atomic_flag suggests, not all of the atomic types can be implemented using hardware facilities – some are not lock free. To find out which are implemented as lock free types you can use:

```
var=atomic_is_lock_free( &atomic );
```

which is true if the atomic is lock free.

Usually, simple variables and simple structs are implemented without using locks but most compilers will eventually resort to using locks if things get complicated.

Atomic Structs

You can use Atomics with structs but there are pitfalls that aren't easy to find out about. An atomic struct is defined just like an atomic int.

For example:

```
_Atomic struct person {
    char name[25];
    int age;
};
```

The most important thing to know about an atomic struct is that you cannot access any of its fields. This at first makes atomic structs seem pointless – what can you do with them if you cannot access individual fields?

The answer is that you can use functions like atomic_fetch and atomic_store to atomically transfer the contents of an atomic struct to a non-atomic struct. The basic idea is that the atomic struct acts as the shared resource and threads fetch the data to a non-atomic copy that they can work with, and then store back to the shared atomic.

This means that for every struct you are going to need to use atomic and non-atomic versions.

For example, let's implement the simple record modifying program given earlier in the chapter. Because of the need to copy to and from non-atomic structs the program is slightly different from the one that uses locks. First we need an atomic struct to share:

```
struct person {
    char name[25];
    int age;
};
_Atomic struct person me;
```

The thread function has to transfer a complete non-atomic struct to the atomic struct:

```
void * resetRec(void *p) {
    struct person blank = {.name = "xxxx", .age = 0};
    for (j = 1;; j++) {
        atomic_store(&me, blank);
    }
}
```

The store is completed as one indivisible action and so no other thread can interfere and create an invalid struct.

The main program does the same sort of thing:

```
int main(int argc, char** argv) {
    pthread_t pthread;
    int id = pthread_create(&pthread, NULL, resetRec, NULL);
    struct person metemp = {.name = "Harry", .age = 18};
    struct person metest;
    for (int i = 0;; i++) {
        atomic_store(&me, metemp);
```

Again the non-atomic metemp is moved into the atomic me in an indivisible operation. This again means that no other thread can intervene and create an invalid struct.

Now we have to test to make sure that the contents of the atomic struct really are valid and not a mixture of the two possible states. Once again we can't simply access the atomic struct so we need to copy it atomically into another struct:

```
        metest=atomic_load(&me);
        if (strcmp(metest.name, "Harry") == 0 && metest.age != 18) {
            printf("error %s %d %d", metest.name, metest.age,i);
            exit(0);
        }
    }
```

This is now as good as the first version that used a mutex. Of course there is the possibility that that a lock is being used. If you add:

```
printf("%d",atomic_is_lock_free( &me ));
```

you will discover if a lock is used. On x86 and ARM a lock is used on this simple struct.

If you try the program out you will most likely find out that it doesn't work. The reason is that for anything except integer atomics a library file is needed. This varies according to the system and compiler but for GCC you simply need to add the library file atomic to the Netbeans properties or add -latomic to the compiler command line.

The complete program is:

```c
#include <stdio.h>
#include <stdlib.h>
#include <stdatomic.h>
#include <pthread.h>

struct person {
    char name[25];
    int age;
};
_Atomic struct person me;

void * resetRec(void *p) {
    struct person blank = {.name = "xxxx", .age = 0};
    for (j = 1;; j++) {
        atomic_store(&me, blank);
    }
}

int main(int argc, char** argv) {
    pthread_t pthread;
    int id = pthread_create(&pthread, NULL, resetRec, NULL);
    struct person metemp = {.name = "Harry", .age = 18};
    struct person metest;
    for (int i = 0;; i++) {
        atomic_store(&me, metemp);

        metest=atomic_load(&me);
        if (strcmp(metest.name, "Harry") == 0 && metest.age != 18) {
                printf("error %s %d %d", metest.name, metest.age,i);
                exit(0);
            }
    }
    return (EXIT_SUCCESS);
}
```

You can also replace the calls to load and store by assignment as this is atomic i.e.:

```c
me=blank;
```

is atomic.

C11 Memory Models and Barriers

It is important to know and remember that all of the atomics so far described impose full memory barriers that stop the compiler or the hardware from reordering instructions across the atomic operation. This is safe and in most cases you should stay with it. If you do want to relax the ordering constraints to gain increased efficiency then start from the default memory model and relax the constraints stepwise and make sure to test that there are no problems. Of course how you test is an interesting question given that reordering problems can be such that they show themselves very infrequently.

There are six memory orderings defined by C11 and they impose constraints on how memory operations can be moved relative to atomic operations:

`memory_order_relaxed`	no synchronization or ordering constraints imposed on other reads or writes.
`memory_order_consume`	no reads or writes in the current thread dependent on the value currently loaded can be reordered before this load. Mostly unimplemented.
`memory_order_acquire`	no reads or writes in the current thread can be reordered before this load.
`memory_order_release`	no reads or writes in the current thread can be reordered after this store.
`memory_order_acq_rel`	no memory reads or writes in the current thread can be reordered before or after this store.
`memory_order_seq_cst`	This is the default ordering – sequentially consistent.

To use any of these you simply have to call the atomic function but with _explicit as a postfix and a final memory order parameter. For example:

```
atomic_load_explicit(&atomic, memory_order_acq_rel );
```

would perform the atomic load and forbid any reads or writes to be moved across the load.

There are also two memory barrier functions:

```
atomic_thread_fence( memory_order order );
```

which is a physical barrier and:

```
atomic_signal_fence(memory_order_acq_rel);
```

which is a software barrier.

Summary

- Even small machines now have multi-core processors and this introduces true parallelism. You can take control of how threads are allocated to processing units but it isn't standard.

- Another problem for the multi-threaded program is the reordering of instructions by the processor or by the compiler. To control this we can use memory barriers and fences.

- C11 introduces atomics which can be used to create safe programs that don't use explicit locks. If the processor has the facilities to support atomics this can be much faster.

- C11 also introduced a memory model which provides a standard way to control instruction reordering. In practice this is not much used.

Chapter 14

Interrupts & Polling

Asynchronous programming is very much a part of interfacing with the real world. Things that happen in the real world happen much slower than the processor can obey instructions. When you initiate an external task such are reading a file or waiting for a switch to close, you cannot afford to keep the processor idle waiting for something to happen. The usual solution is to associate an interrupt with the completion of the event. When the interrupt occurs the processor stops what it is doing and attends to whatever caused the interrupt – it generally runs an interrupt routine.

Interrupts are common in low level programming but under Linux they are less common. It is also true that it is often better to keep the processor waiting in a loop to service the external world event in as short a time as possible. Interrupts are also very prone to the same sort of problems that a multi-threaded program has. As a result many organizations ban the use of any sort of interrupt so that the behavior of the processor is fully deterministic.

However, there are times when an interrupt is a good way to approach a problem, and in this chapter we look at the facilities that Linux provides for handling user space interrupts.

Interrupts and Poll

The first thing to make clear is that Linux/POSIX doesn't support anything that looks like a hardware interrupt in user space. To find true hardware interrupts you have to write code for the kernel.

There are two sorts of features that are often interpreted as interrupts in user space – signals which we have already met, and select/poll on file descriptors. In many ways this is an area that is evolving and it is far from solved. However, you need to know a little about how select/poll works.

The basic idea is that a user mode program can wait for a file operation to complete. Linux will suspend the thread concerned and restart it only when the file operation is complete. This is a completely general mechanism and you can use it to wait for any file based operation to complete, including file operations in sysfs and this means we can wait for hardware that is packaged as a file or socket or a pipe or a... Recall that in Linux/Unix everything is a file.

The function we need is poll and we need to include poll.h to use it:

```
int poll(fdset[],n,timeout)
```

where fdset is a struct that specifies the file descriptor and the event you want to wait for, n is the size of the fdset array and timeout is the timeout in milliseconds. You can specify a negative timeout if you want to wait indefinitely or a zero timeout if you don't want to wait at all.

A return value of zero indicates a timeout, otherwise the return value is the number of file descriptors that fired the event specified.

The format of the struct is:

```
struct pollfd {
          int   fd;          /* file descriptor */
          short events;      /* requested events */
          short revents;     /* returned events */
          };
```

The fd field is just the file descriptor you want to wait for, and events specifies what sort of event you want to wait for. There is a range of possible events but the ones you use most often are:

POLLIN   There is data to read
POLLOUT   Ready to accept data
POLLPRI   There is some exceptional condition.

The revents field returns the event that occurred which can be any of the above plus:

POLLERR   Error condition
POLLHUP   Hang up
POLLNVAL   Invalid request.

Notice that in general the fdset array can contain more than one file descriptor and poll will wait until the specified events occur on one of them. This makes it possible to start multiple transfers in progress and service each one as it becomes ready. In the following example we will only poll a single file descriptor, but the extension to multiple descriptors is obvious. To find which descriptors have triggered the event you simply scan the fdset array and examine each revents field to see if it returned the value you are looking for.

If you call poll then it will wait for the specified event on the file descriptors until the timeout is up when it returns. In fact what actually happens is a little more complicated. The thread that called poll is suspended until the event occurs and then the system restarts it. This is not really an interrupt, as in a true interrupt the thread would continue to execute until the interrupt occurred when it would run the ISR specified. This may not be an interrupt proper, but with a little more work it can provide more or less the same behavior. Notice that poll is badly named because it isn't implemented as a polling loop.

When you poll on a set of file descriptors the call only returns when:

- ◆ any file descriptor is ready
- ◆ the call is interrupted by a signal handler

or

- ◆ the timeout occurs.

Notice that this means that when the poll returns there is a possibility that the event that you are waiting for has not occurred.

An Event Driven Socket Server

As an example of using poll let's return to the socket server described in the previous chapter. If this isn't the case we need to make the call to accept non-blocking. The simplest way of doing this is to OR SOCK_NONBLOCK in the call to socket:

```
int sockfd = socket(server→ai_family,
                    server->ai_socktype| SOCK_NONBLOCK,
                    server->ai_protocol);
```

This change makes the attempt to read from the socket:

```
int client_fd = accept(sockfd,
            (struct sockaddr *) &client_addr, &addr_size);
```

return immediately but with -1 if there is no data to read. Our only solution is to repeatedly attempt to read the data using accept:

```
for(;;){
int client_fd = accept(sockfd,
    (struct sockaddr *) &client_addr, &addr_size);
if(client_fd>0){
 process the data;
}
```

You can see that this keeps the thread busy in a tight polling loop.

A much better solution is to use poll to suspend the thread until there is data to read:

```
struct pollfd fdset[1];
fdset[0].fd = sockfd;
fdset[0].events = POLLIN;
fdset[0].revents = 0;
poll(fdset, 1, 10000);
```

The call now waits until there is data read to read from the socket or timeout occurs after 10 seconds. This means we can follow the call with code to read the data, but only after checking that the event occurred and it wasn't a timeout or a signal:

```
if (fdset[0].revents & POLLIN) {
  int client_fd = accept(sockfd, (struct sockaddr *) &client_addr,
                                                       &addr_size);
    process data:
```

Of course this only allows one client to use the server. We still need to put the poll and the processing in a loop:

```
struct pollfd fdset[1];
for (;;) {
   fdset[0].fd = sockfd;
   fdset[0].events = POLLIN;
   fdset[0].revents = 0;
   poll(fdset, 1, 10000);
   if (fdset[0].revents & POLLIN) {
     int client_fd = accept(sockfd,
                 (struct sockaddr *) &client_addr, &addr_size);
     int n = read(client_fd, buffer, 2048);
     printf("%s", buffer);
     n = write(client_fd, data, strlen(data));
     close(client_fd);
     printf("client request");
     fflush(stdout);
   }
   if (fdset[0].revents == 0) {
     printf("timeout");
     fflush(stdout);
   }
}
```

Notice that you have to initialize the struct for each call to poll and you can also add a check for a timeout.

You can make this much more sophisticated but this is the basic idea. It is common for example to pass the request on to a separate thread so that the loop can go back to waiting for the next client.

The complete program is:

```c
#define _GNU_SOURCE
#include <stdio.h>
#include <stdlib.h>
#include <unistd.h>
#include <sys/socket.h>
#include <string.h>
#include <sys/types.h>
#include <netinet/in.h>
#include <netdb.h>
#include <poll.h>

int main(int argc, char** argv) {

    struct addrinfo hints, *server;
    memset(&hints, 0, sizeof hints);
    hints.ai_family = AF_INET;
    hints.ai_socktype = SOCK_STREAM;
    hints.ai_flags = AI_PASSIVE;
    getaddrinfo(NULL, "1024", &hints, &server);

    int sockfd = socket(server->ai_family,
                        server->ai_socktype| SOCK_NONBLOCK,
            server->ai_protocol);
    bind(sockfd, server->ai_addr, server->ai_addrlen);

    listen(sockfd, 10);

    struct sockaddr_storage client_addr;
    socklen_t addr_size = sizeof client_addr;
    char buffer[2048];


    char headers[] = "HTTP/1.0 200 OK\r\nServer:C\r\n
                        Content-type: text/html\r\n\r\n";
    char html[] = "<html><head><title>Hello HTTP World </title>
        </head><body><p>Hello HTTP World</p></body></html>\r\n";
    char data[2048] = {0};
    snprintf(data, sizeof data, "%s %s", headers, html);
```

```
struct pollfd fdset[1];
    for (;;) {
        fdset[0].fd = sockfd;
        fdset[0].events = POLLIN;
        fdset[0].revents = 0;
        int rc=poll(fdset, 1, 10000);
        if (fdset[0].revents & POLLIN) {
            int client_fd = accept(sockfd,
                (struct sockaddr *) &client_addr, &addr_size);
            int n = read(client_fd, buffer, 2048);
            printf("%s", buffer);
            n = write(client_fd, data, strlen(data));
            close(client_fd);
            printf("client request");
            fflush(stdout);
        }
        if (rc == 0) {
            printf("timeout");
            fflush(stdout);
        }
    }
    return (EXIT_SUCCESS);
}
```

GPIO Interrupts and Poll

The important thing about poll is that it can be used to wait for an event on any file descriptor and as we already know, in Linux/Unix everything is a file. This example of using sysfs, introduced in Chapter 9, with poll to respond to a GPIO interrupt applies to the Raspberry Pi and is taken from *Raspberry Pi IoT in C* (ISBN: 978-1871962604).

Any GPIO line that is capable of generating an interrupt has an edge directory in sysfs. This can be set to none, rising, falling or both to set the corresponding edge interrupt.

So the first thing we need is a sysfs function to set the edge by writing to it:

```
int setEdgeGPIO(int gpio, char *edge)
```

This simply writes whatever edge is to the edge directory. Notice that, for simplicity, no checks are included for the GPIO pin being exported and set to input, i.e. that it has been set up to generate an interrupt. The details of the function are given in the complete listing.

So now we can set the interrupt we want to use, but how do we wait for it to happen?

Let's construct the simplest possible example using poll to wait for a raising edge on GPIO 4 (pin 7). First we need to open GPIO 4 and set edge to rising:

```
openGPIO(4, 0);
setEdgeGPIO(4, "rising");
```

The details of the openGPIO function are given in the complete listing but it stores the file descriptor in a global array `fd[gpio]` so in `fd[4]` in this case. Note that you don't have to use these sysfs functions, you can do the job any way that works, but you must use sysfs because you need a file descriptor to pass to the `poll` function in the `fdset` struct:

```
struct pollfd fdset[1];
for (;;) {
            fdset[0].fd = fd[4];
            fdset[0].events = POLLPRI;
            fdset[0].revents = 0;
```

In this case we are only polling on a single file descriptor and this is stored in the `fd` field. The events field is a bit mask, set in this case to `POLLPRI`, which is defined as "there is urgent data to read".

Now everything is in place to call `poll` to wait for the event, which might already have happened:

```
int rc = poll(fdset, 1, 5000);
```

The timeout is set to five seconds. The `rc` return value is either `0` for a timeout, a positive value giving the number of file descriptors that fired the interrupt, or a negative error value.

```
    if (rc < 0) {
        printf("\npoll() failed!\n");
        return -1;
    }
    if (rc == 0) {
        printf(".");
    }
    if (fdset[0].revents & POLLPRI) {
        lseek(fd[4], 0, SEEK_SET);
        int val=readGPIO(4);
        printf("\npoll() GPIO 4 interrupt occurred %d\n\r",val);

    }
        fflush(stdout);
}
```

If the event has occurred on the file descriptor we set, then to clear the interrupt we seek to the start of the file. You can also read the current value of the GPIO line.

If you try this out you will discover that when pin 7 is toggled from low to high you get an interrupt.

Complete Listing

```c
#include <stdio.h>
#include <string.h>
#include <bcm2835.h>
#include <fcntl.h>
#include <unistd.h>
#include <poll.h>

#define BUFFER_MAX 50
int fd[32] = {0};

int openGPIO(int pin, int direction);
int writeGPIO(int gpio, int value);
int readGPIO(int gpio);
int setEdgeGPIO(int gpio, char *edge);

int main(int argc, char** argv) {
    if (!bcm2835_init()) return 1;
    openGPIO(4, 0);
    setEdgeGPIO(4, "rising");
    struct pollfd fdset[1];
    for (;;) {

        fdset[0].fd = fd[4];
        fdset[0].events = POLLPRI;
        fdset[0].revents = 0;

        int rc = poll(fdset, 1, 5000);
        if (rc < 0) {
            printf("\npoll() failed!\n");
            return -1;
        }
        if (rc == 0) {
            printf(".");
        }
        if (fdset[0].revents & POLLPRI) {
                lseek(fd[4], 0, SEEK_SET);
                int val=readGPIO(4);
            printf("\npoll() GPIO 4 interrupt occurred %d\n\r",val);

        }
        fflush(stdout);
    }
    return 0;
}
```

```c
int openGPIO(int gpio, int direction) {
    if (gpio < 0 || gpio > 31) return -1;
    if (direction < 0 || direction > 1)return -2;
    int len;
    char buf[BUFFER_MAX];
    if (fd[gpio] != 0) {
        close(fd[gpio]);
        fd[gpio] = open("/sys/class/gpio/unexport", O_WRONLY);
        len = snprintf(buf, BUFFER_MAX, "%d", gpio);
        write(fd[gpio], buf, len);
        close(fd[gpio]);
        fd[gpio] = 0;
    }
    fd[gpio] = open("/sys/class/gpio/export", O_WRONLY);
    len = snprintf(buf, BUFFER_MAX, "%d", gpio);
    write(fd[gpio], buf, len);
    close(fd[gpio]);
    len = snprintf(buf, BUFFER_MAX,
            "/sys/class/gpio/gpio%d/direction", gpio);
    fd[gpio] = open(buf, O_WRONLY);
    if (direction == 1) {
        write(fd[gpio], "out", 4);
        close(fd[gpio]);
        len = snprintf(buf, BUFFER_MAX,
            "/sys/class/gpio/gpio%d/value", gpio);
        fd[gpio] = open(buf, O_WRONLY);

    } else {
        write(fd[gpio], "in", 3);
        close(fd[gpio]);
        len = snprintf(buf, BUFFER_MAX,
                "/sys/class/gpio/gpio%d/value", gpio);
        fd[gpio] = open(buf, O_RDONLY);
    }
    return 0;
}

int writeGPIO(int gpio, int b) {
    if (b == 0) {
        write(fd[gpio], "0", 1);
    } else {
        write(fd[gpio], "1", 1);
    }

    lseek(fd[gpio], 0, SEEK_SET);
    return 0;
}
```

```
int readGPIO(int gpio) {
    char value_str[3];
    int c = read(fd[gpio], value_str, 3);
    lseek(fd[gpio], 0, SEEK_SET);

    if (value_str[0] == '0') {
        return 0;
    } else {
        return 1;
    }

}

int setEdgeGPIO(int gpio, char *edge) {
    char buf[BUFFER_MAX];
    int len = snprintf(buf, BUFFER_MAX,
                    "/sys/class/gpio/gpio%d/edge", gpio);
    int fd = open(buf, O_WRONLY);
    write(fd, edge, strlen(edge) + 1);
    close(fd);
    return 0;
}
```

Poll on Another Thread

The poll function gets you as close to an interrupt handler as you can get in user mode, but there is one thing missing - the thread is suspended while waiting for the interrupt. This is generally not what you want to happen.

You can create a better approximation to a true interrupt by running the poll function on another thread. That is, if the main program wants to work with an interrupt you have to define an interrupt handling function that will be called when the interrupt occurs. Next you have to create a new thread that sets everything up and then calls poll on the file descriptor. This causes your new thread to be suspended, but you don't care because its only purpose is to wait for the interrupt, and meanwhile your program's main thread continues to run and do useful work. When the interrupt occurs, the new thread is restarted and it checks that the interrupt was correct and then calls your interrupt handler. When the interrupt handler completes, the thread cleans up and calls poll again to wait for another interrupt.

In the following program the basic skeleton of an interrupt handling framework is developed, without error checking or error recovery. If you are going to use this sort of approach in the real world you would have to add code that handles what happens when something goes wrong, whereas this code works when everything goes right.

To make the idea work we need two new functions, one to create a new thread and run the second, which sets up the interrupt and waits using poll.

The first is called `attachGPIO` because it attaches a specified GPIO line, edge event and interrupt handler and it makes use of the function defined in the previous section:

```
int attachGPIO(int gpio, char *edge, eventHandler func) {
    openGPIO(gpio, 0);
    setEdgeGPIO(gpio, edge);
    readGPIO(gpio);
    intData.fd = fd[gpio];
    intData.gpio=gpio;
    intData.func = func;
    pthread_t intThread;
    if (pthread_create(&intThread,
            NULL, waitInterrupt, (void*) &intData)) {
        fprintf(stderr, "Error creating thread\n");
        return 1;
    }
    return 0;
}
```

The first part of the function sets up the specified GPIO as an input and sets the edge event you want to respond to. It then does a read to clear any interrupts. Then it creates a new thread which runs the second function `waitInterrupt`, which waits for the interrupt and calls the interrupt function passed as the third parameter as a function pointer.

To make this work we need to define the `eventHandler` type:

```
typedef void (*eventHandler)();
```

which simply defines the function used for the event handler as having no result and no input parameters. We also need to pass some data to the `waitInterrupt` function.

We need to pass the file descriptor and the interrupt function to call to `waitInterrupt` so we have to pack them into a struct. What is more this struct has to be available after the `attachGPIO` function has terminated since the new thread keeps `waitInterrupt` running long after `attachGPIO` has completed.

The correct solution is to get the function to create the struct on the heap, but a simpler and workable solution is to create it as a global variable which lives for the entire life of the program:

```
typedef struct {
    int fd;
    int gpio;
    eventHandler func;
} intVec;

intVec intData;
```

It is this structure that is passed to waitInterrupt with the file descriptor and function pointer.

Next we have to write waitInterrupt:

```
void *waitInterrupt(void *arg)
    intVec *intData = (intVec*) arg;
    int gpio=intData->gpio;
    struct pollfd fdset[1];
    fdset[0].fd = intData->fd;
    fdset[0].events = POLLPRI;
    fdset[0].revents = 0;
    for (;;) {
        int rc = poll(fdset, 1, -1);
        if (fdset[0].revents & POLLPRI) {
            intData->func();
            lseek(fdset[0].fd, 0, SEEK_SET);
            readGPIO(gpio);
        }
    }
    pthread_exit(0);
}
```

This unpacks the data passed to it using the arg pointer into a pollfd struct as before. Then it repeatedly calls poll which suspends the thread until the interrupt occurs. Then it wakes up and checks that it was the correct interrupt and if so it calls the interrupt routine and when this has finished resets the interrupt.

To try this out we need a main program and an interrupt function. The interrupt function simply counts the number of times it has been called:

```
static int count;
void myIntHandler() {
    count++;
};
```

The main program to test this is something like:

```
int main(int argc, char** argv) {
    attachGPIO(4, "both", myIntHandler);
    for (;;) {
      printf("Interrupt %d\n\r",count);
      fflush(stdout);
    };
    return 0;
}
```

It simply attaches the handler to the GPIO line and then prints the count variable in an infinite loop.

When you run the program you will see count increment every time there is an interrupt. Notice the count is incremented while main repeatedly prints the count; the use of a second thread really does let main get on with other work. You can also use the core affinity functions to make sure that the interrupt thread runs on a different core to the main thread if you want to make sure that they don't interfere with each other.

It is often argued that this approach to interrupts is second class, but if you think about how this threaded use of poll works, you have to conclude that it provides all of the features of an interrupt. The interrupt routine is idle and not consuming resources until the interrupt happens when it is activated and starts running. This is how a traditional interrupt routine behaves.

There are other disadvantages of this approach. The main one is that the interrupt routine is run on a different thread and this can cause problems with code that isn't thread-safe - UI components, for example. It also more difficult to organize interrupts on multiple GPIO lines. It is generally said that you need one thread per GPIO line, but in practice a single thread can wait on any number of file descriptors and hence GPIO lines.

Finally, the big problem with this approach to interrupts is speed. Interrupt handling times are of the order of 50 to 100 milliseconds on a Raspberry Pi. This makes this approach to interrupts suitable for infrequent non-urgent events and unsuitable for fast protocols or high priority tasks.

At the moment polling - real polling - is faster. In fact, it would be faster to use the second thread to poll the GPIO state and run the interrupt handler directly without the help of sysfs and its interrupt facilities.

Summary

- Under Linux the closest you can get to an interrupt in user space is to use the poll or select function to wait on a file descriptor.

- This might seem restrictive, but as most things in Linux are presented as files it usually provides a way of achieving the same result as a true interrupt.

- If you use poll or select on a thread then the thread is suspended until the file descriptor is ready to be processed. This looks wasteful, but the system can run another thread while the original is waiting.

- The closest you can get to an interrupt in user space is to poll or select on a new thread. The new thread waits for the event and then runs the equivalent of the interrupt handler.

Chapter 15

Assembler

This is a book on using C in a POSIX or Linux environment so why should we end with a chapter on assembly language? The reason is that C is close to the machine and this means that your C program isn't that far away from the assembly language the compiler creates. In other words, there is a strong affinity between C and assembler. This book is also about low-level programming as encountered in the IoT, and embedded applications in general, and in this area assembler is sometimes the only way to achieve a result that needs speed or access to hardware that the software makes difficult to get at.

Of course, we have a problem in that if you are going to write assembly language then you need to know how. The good news is that it isn't difficult to learn assembler. The only slight problem is that are two common dialects for the x86 - AT&T and Intel, and there are differences between x86 and x64. There are similar variations for the ARM and other processors.

C Assembler as Text Insertion

The most important thing to remember is that GCC compiles your C program to human-readable assembler. The simplest way to add custom assembly language code into your program would be to simply insert the text into the assembly language file that the compiler creates. You could manually edit the assembler, but you would have to do this following each fresh compile. What the GCC compiler provides is a way for you to tell it what assembly language you want to insert.

The C standard way of doing the job is to use the basic `asm` command:

```
__asm__ (assembler instructions);
```

The assembler instructions are represented by a single string or a set of strings, one for each line of assembler. You have to terminate each line correctly for the assembler in use. The GCC assembler is happy with \n\t i.e. newline and tab or a semicolon. Basically, you have to conform to the rules of the assembler that is in use. The text that you write as assembler instructions is inserted into the compiler's assembly language output at the point it is encountered. So what you need to write in is governed by the assembler. You can generally find out what the conventions are by simply writing a small C program and compiling it with the -S option to generate an assembler file with extension .s. Using the compiler's assembly language output you can see what effect your inline assembler is having and this is the simplest way of finding out how to modify it to make it work.

The basic assembler command is limited to being run at the top level, which means you can't put it into a function, and there are no facilities to let you work with variables in your C code. There may be no facilities, but you can still do the job if you examine the assembler output of the compiler.

For example, most C compilers do not mangle the names of C variables, as C++ does. At worst, a compiler might add an underscore to the start of the name. You can find out what happens in a particular case by declaring a global variable and looking at the assembler generated. GCC on x86 and ARM doesn't mangle names, so you can simply use C variable names in your assembler. Notice that local variables are stored on the stack, and names are not retained in the assembler output. You can access local variables from assembler, but it is more difficult.

If you place a basic asm block into a function, including main, then it is automatically treated as an extended asm block, as covered in a later section. However, if you don't take advantage of its extra features, it just looks like a basic asm block.

Addition

As an example, let's write an assembly language program that adds 1 to a C variable myA and stores the result in myB. Of course, the code depends on what system you are using. For an x64 processor we have, (the code for a 32-bit processor is slightly different):

```
#include <stdio.h>
#include <stdlib.h>
int myA = 1;
int myB;

int main(int argc, char** argv) {
    __asm__ (
            "pushq %rax \n\t;"
            "pushq %rbx \n\t"
            "movl myA(%rip),%eax \n\t"
            "movl $01, %ebx\n\t"
            "addl %ebx, %eax\n\t"
            "movl %eax,myB(%rip) \n\t"
            "popq %rbx \n\t"
            "popq %rax \n\t"
            );
    printf("%d", myB);
    return (EXIT_SUCCESS);
}
```

If you know x86 or x64 assembler, this should be easy to understand. Notice that by default, GCC generates AT&T-style assembly language, but you can set an option to generate Intel style. The main difference is that AT&T has the source first and the destination second, whereas Intel uses the opposite order. So:

```
"movl myA(%rip),%eax \n\t"
```

stores the contents of the C variable myA into the eax register. In x64 compiled assembler all globals are addressed relative to the rip register. There is no way you can work this out from first principles, you just have to look at the assembly output and see how it is done in any particular case. After this we store 1 in the ebx register and then add ebx to eax. The final instruction stores eax into the C variable myB. Notice that, to avoid interfering with the rest of the program, we have to save and restore the two registers we use.

The same program is easy enough to create for ARM, but the conventions are different and, again, you need to look at the assembler output to find out how the compiler does things. The same program for the Raspberry Pi's ARM is:

```
#include <stdio.h>
#include <stdlib.h>
int myA = 1;
int myB;
int main(int argc, char** argv) {
    __asm__ (
                "PUSH {r1,r2,r3,r4} \n\t"
                "ldr r4,=myA \n\t"
                "ldr r2,[r4] \n\t"
                "mov r3,#1 \n\t"
                "add r1,r2,r3 \n\t"
                "ldr r4,=myB \n\t"
                "str r1, [r4] \n\t"
                "POP {r1,r2,r3,r4} \n\t"
                );
    printf("%d", myB);
    return (EXIT_SUCCESS);
}
```

It is slightly more complicated because of the structure of the ARM processor. The PUSH and POP are macros that the assembler converts into a set of equivalent instructions. The instruction:

```
"ldr r4,=myA \n\t"
```

is a GCC-specific extension that loads a register with a relative reference to the variable into the register. This is then used in:

```
"ldr r2,[r4] \n\t"
```

to store the value at the address in r4 into r2. We then load r3 with 1 and add r2 to r3, storing the result in r1. Finally, the same GCC-specific instruction is used to get the address of myB into r4 and then a str instruction is used to store the contents of r1 into the location given by the address in r4. If you are not familiar with ARM assembler, it is worth saying that in str the source and destination are the other way round - presumably so that the register can be specified first.

Rotate a Global

Another good example is adding a rotate command to C. For x64 this is fairly easy and to rotate right by two bits you would use:

```
#include <stdio.h>
#include <stdlib.h>
int myA = 1;
int main(int argc, char** argv) {
    __asm__ (
            "pushq %rax \n\t;"
            "movl myA(%rip),%eax \n\t"
            "ror $2,%eax\n\t"
            "movl %eax,myA(%rip) \n\t"
            "popq %rax \n\t"
            );
    printf("%X", myA);
    return (EXIT_SUCCESS);
}
```

Notice that you still have an overhead of pushing and popping the register, getting the value from the variable and putting it back again. If the compiler you are using recognizes the usual idiom for rotate then it is likely to generate faster code.

For the ARM, specifically Raspberry Pi:

```
#include <stdio.h>
#include <stdlib.h>
int myA = 1;

int main(int argc, char** argv) {
    __asm__ (
            "PUSH {r1,r2} \n\t"
            "ldr r2,=myA \n\t"
            "ldr r1,[r2] \n\t"
            "ror r1,r1,#2 \n\t"
            "str r1, [r2] \n\t"
            "POP {r1,r2} \n\t"
            );
    printf("%X", myA);
    return (EXIT_SUCCESS);
}
```

Again, if the compiler recognizes the usual idiom for ror in C, it is likely to generate faster code.

You can carry on in this way, using the assembler output to guide how you should integrate your code with the generated code, but it isn't the best way to do the job. The problem is that it depends on the way the compiler works and this can change. Optimizations can also change the assembler output in ways that can break your code. A better way to do any complicated assembler task is to use the extended inline assembler command.

Extended Asm

As the asm commands we have been using so far have been within a function, i.e. `main`, we are already using extended asm blocks, but there are some extras we can take advantage of. You can use special symbols to get the compiler to insert variable references, and even select registers, for you. In other words, you don't write finished, complete assembler to be inserted into the generated assembly language, you write an assembler template that the compiler completes for you.

The simplest of the extended forms of asm is:

```
__asm__ ( code template
        : output operand list
        : input operand list
      )
```

This can only be used inside a function and it needs to be marked as `volatile` if it has no outputs as otherwise the compiler might optimize it away. The lists following the colons are optional. You can leave out a list by simply writing an empty list.

You might think that the operand lists would just be names of variables, but extended asm is more sophisticated and hence initially more confusing. It uses a system of "constraints" to help the compiler work out how to deal with the C variable. For example, a constraint of r tells the compiler to use a register for the operand. The compiler keeps a table of which registers are in use so that it can allocate a register to use to store the value without having to save and restore the register.

The code template can contain any valid assembler, just as in the case of the basic asm, but you can also include tokens that the compiler will replace with registers or references to variables. All of the tokens start with % and if you need to include a % symbol in your assembler simply double it up to %%. Also if you need to include {, } or | in the code then put a % in front.

The main use of tokens is to identify the operands defined in the output and input operand lists, and to understand how this works we have to look at the way these lists are constructed.

Operands in the input or output lists take the form:

`[assembler name] constraint (variable name)`

where the variable name is the name of the variable in the C program you want to use. The assembler name is the name that will be used in the assembler code for the same variable. The constraint specifies how the variable is to be handled.

If you don't specify an assembler name then you have to refer to operands using their position in the list. For example, %0 is the first operand in the list, %1 the second and so on. For readability you should always specify an assembler name and it is a good idea to make it the same as the variable name. At the moment the limit is no more than 30 operands in total.

The rules for input and output operands are slightly complicated.

Output operands have an initial constraint modifier of =, which means you can only use them as a destination in an instruction. You can use + in place of =, which means they are also input operands and can be used as source in an assembler instruction.

An output operand is automatically transferred to the C variable when the assembler ends. An input operand is automatically transferred from the C variable to a register at the start of the assembler. An output operand that has a + modifier is transferred from and to the C variable when the assembler starts and ends.

If you use an output-only operand as a source in an assembler instruction you cannot be sure it will have the same value as the variable in the C program, as the compiler doesn't bother generating an instruction to initialize the operand from the C variable. This means that there are three types of operand:

output only	included in the output operand list with a modifier of =
output and input	included in the output operand list with a modifier of +
input only	included in the input operand list

As already mentioned, a constraint of r means use a register for the operand. It is the most commonly used constraint, but there are many others including a lot that are machine-specific. For example, m means use a memory location. If you specify rm this means the compiler can use either a register or a memory location according to what is optimal. In general it is better to use as many constraints as allowed to let the compiler work out the best way to do the job. However, it is also possible for the compiler to get it wrong and create an illegal instruction.

Adding Two Values

As an example, let's implement a function that adds two numbers together:

```
int sum(int myA, int myB){
    int myC;
    __asm__ (
                "addl %[myA],%[myB]\n\t"
                "movl %[myB],%[myC] \n\t"
                :[myC] "=r" (myC)
                :[myA] "r" (myA),
                 [myB] "r"  (myB)

    );
    return myC;
}
```

You can see that the C variable myC is an output operand and this means that its current value is not loaded into a register for use by the program. The two input operands are loaded into registers. This makes it possible to write:

```
"addl %[myA],%[myB]\n\t"
```

and the compiler substitutes the registers it selects for myA and myB. The final instruction:

```
"movl %[myB],%[myC] \n\t"
```

stores the value in myB into the register assigned to myC. The compiler then generates the extra instruction to transfer the value in the register into the C variable myC.

You might be surprised at how short the assembler is. Extended asm does all of the work in connecting the C variables and registers for you and you don't have to push and pop any registers as the compiler makes sure that they aren't being used for anything else.

The code generated on an x86 Linux system is:

```
mov     -0x14(%rbp),%eax
mov     -0x18(%rbp),%edx
add     %eax,%edx
mov     %edx,%eax
mov     %eax,-0x4(%rbp)
```

You can see that the compiler has picked the eax and edx registers to use to hold the input operands. It also reuses the eax register as the one to stand in for the myC variable. At the end of the program the compiler has also generated an instruction to transfer the eax register to the C variable myC.

This is a little inefficient as the result is moved to a different register and then stored back in memory. It would be much simpler to store the original register to memory and this can be done using an output operand that is also set to be an input operand:

```
int sum(int myA, int myB){
    __asm__ (
                "addl %[myA],%[myB]\n\t"
                :[myB] "+r" (myB)
                :[myA] "r"  (myA)
        );
    return myB;
}
```

Notice that now myB is an output and an input operand due to the use of the +. This means that the compiler now generates an instruction that loads a register from myB and at the ends stores that register back into myB. The generated code is:

```
mov     -0x4(%rbp),%edx
mov     -0x8(%rbp),%eax
add     %edx,%eax
mov     %eax,-0x8(%rbp)
```

which you can see does exactly what you would expect and uses only two registers.

What if we ask the compiler to use a memory reference for myB:

```
int sum(int myA, int myB){
    __asm__ (
                "addl %[myA],%[myB]\n\t"
                :[myB] "+m" (myB)
                :[myA] "r"  (myA)
        );
    return myB;
}
```

The generated code is now:

```
mov     -0x4(%rbp),%eax
add     %eax,-0x8(%rbp)
```

which as you can see now directly addresses myB rather than using a register.

If you change the memory constraint on myA to m then you will simply get an error as there is no add instruction that works with two memory references.

If you use the rm constraint on both variables and let the compiler pick how to implement the instruction the result is:

```
mov    -0x8(%rbp),%eax
add    -0x4(%rbp),%eax
mov    %eax,-0x8(%rbp)
```

which of course might change according to the version of the compiler in use.

You can see that how you specify constraints really does alter the nature of the assembly language code the compiler generates.

The same example implemented in ARM assembly language is:

```
int sum(int myA, int myB) {
    __asm__ (
            "add %[myB],%[myA],%[myB] \n\t"
            : [myB] "+r" (myB)
            : [myA] "r" (myA)
            );
    return myB;
}
```

Notice that it is considerably simpler than implementing all of the variable-to-register and register-to-variable transfers yourself. The generated code is also simpler because the compiler selects registers that it doesn't have to save and restore and it knows the offsets of the variables in memory.

```
ldr   r2, [r11, #-8]
ldr   r3, [r11, #-12]
add   r3, r2, r3
str   r3, [r11, #-12]
```

Rotate a Variable

Suppose you want to implement a function that rotates a value a specified number of bit positions. You could write a loop using a ror 1 instruction, but the x64 has a variable rotate using the cl register. That is:

```
ror %cl,%eax
```

right-rotates eax the number of times specified by the value in cl.

The number of rotates has to specified in the cl register - no other register will do - but there are a number of ways of doing this.

The first is to not rely on the compiler to allocate registers but to explicitly use cl. For example:

```
int ror(unsigned int value, unsigned char n) {
    __asm__ (
            "mov %[n],%%cl\n\t"
            "rorl %%cl,%[value]\n\t"
            : [value] "+r" (value)
            : [n] "m" (n)
            );
    return value;
}
```

The first instruction moves the C variable n into the cl register. The second performs the rotate using it. Notice the use of %% to make sure that we have %cl in the instructions. Also notice the way n is constrained to be a memory reference - what is the point in moving n into a register and then moving it to another register? This function produces the following assembler:

```
mov     -0x4(%rbp),%eax
mov     -0x8(%rbp),%cl
ror     %cl,%eax
mov     %eax,-0x4(%rbp)
```

The Clobber List

The only problem with this is that you are using cl without knowing if it is free to be used. You could push it at the start of the function and then pop it at the end, but it is much easier to use the clobber list. This is an optional final list in the extended asm which you can use to specify registers that are not input or output registers, but which you still make use of in your program. The compiler checks that any registers that you include in the clobber list are available for your use and will save and restore if necessary.

So to make sure the use of cl is trouble free you need to add a clobber list:

```
int ror(unsigned int value, unsigned char n) {
    __asm__ (
            "mov %[n],%%cl\n\t"
            "rorl %%cl,%[value]\n\t"
            : [value] "+r" (value)
            : [n] "m" (n)
            : "cl"
            );
    return value;
}
```

The rule is that any registers that you use, but aren't input or output registers, should be included in the clobber list to make sure the compiler knows about them and takes care of them.

As well as register names, there are also other resources that can be placed in the clobber list. The name cc stands for the condition code register and including it tells the compiler that it has been modified by your program. If you used any memory that isn't a C variable, i.e. if you have directly accessed memory without it being in the input or output list, then you need to include memory in the clobber list. This also implements a software read/write memory barrier. This is the reason that you can use:

```
asm(:::memory)
```

as a software memory barrier even when you are not using inline assembler.

Processor-Specific Constraints

A second way of specifying a particular register is to use one of the many processor-specific constraints. The x86 processor supports constraints for specific registers and c specifies the c register. This means we could write the function as:

```
int ror(unsigned int value, unsigned char n) {
    __asm__ (
            "rorl %[n],%[value]\n\t"
            : [value] "+r" (value)
            : [n] "c" (n)
            );
    return value;
}
```

This produces:

```
movzbl  -0x8(%rbp),%edx
mov     -0x4(%rbp),%eax
mov     %edx,%ecx
ror     %cl,%eax
mov     %eax,-0x4(%rbp)
```

which is perhaps not what you might expect. Why the compiler uses edx rather than ecx to load n and convert from a byte to 32 bits is a mystery.

Register Variables

The third and final way is to use register variables. You can declare a local variable and assign it a register using:

```
register type variable __asm__("register");
```

where type and variable are the usual declarations and register is the name of the register to use. You can only reliably use this in conjunction with an extended asm block. Notice that this is not the same as the register type modifier which usually has no effect on what the compiler does.

For example:

```
int ror(unsigned int value, unsigned char n) {
    register  unsigned char count __asm__("cl");
    count = n;
    __asm__ (
            "rorl %[count],%[value]\n\t"
            : [value] "+r" (value)
            : [count] "r" (count)
            );
    return value;
}
```

generates:

```
 movzbl -0x8(%rbp),%ecx
```

for the assignment to count and then:

```
 mov    -0x4(%rbp),%eax
 ror    %cl,%eax
 mov    %eax,-0x4(%rbp)
```

This has the advantage in transferring n directly into the ecx register. However, the documentation warns that the register may be used by functions called in the code following the use of the register variable. That is, the register is not protected in any way and if you need to maintain its value you need to save and restore it.

You can declare register variables at a global level, but they cannot have initial values and they are subject to the same problem as local register variables. However, the values of global register variables are saved by setjmp and restored by longjmp - but not on all machines.

ARM Rotate and Portable Code

The ARM processor also has a `ror` instruction that allows the number of rotates to be specified in a register but, unlike the x86, it can be any register. This means we can allow the compiler to do all of the register allocation without having to worry about clobber lists, constraints or register variables.

For example:

```
int ror(unsigned int value, unsigned char n) {
    __asm__ (
            "ror %[value],%[value],%[n] \n\t"
            : [value] "+r" (value)
            : [n] "r" (n)
            );
    return value;
}
```

generates:

```
 ldrb  r2, [r11, #-9]
 ldr   r3, [r11, #-8]
 ror   r3, r3, r2
 str   r3, [r11, #-8]
```

which is exactly what you would expect.

When you opt to write assembler you have to put up with very large changes in the code you write and how you specify register use. It is difficult to see how you could write portable code, but GCC provides a way you can attempt such a feat.

Goto Labels

In most cased the assembler blocks that you put into your code are self-contained in terms of execution path. That is, the flow of control enters the assembler code and while it may loop or branch within itself, it usually doesn't jump to other parts of your C program. However, you can make it do this if you really have to.

If you add the `goto` modifier at the start of the extended assembler block you can add a comma separated list of C labels at the end. You can use these C labels in assembler by `%l` (l for label) followed by either an integer giving the position in the list or [*label*] i.e. the C label you want to use.

For example:

```
int test(int value1,int value2) {
    __asm__   goto(
            "cmp %[value1],%[value2]\n\t"
            "jg %l[bigger]\n\t"
            : //no outputs
            : [value1] "r" (value1),[value2] "r" (value2)
            : // no clobbers
            : bigger
            );
    return 0;
bigger:
    return 1;
}
```

The cmp (compare) instruction sets the condition code register and the jg (jump if greater) transfers control to the label bigger if value2 is bigger than value1.

In most cases goto between assembler and C is better avoided as it ties the two types of code together too tightly. It is safer to consider your assembler block as a self-contained unit which has specific inputs and outputs.

Using the Condition Code Register

One of the common uses of inline assembly is to access the condition code register. This is simple in theory, but difficult in practice.

In the case of an x64 machine, the condition code register is 64 bits and you have no choice but to use a 64-bit push to pop it into another 64-bit register. A function to retrieve its value is:

```
int cc() {
    long long ccr;
    __asm__ (
            "pushfq \n\t"
            "popq %[ccr]\n\t"
            : [ccr] "=r" (ccr)
            : // no inputs
            );
    return ccr;
}
```

If you want a 32-bit version you need to modify the variable to be a 32-bit int and you need to change pushfq into a 32-bit flag register push.

You can use this to check for unsigned overflow or rollover by testing the carry flag, which is bit 0 in the condition code register:

```c
int main(int argc, char** argv) {
    unsigned int result = UINT_MAX;
    result++;
    int carryFlag = cc()& 0x01;
    printf("%X", carryFlag);
    return (EXIT_SUCCESS);
}
```

This prints 1 and if you change result++ to result-- it prints 0.

The problem with using this in practice is that you have to test after every arithmetic operation because the carry bit is set appropriately by every arithmetic operation. The act of calling a function between each arithmetic operation is an overhead that usually cannot be tolerated. To enable the assembler to be reused efficiently, it is better to define a macro:

```c
#define carryCheck      __asm__ ( \
            "pushfq \n\t" \
            "popq %[ccr]\n\t" \
            : [ccr] "=r" (ccr) \
        ); \
            if(ccr & 0x01) printf("overflow");
```

Notice that this macro assumes that there is a long long called ccr.

Now you can write code which tests for rollover after each arithmetic operation:

```c
int checkedArith() {
    long long ccr;
    unsigned int blowUP = UINT_MAX;
    unsigned int result = 1 + 2;
    carryCheck;
    result = result + blowUP;
    carryCheck;
}
```

Now there is no function call overhead but, of course, there is slightly more code. The macro can be made much more sophisticated than this.

Implementing the same thing for ARM is more difficult because the condition codes are only set by arithmetic operations with the S suffix. If you simply write:

```
result=result+1;
```

then the compiler will generate:

```
ADD R1,R1,#1
```

It doesn't need to set the condition codes as no test follows. It doesn't seem possible to force the compiler to use ADDS as it prefers to perform a CMP to set the condition codes.

The only way that you can make use of the condition codes is to write everything in assembler:

```
int checkedArithmetic() {
    unsigned int ccr;
    unsigned int result = 0xFFFFFFF0;
    __asm__ (
            "ADDS  %[result],%[result],$1  \n\t"
            "MRS   %[ccr], CPSR  \n\t"
            : [ccr] "=r" (ccr), [result] "+r" (result)
            :
            );
    return ccr;
}
```

You can check for the carry bit using:

```
 int carryFlag = checkedArithmetic() & 0x020000000;
```

This will be zero if there is no carry and non-zero if there is. You can check the program by changing 0xFFFFFFF0 to 0xFFFFFFFF.

When it comes to ARM, trying to use the carry flag to detect overflow is difficult and in most cases not worth pursuing.

Assembler or C

If programming low level code in C feels like fighting the compiler, then moving to assembler is more so. The compiler tries to organize things so that you get efficient code, but often at the expense of the code doing what you actually want it to. Since the first compiler removed a loop that didn't appear to be doing anything, timing is of not importance to a program after all, optimizations have been increasingly changing what programs actually do – and, of course, it is always the programmer's fault for not writing standard code.

When you take on assembler you have the additional problem of the different dialects of assembly language and even different versions of the assembly language - x86 v x64 say. And you still have the problem of fighting the compiler to get it to integrate your code with the assembler it produces from your C code.

Then there is the question of is it worth it?

Trying to get increased performance used to be a good argument for hand-coded assembler. In this area compilers have now developed to the point where, although you might not always understand why some particular code has been generated, it nearly always runs faster. In this area human programmers have lost the war with the compiler.

So why write assembler at all?

A good question and the honest answer is that you should avoid doing it until you have no other choice. You need to be dragged, kicking and screaming, to an assembler project and it really should be the last resort. Today about the only thing that justifies the complexity of assembler is when C doesn't support the hardware adequately. In such cases you can just write a few lines of assembler to make up the deficiency. If you really do have to support something large in assembler then it is often better to write a complete standalone function which can be called as if it was a C function. If you look up how to do this, you will find lots of explanations of different calling conventions and how to implement them. The simplest solution, however, is to write a C function with the required name and parameters and a dummy body - it may also have to have some instructions to stop the compiler optimizing it away. Then compile the function with -S or equivalent for another compiler to create an assembler .s file. Use this file as your template and fill in the body of the function using as much assembler as you like. The compiler will have generated the calling convention boilerplate code for you - just use it.

Summary

- The GCC compiler outputs assembly language code, which is then processed by an assembler to produce executable code.

- The asm command allows you to insert your own assembly language instructions into the compiler's output.

- The rules for writing assembly language depends on the processor you are using, the exact dialect of assembler and the assembler itself. These are all very platform-dependent.

- Basic asm allows you to insert assembler at the top-most level and is very limited.

- Extended asm can be used within functions and allows you to get the compiler to make connections between C variables and registers.

- Used in the simplest way, extended asm demands that you work out your own ways of connecting to C variables. Used in extended form you can specify an input and an output list which can be used to specify which C variables should be in registers or in memory.

- Exactly how C variables are treated depends on the constraints you supply.

- If you use any variables or memory locations not included in the input or output list then you have to include them in the clobber list so that the compiler knows what you are doing.

- You can also specify a list of goto labels, which correspond to labels in your C program which the assembler can transfer control directly to.

- Avoid using assembler if at all possible. It is usually not the case that your hand-crafted assembler will be faster than the compiler-created equivalent code.

- The only situation in which assembler is really needed is to gain access to hardware features that C ignores, such as the condition code register.

Index

accept..216
active type conversion..132
addrinfo..223
AF_INET...214
affinity..266
Android Things...165
anonymous pipes...152
ANSI C..14
Apache..213
ARM...111, 299, 308, 312, 314
ASCII...71
asm..300
assembler...19, 83
assembler template..304
asynchronous..19, 49, 201
AT&T-style..299, 301
atomic..152, 243
atomic struct...280
atomics...274

BCD arithmetic...76
biased representation..123
Binary Coded Decimal (BCD)...67, 70, 91
binary fractions..133
binary point..102
bind...215
bit rot..12
BlackPixel...196
block...52
boot loader..269
bounce...185
broadcast...249
brush...197
built-ins..79

C11...14, 24, 233, 242, 272
C11 Memory Models and Barriers..282
C89..14
C99...14, 126, 129
cache...264, 265
cache coherency mechanisms...264
carry bit..68
cast...132
cat...160
Celsius..104

chmod...29
CLang...16
client socket..214, 215
client-server architecture..194
clobber list...309
close..140
closedir...155
coherency mechanisms..264
cold cache..265
color..199
compiler writers..13
compiling the kernel...26
condition code register...313
condition variable...246, 248
connect...215
constraint...305, 308
containers...205
context switch..22
cores...235
cpuset...269
cron..40
Ctrl-\...48
Ctrl-C...48
current directory...31
CygWin...16, 213

d_ino...155
d_name...155
Debian..16
debugfs..160
Decimal Fixed Point...117
DefaultColormap...199
DefaultScreen...196
denormalized...127
detached..239
digit extraction...92
Directory function...154, 156
dirent..155
display...179
division by zero...92, 129
DNS..222
double..124
driver...12
dup...141

Earliest Deadline Scheduling (EDS)...15, 255
EBUSY...257
Eclipse...15

embedded applications...299
end around carry...75
event handling...228
events..200
exception...64, 130
exec..234
execute bit...29
exit...237
exponent..123
export...163
extended inline assembler...304
extended precision...125

F_GETLK...145
F_OFD_GETLK..148
F_OFD_SETLK...148
F_OFD_SETLKW..148
F_SETLK..145
F_SETLKW...145
Fahrenheit..104
FBIO_WAITFORVSYNC..188
fclose..138
fcntl..143
fdopen..142
feenableexcept...131
fence..271
feof..138
fflush..138, 165, 237
fgetc...138
fgets...138
FIFO..149, 253
file descriptor...139
file descriptor functions...188
file handling...17
fileno..142
fixed point arithmetic..17, 99,101
fixed point overflow..107, 110, 111
flag field...53
float..124
floating point..17, 67, 99, 121
FLT_EPSILON..134
FLT_EVAL_METHOD...126
fopen..138
fork...58, 234
FOURCC...183
FPE_INTDIV..95
fprintf..138
fputc...138

fputs..138
fractional..123
framebuffer...18, 179, 180, 187
frameworks..203
fread...138
fscanf...138
fseek..138
ftell...138
ftrapv..78
ftruncate...171
full adder..68
fwrapv..78
fwrite...138

g_application_run...204
GCC...16, 79, 111, 299
GET...218, 226
getaddrinfo...222, 225
getaffinity...266
getc...138
getcwd..154
getpid..161
getppid...161
GIMP Toolkit...203
Glade...203, 207, 210
glibc...17, 24
global variable..241, 301
GNU (Gnu Compiler Collection)..16, 79, 111, 299
goto...312
GPIO...22, 163, 164, 179, 290
gradual underflow..127
graphics context...197
GTK..18, 179,180, 203, 210
gtk_application_new...204
GTK+..180
GtkButtonBox...206
GUI designer...207
GUI frameworks...203
gz functions...188
gzclose...188
gzipped...188
gzread..188

half adder..68
headers..219
hints..222
HTTP...217, 218
hyperthreading...263, 268, 264

322

I/O ports...167
IEEE standard floating point..124
implementation-dependent..12
increased Precision..82
inf..127, 128
insmod..26
integer arithmetic..17, 67
Intel..299
Intel style...301
Inter Process Communication...58
interrupt..19, 27, 270, 285, 297
ioctl...182
iomem..160, 166
IoT...299
IPC..58
isnan...128
isolcpus..269

joinable..239
journal..36

Kahan Summation...135
kernel mode...21, 26
kill...48

libfixmath..113
LibGD...210
library...114
listen..216
lock file...145
lockf...145
locking...17, 144, 241, 244
long double...126
long long..73
longjmp..62
lseek...140
lsmod..26
lstopo..264

magnitude...122
malloc..172
man pages...161
MapNotify...201
mask..130
mask field...52
mbed...31
mean..134

mem...168
meminfo..160
memory barrier..271
memory map..167
memory mapping...166, 167
MicroPython...12
Microsoft's C compiler...16
MinGW...126, 213, 220, 223
mkdir...154
mkfifo..149
mmap...167, 169
mod operator (%)..89
modprobe...26
modular arithmetic..89
monitor...248
multi-core..263
multi-threaded...233
munmap..169
mutex..245, 248, 249
mysterious "6"...72

named pipe..149
NaN (Not a Number)...127
nanosleep..188
nasal demons..13
NetBeans...15, 51, 203, 260
nibble..70, 72
nice...252
non-local jumps..17
normalized...123
numerical analysis...122

O_NONBLOCK..151
open...139
OpenCV..210
opendir..154
OpenGL..210
operand..305
overflow...70, 103
overflow detection...79

packed BCD..73
page size..167
pairwise summation...135
parallelism...19
PATH..31
Patriot missile system...133
pause...57, 60

pen...197
Periodic Execution...40
permissions..29
physical barrier...277
PID...37, 58, 161, 234
pipe...17, 149, 152, 195
pipefs...160
pkg-config...203
poll..19, 216, 285, 286, 288, 290, 294
polling loop...297, 228
port..167, 217
POSIX..................14, 24, 29, 47, 51, 139, 213, 220, 233, 242, 252, 255, 265, 285
POSIX record lock...145
power...160
precision...122
print a fixed point value..105
printf...91, 236
priority..253
process identification number..37
processing unit...264
processor...264
processor-specific constraints...310
procfs...159
ps ax...51
pseudo directories...59
pseudo file system...18, 159
PSF 2...193
PSF format...188
pthread_create..236
pthread_detach..240
pthread_exit..237
pthread_join..239
pthread_kill..56
pthreads..15, 235, 236
putc...138
Python...12

Qt...179

raise...56
Raspberry Pi..16
read...140
readdir...155
reader lock...144
real-time signals...57
recv...215
register...306, 307
register variables..311

remove..154
rename..154
representation of zero................................123
restart...37
result bit..68
rewind..138
rewinddir...155
RGBA..183
rings...23
rmmod...26
rollover.............................74, 75, 76, 77, 314
root..259
rotate....................................303, 308, 312
Round Robin...253
rounding..102
running a program.....................................30

SA_RESTART..53
SA_SIGINFO..55
saturation arithmetic............................77, 112
SBCs..11, 22
scale factor..100
SCHED_OTHER...252
SCHED_RR..253
sched_yield...255
scheduling.......................18, 22, 252, 256, 265
scientific notation...................................123
screen dump...180
sd_notify...40
security..27
seekdir...155
select..285
sem_close...172
sem_destroy...172
sem_init..172
sem_open..172
sem_post..172
sem_wait..172
semaphore..172, 245
send..215
sequence point..273
server..225
server socket....................................214, 215
service unit..32
setaffinity...265
setdetachstate..240
setjmp..62
setlongjmp..94

setpriority..252
shift left...103
shm_open...169
SIGABRT...48, 49, 78, 83, 85
sigaction...50
SIGCONT...49
SIGFPE...95
SIGINT..48, 54
SIGKILL...48
siglongjmp...63
signal..17, 47, 50, 249
signal handler...84
signal state..62
signalfd...61
signalfd_siginfo..61
signals and threads..55
signed overflow..65
SIGPIPE..151
sigqueue...56
SIGQUIT..48
SIGRTMAX..58
SIGRTMIN...58
sigset...52
sigsetjmp...62, 63
SIGSTOP...48, 49
sigsuspend...57
sigtimedwait..57
sigwait...57, 60
sigwaitinfo...57
Single Board Computers...11, 22
single precision..124
sleep..250
SOCK_NONBLOCK...227, 287
sockaddr..216
sockets...18, 195, 213, 214, 217
software interrupt...47, 83
software memory barrier..274, 310
sprintf...91
SSH...259, 260
standards-based..12
starvation..246, 248
status..36
status register..83
STDERR..139
STDIN_FILENO..139
stdout..25
STDOUT_FILENO...139
stride...182

struct...243, 279
struct flock..145
struct sigaction...50
StructureNotify...201
SUID bit..30
supervisor mode...23
sync_synchronize..272
synchronous...49
synthetic file system...159
syscall...23, 25, 256
sysfs..159, 164, 290
system call..23
systemctl..34
systemd...17, 29, 31

TCP..217
telldir...155
ten's complement..73, 76
test for overflow...80
testing for equality..134
thread...234, 235, 252, 294
thread attributes...238
thread creation..236
thread local..241
thread-safe...297
threads..55
time intervals..43
timer..40
tmpfile..154
tmpfs...160
tmpnam...154
tokens...304
toolchain..15
trap..83
trap a division by zero...93
Truetype..192
try-catch..62, 63, 94
trylock...248
two's-complement arithmetic...90
two's-complement representation...74

Ubuntu...16
undefined behavior...12, 77, 92, 133, 278
unexport...163
ungetc..138
unistd.h..25
unit file..32
unlock...245

unsigned overflow...314
unsigned rollover..88
user interface...179

volatile...266, 273

warm cache..265, 275
watchdog...38
web client...217
WhitePixel...196
WinSock...213, 220, 229
wrapper functions...24
write..140
writer lock...144

X-Windows..180, 194
X11...18, 194
XAllocColor...199
XAllocNamedColor...200
XCB..195
XColor..199
XCreateGC...197
XCreateSimpleWindow...196
XDrawArc...197
XDrawLine..197
XDrawPoint..197
XDrawRectangle...197
XDrawString...197
XEvent..202
Xflush...195
Xlib...195
XNextEvent..200
XOpenDisplay...196
XPeekEvent..200
XSelectInput..200
XSetForeground...197
Xsync...195

yield...246, 253

zlib library..188

Other Books by Harry Fairhead

Fundamental C: Getting Closer To The Machine
ISBN: 978-1871962604

Although by no means a prerequisite, this is the companion book at introductory level that has been referred to in earlier chapters. It explores C from the point of view of the low-level programmer that keeps us close to the hardware. It covers addresses, pointers, and how things are represented using binary and emphasizes the important idea is that everything is a bit pattern and what it means can change.

As a C developer you need to think about the way data is represented, and Harry Fairhead encourages this. He emphasizes the idea of modifying how a bit pattern is treated using type punning and unions.

This power brings with it the scourge of the C world – undefined behavior - which is ignored in many books on C. Here, not only is it acknowledged, it is explained, together with ways to avoid it. A particular feature of the book is the way C code is illustrated by the assembly language it generates. This helps you understand why C is the way it is.

For beginners, the book covers installing an IDE and GCC before writing a Hello World program and then presents the fundamental building blocks of any program - variables, assignment and expressions, flow of control using conditionals and loops.

Once the essentials are in place, data types are explored before looking at arithmetic and representation. We then go deeper into evaluating expressions before looking at functions and their scope and lifetime. Arrays, strings, pointers and structs are covered in separate chapters, as is bit manipulation, a topic that is key to using C, and the idea of a file as the universal approach to I/O. Finally, he looks at the four stages of compilation of a C program, the use of static and dynamic libraries and make.

This is C as it was always intended to be written - close to the metal.

Raspberry Pi IoT in C
ISBN: 978-1871962468

The Raspberry Pi makes an ideal match for the Internet of Things. To put it to good use in IoT you need two areas of expertise, electronics and programming in the C language and, because of the way hardware and software engineering tend to occupy separate niches, you may need help with combining the two. This book teaches you to think like an IoT programmer. After reading it you will be in a better position to tackle interfacing anything-with-anything without the need for custom drivers and pre-built hardware modules.

If you want to know how to work with the GPIO lines directly, how to work with near realtime Linux, and generally take control of the Pi, this is the book you need. It explains how to use the standard bus types - SPI, I2C, PWM - and with custom protocols including an in-depth exposition of the 1-wire bus. You will also discover how to put the Internet into the IoT using sockets and the low cost ESP8266. Throughout the book takes a practical approach, helping readers to understand electronic circuits and datasheets and translate this to code, specifically using the C programming language.

The main reason for choosing C is speed, a crucial factor when you are writing programs to communicate with the outside world. If you are familiar with another programming language, C shouldn't be hard to pick up. Here it is used in conjunction with NetBeans and with the bcm2835 library.

The main idea in this book is to not simply install a driver, but to work directly with the hardware. So rather than using Raspberry Pi HATs or other expansion boards we use the Pi's GPIO and connect off-the-shelf sensors.

Micro:bit IoT In C
ISBN: 978-1871962451

Harry Fairhead   THE I PROGRAMMER LIBRARY
PUBLISHED BY IO PRESS

The BBC micro:bit is capable of taking on a variety of roles including that of a powerful IoT device. In order to gain full access to its features and to external devices, however, you need to use C. which delivers the speed crucial to programs that communicate with the outside world. This book, written for the electronics enthusiast with a programming background, presents details of sensors and circuits with several complete programs.

A first "Hello Blinky" C program introduces the mbed online compiler, after that an offline approach using the yotta development environment plus NetBeans is used to discover how to control the micro:bit's I/O lines and explore the basis of using the GPIO. For speed we need to work directly with the raw hardware and also master memory mapping and pulse width modulation.

Sensors are connected using first the I2C bus, then by implementing a custom protocol for a one-wire bus, and eventually adding eight channels of 12-bit AtoD with the SPI bus, which involves overcoming some subtle difficulties and serial connections. The micro: bit lacks WiFi connectivity but using a low-cost device it can become an Internet server via its serial port.

To conclude we look at the micro:bit's LED display. This may only be 5x5, but it is very versatile, especially when you use pulse width modulation to vary the brightness level, something demonstrated in the classic game Commando Jump, written in C.

Printed in Great Britain
by Amazon

22007981R00185